A HISTORY *of*

US

CONCISE EDITION

Front Cover
Children recite the Pledge of Allegiance.

Compilation Copyright © 2011 K12 Inc.
Text Copyright © 1993, 1999, 2003, 2006, 2010 by Joy Hakim
Adapted with permission of Oxford University Press, Inc.

ISBN-13: 978-1-60153-184-1

Printed by LSC Communications, Willard, OH, May 2019.

VOLUME **D** 1929 TO PRESENT

Joy Hakim

A HISTORY of US

CONCISE EDITION

K12

Editors of the K^{12} Concise Edition

John Holdren and Patricia O'Connell Pearson

Concise Edition Volume D Staff and Contributors

Allyson Jacob, Kay McCarthy, Jill Tunick *Text Editors*
Suzanne Montazer *Creative Director, Print and ePublishing*
Stephanie Shaw Williams *Print Visual Designer*
The Quarasan Group, Inc. *Interior Design and Composition*
Kim Barcas, Carol Leigh *Cover Designers*
Meredith Condit, Charlotte Fullerton *Picture Editors*
Jean Stringer *Rights Manager*
David Swanson *Cartographer*
Jay White *Contributing Instructional Designer*
Susan Raley *Senior Manager, Editors*
Candee Wilson *Senior Project Manager*

Maria Szalay *Senior Vice President, Product Development*
John Holdren *Senior Vice President, Content and Curriculum*
David Pelizzari *Vice President, Content and Curriculum*
Kim Barcas *Vice President, Creative*
Laura Seuschek *Vice President, Instructional Design and
    Evaluation & Research*
Aaron Hall *Vice President, Program Management*

Lisa Dimaio Iekel *Senior Production Manager*

About K12 Inc.

K12 Inc., a technology-based education company, is the nation's leading provider of proprietary curriculum and online education programs to students in grades K–12. K^{12} provides its curriculum and academic services to online schools, traditional classrooms, blended school programs, and directly to families. K12 Inc. also operates the K^{12} International Academy, an accredited, diploma-granting online private school serving students worldwide. K^{12}'s mission is to provide any child the curriculum and tools to maximize success in life, regardless of geographic, financial, or demographic circumstances. K12 Inc. is accredited by CITA. More information can be found at www.K12.com.

A Note from the Author

This fourth book in the concise edition of *A History of US* takes us to a time—right now—when much of the world is struggling to achieve what we often take for granted: democracy. It's a messy kind of government, not easy to maintain, but better than any other that has been tried. As James Madison said, "If men were angels, no government would be necessary." He also said that, "religion and Government will both exist in greater purity, the less they are mixed together."

Separation of church and state, conceived by Jefferson and Madison and formalized in the First Amendment to the Constitution, is our unique contribution to political thought. Our government encourages us to think for ourselves, pray as we wish, and work where we want. There's a downside to freedom and democracy: all kinds of ideas get an audience. Some of those ideas—like segregation—have been horrendous. But our Founders were wise enough to give us a system that can improve itself. We the people are in charge, and when we are smart enough to realize that, and take advantage of our people power, well, this nation's achievements become awesome.

—Joy Hakim

Contents

PART 2

POSTWAR AMERICA

PART 3
CONFLICT AT HOME AND ABROAD

PART 4

NEW CHALLENGES, NEW DIRECTIONS

PART 1

FACING THE DEPRESSION AND FIGHTING WORLD WAR II

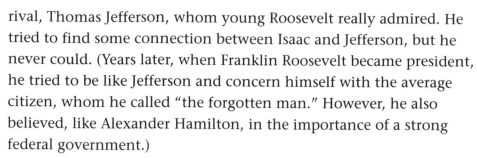

Franklin Roosevelt, age 5, poses with his mother, Sara Delano Roosevelt. ▼

James Roosevelt helped inspire his young son's love of history. ▶

rival, Thomas Jefferson, whom young Roosevelt really admired. He tried to find some connection between Isaac and Jefferson, but he never could. (Years later, when Franklin Roosevelt became president, he tried to be like Jefferson and concern himself with the average citizen, whom he called "the forgotten man." However, he also believed, like Alexander Hamilton, in the importance of a strong federal government.)

Franklin's father wasn't the only one with stories to tell. His mother talked of her family, the Delanos. The first American Delano was French, and a Huguenot, and he arrived at the Plymouth Colony in 1621. (He missed the *Mayflower* by a year.) It was love that brought him to America. He was in love with Priscilla Mullins. She must have been special; Myles Standish and John Alden loved her, too. She married Alden and rejected the Frenchman, Philippe de la Noye, who, some years later, married an Englishwoman named Hester. Then he dropped the *ye* from his name and became Delano.

The Roosevelts and Delanos prospered in America. Most of them, like Theodore Roosevelt, became Republicans. But James Roosevelt, Franklin's father, was a Democrat.

When Frank was five years old, in 1887, his father took him to meet President Grover Cleveland. Cleveland was the first Democrat to be president in 28 years. James Roosevelt had contributed money to help get him elected. But being president is no easy job; the day young FDR visited, the chief executive was tired. "My little man," said the huge president to the small boy dressed in a sailor suit standing in front of him, "I am making a strange wish for you. It is that you may never be president of the United States."

Well, you know how kids are. Just tell them what you don't want them to do, and that is what they will go for. So it may have been that day that Franklin Delano Roosevelt first got the idea that he would like to be president.

How About This?

CHAPTER 2

How would you like this: a house in New York City, a country house overlooking the Hudson River at Hyde Park, New York, and a summer house in Campobello, New Brunswick, by the sea? Now, just for variety you'll take plenty of trips: Paris this year, England the next. You'll be surrounded by servants: cooks, drivers, gardeners, a laundress, and your own private teachers. You'll have a pony and dogs and just about everything you want. In addition, you'll have loving parents who adore you and see that children come to play with you. When you finally go off to school—at age 14—your parents will take you in their own railroad car; it has a bedroom and living room.

Sounds pretty terrific? Well, it wasn't bad—and that was what Franklin Delano Roosevelt's childhood was like. No, he wasn't a prince; he just lived like one. So did other children of the wealthy American upper class in the late 19th century. That was at a time when 11 million of the 12 million families in America had an average income of $380 a year. Only a few thousand families could be called rich. And, compared with the really wealthy Vanderbilts or Astors, the Roosevelts were no big deal. How do you think you would turn out if you had everything you wanted? Do you think you might be vain, arrogant, spoiled, and worthless? Well, that is just how some of those rich kids turned out. (Some poor kids probably turned out that way, too.) But not Frank Roosevelt.

▲ Franklin Roosevelt in 1898, with his Newfoundland, Monk, at the family's country home in Hyde Park, New York

The Vanderbilts had a huge king's palace of a mansion in Hyde Park just down the road from the Roosevelts' house. Maybe that was why Franklin Roosevelt never thought of himself as rich. Today, both houses are museums, and you can walk from one to the other on a special hiking trail that meanders alongside, affording a spectacular view of the Hudson River.

The Roosevelt mansion in Hyde Park is now a national historic site and museum. ▶

His parents gave him good values. They expected him to behave like a gentleman: to be kind, considerate, and honest. They gave him a strong religious faith. (He was an Episcopalian.) That faith gave him courage when he needed it.

He needed courage many times in his life. First, when he went away to Groton. Groton was a rich boys' school (now there are girls, too), but the headmaster didn't believe in pampering. Every boy was expected to take a cold shower each morning. That wasn't really hard, if you gritted your teeth and showered fast; it was much harder trying to be just one of the group when you had always been the center of attention. Franklin was handsome, charming, and friendly—but he never got along with people his age as well as he did with those older and younger. At Groton he didn't get picked for awards and teams he really wanted, and that hurt, but he had been taught not to complain.

It became a part of his character, not complaining. He would be enthusiastic and act as if everything was fine, even if it wasn't. It made him pleasant to be around, but it also made some of his friends uneasy. They never knew how he really felt.

Franklin went to Harvard, as his parents expected him to do, and to Columbia Law School. His mother intended him to live the comfortable life of a country squire, as his father had before him. After all, with the family money, he had no need to work hard. He didn't have to concern himself with others, but he did. When he was a student himself he wrote to segregated Southern colleges appealing to them to do as Harvard did and accept black students.

He may have been concerned with those who were less fortunate than himself because of an important influence in his life, a man he admired more than anyone else. A man who cared about people and wanted to make the world better than he had found it. It was the president of the United States, his cousin Theodore.

When Frank was a child he loved to visit Sagamore Hill, TR's Long Island home in Oyster Bay. There he could romp and run with energetic, fun-loving Teddy and his five children. Frank decided that someday he, too, would have a big family and play with his family as TR did.

Roosevelt learned to sail as a boy and loved being on the water. After his graduation from Harvard in 1904, he took the family yacht for a trip on the Bay of Fundy in Canada. ▼

When this picture was taken in 1919, FDR was the assistant secretary of the navy under President Woodrow Wilson. Roosevelt and his wife, Eleanor, had six children; one of their sons died in infancy.

He also decided he would serve his country—and he set out to do it. First he became a New York state senator. Then Woodrow Wilson made him assistant secretary of the navy. (TR had held that job.) In 1920, he ran for vice president with James Cox against Warren Harding and Calvin Coolidge. He lost, but people began to talk of him as a politician to watch.

He soon had a fine family: a busy wife, a daughter, and four sons. He was an energetic father, full of good spirits, who loved to sail and hike. Yale's football coach watched him exercise and said,

> *"Mr. Roosevelt is a beautifully built man with the long muscles of an athlete."*

But what he wanted most of all was to be president. He told that to a classmate while he was still in college. And it looked as if he had a good chance to fulfill his ambition.

Then tragedy struck. He went to bed one night, not feeling well; the next morning, he couldn't move. He was 39 and he had a dreaded disease: *poliomyelitis* (PO-lee-o-my-uh-LY-tiss). Usually it struck

After contracting polio in 1921, Roosevelt worked tirelessly to regain his physical strength. He was never able to walk unaided again, but his energy and optimism were apparent when he attended the New York State Democratic Convention in 1926.

children: its common name was *infantile paralysis*. It was especially hard on adult victims. (Later, Jonas Salk and Albert Sabin developed vaccines to prevent polio, but that was still 20 years in the future.)

Imagine you're an active man, father of five children, with big ideas. Then, overnight, you're crippled. At first Roosevelt couldn't move at all. Slowly, with painful therapy and concentration, he regained the use of his upper body. He would never run again. When he walked it was in heavy braces with agonizing steps. Would you have the courage to go on with your plans? Would you feel sorry for yourself? Would you take it easy and let people wait on you?

At first, everyone was sure his career was finished. Franklin's mother expected him to live the life of a wealthy invalid. But Franklin was determined to live normally. He was a cheerful man, and an optimist. Where others saw problems, he saw challenges.

His parents had trained him not to complain, and, even when he was in great pain, he didn't. As it turned out, he gained something from his terrible illness. It taught him patience and made him more determined. It made him know frustration, and sorrow, and anguish. He—the boy who had had everything—learned to understand those who had troubles.

On top of all that, he was married to a very unusual woman. She, too, was determined that he should not change his goals. Her name was Eleanor.

While campaigning, FDR shakes hands with farmers in Georgia. Roosevelt was always eager to meet and learn from people from every walk of life. ▶

A Lonely Little Girl Grows Up

Eleanor Roosevelt once described her childhood self as "an ugly little thing." She wasn't ugly, but she thought she was, perhaps because her mother was a great beauty. Eleanor had long blond hair, blue eyes, a plain face, and teeth that seemed too big for her mouth. She was shy, easily frightened, and serious. Sometimes she told little lies because she was afraid people would not want to hear the truth.

▲ Eleanor Roosevelt at about age 3

She had a dreadful childhood. Not an ordinary unhappy childhood; a horrible, awful, terribly lonely one.

She adored her father, Theodore Roosevelt's handsome brother Elliott, but most of the time he wasn't there. He was sweet-natured and charming, but he became an alcoholic. It ruined his life and his family's life, too. Once he took Eleanor and his prize terriers for a walk. They stopped at his men's club and he left Eleanor and the dogs with the doorkeeper while he went inside "for just a minute." Hours later he was carried out—drunk; the little girl was sent home in a taxi.

When she was eight her mother died. When she was nine her brother died. When she was 10 her father died.

When this picture was taken, Eleanor was about 11 years old and had already lost her parents and a brother. ▼

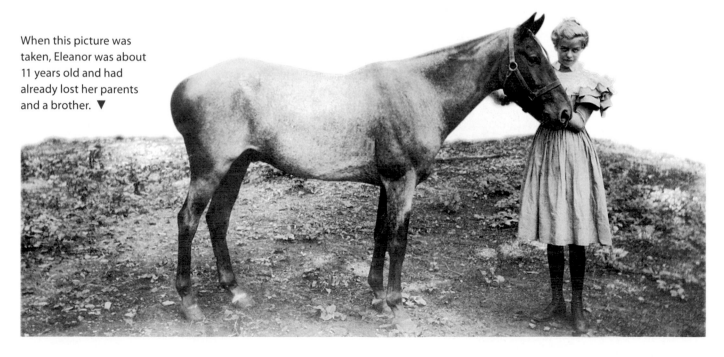

Eleanor's Other Mother

Marie Souvestre was the principal of the school that Eleanor attended in England. She was a strong, proud Frenchwoman, and the girls at Allenswood had to speak French. She taught Eleanor to think for herself, and she taught her that women could become something without the help of men.

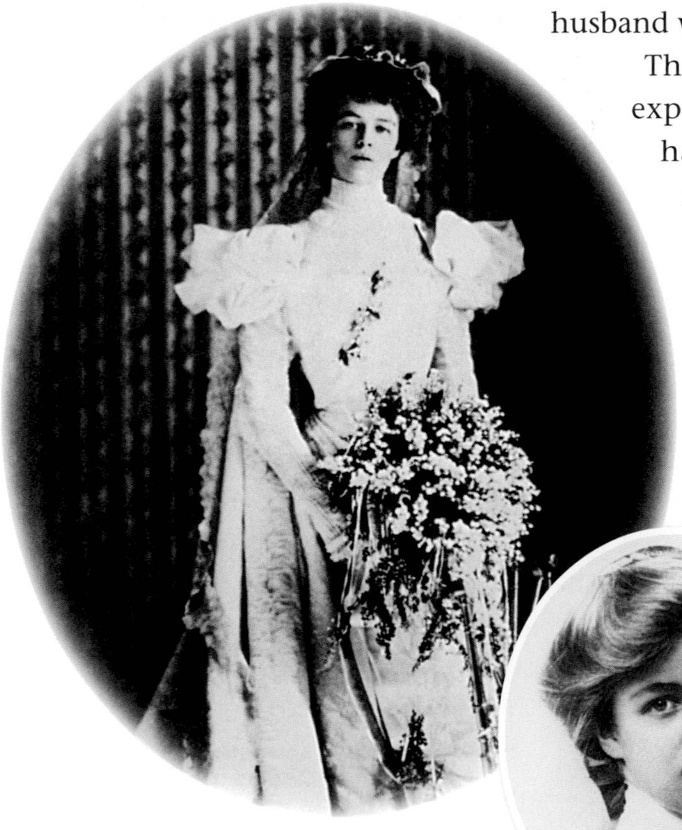

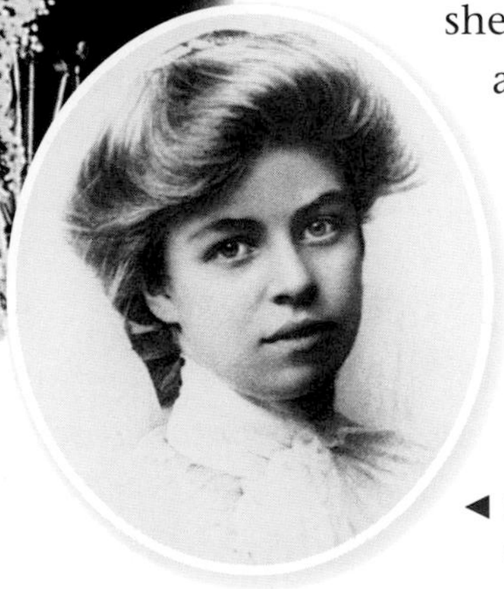

Eleanor and her younger brother, Hall, went to live with their grandmother, who didn't know anything about bringing up children. She lived in a big, spooky house. The noise of children playing bothered her. A governess took care of Eleanor and Hall. The governess was mean to Eleanor.

Then Eleanor was sent away to school in England. Finally, her life took a happy turn. The principal of the school realized that Eleanor had a good mind and a generous, kind nature. Eleanor became her favorite student. She had a talent for leadership. She was able to inspire others to do their best.

When Eleanor came home from England she was tall and willowy. She still thought she was ugly, but other people didn't. Especially her cousin, Franklin, the most dashing of the young Roosevelts. He and Eleanor fell deeply in love.

They were soon married. Before long, Eleanor found herself with five children, three houses that needed managing, and a husband with a busy political career.

Then her husband fell ill with polio. She had had experience with tragedy. Maybe that was why she handled it so well. Her husband's legs would never carry him again. She said that needn't stop him. There was no reason to change his goals. She could become his legs—and his eyes and ears, too.

They were a team, one of the greatest political teams in history. He became president, but she was his link to the people. He stayed in the White House; she went to coal mines and factories and workers' meetings. Then she told the president what people were thinking.

In 1905, Eleanor, seen here in her wedding dress, married Franklin. ▼

◀ Eleanor developed confidence at school in London.

◀ As First Lady, Mrs. Roosevelt worked for many causes, including raising funds to aid children with polio.

Eleanor Roosevelt made regular radio broadcasts for many years. ▼

The first time she spoke before an audience her knees shook. Soon she was one of the most successful speakers of her day. She wrote a newspaper column and a magazine column and books. She was the first First Lady to hold regular press conferences. She served food to needy people, read stories to poor children, visited hospitals, and spoke out for minority rights when few others did.

It is hard for a president—any president—to take time to check out government projects. Besides, everyone knows when a president is coming to visit, so things can be made to look good beforehand. But no one ever knew where Eleanor Roosevelt would pop up. The Secret Service had a code name for her: they called her "Rover."

▲ In 1939, some 75,000 people attended Marian Anderson's performance on the steps of the Lincoln Memorial.

She checked up on government projects and told the president the truth about what was happening. If someone wrote to the president complaining about a problem, Eleanor made sure the letter got answered. Sometimes she invited the letter writer to dinner at the White House. She invited all kinds of people to White House meals: young and old, rich and poor, people of every race and religion.

Always, she fought for the underdog—for those who were persecuted, or treated unfairly. She wanted to see that all people were given an equal opportunity. She worked for women's rights. She worked for minority rights. She stood on the side of truth and justice.

When a women's organization refused to let Marian Anderson, a renowned black singer, use its auditorium, Mrs. Roosevelt resigned from the organization. She encouraged Marian Anderson to sing on the steps of the Lincoln Memorial in Washington, D.C. Marian Anderson sang "America," and more people heard her than could have fit in any auditorium.

Shy, insecure, ugly-duckling Eleanor had grown up to be a strong, sensitive, capable person. She had a kind of no-nonsense wisdom that made her admired around the world. She has been called the outstanding woman of the 20th century.

The Bonus Army returned to Washington when Roosevelt was president. It was called the "Second Bonus Army." He offered the veterans the use of an army camp; sent food, coffee, a convention tent, and doctors; and then added a navy band to entertain them. Mrs. Roosevelt came to visit. "Hoover sent the army," said one Bonus Army man. "Roosevelt sent his wife." Roosevelt did not pay the bonuses, but he did offer the veterans jobs in the Civilian Conservation Corps (CCC), planting trees, creating parks, and so forth. Many went to work.

Handicap or Character Builder?

When Franklin Roosevelt first entered politics he was wealthy, charming, astoundingly good-natured, ambitious, and optimistic—but not very serious. Perhaps everything had come to him too easily. In his boyhood and youth and early manhood he had not known suffering. Now he knew. Now there were steel braces on his legs and a current of steel in his veins.

He had gone through a testing time of great pain when he could hardly move at all. He would never stand by himself again—he always had to call on others for help. Sometimes he crawled to the bathroom. For a proud man it must have been very hard. But if he felt sorry for himself he didn't show it. Even at first, when he was very sick, he made those who came to see him feel good. Everyone remarked on his good spirits, his lighthearted manner, and his great courage.

He was determined to conquer polio, so he worked hard exercising and swimming and learning to manipulate the seven-pound leg braces. His slim, boyish torso became strong, muscular, and powerful. For seven years he stayed away from active political life, trying to learn to walk again, but his weak legs would not respond. If he despaired, if he was sorrowful, he didn't let anyone see it.

He refused to act like an invalid. And so he sailed and went to dances and did everything anyone else would have done. Only he did it with more energy

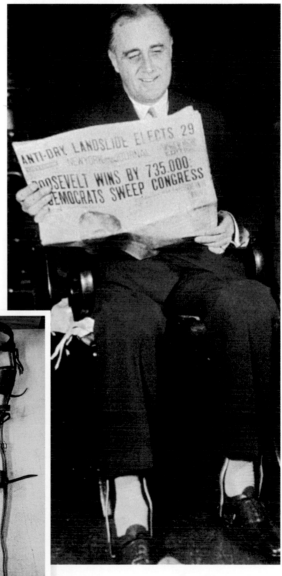

Franklin Roosevelt reads about his election victory in November 1932. (Below: the leg braces that enabled Roosevelt to stand). ▼

Exuberance is joyful enthusiasm.

and exuberance than most people. At a square dance—where he called the dances—others remarked at what a good time he seemed to be having. This was a man who had always loved to dance. How do you think he really felt?

Perhaps, by not showing his inner feelings, he convinced himself, as he convinced others, that he wasn't hurting.

It would have been easier to become president if he had not had polio. And it probably would have happened. After all, he had the Roosevelt name, that incredible energy, and determination. But his disease made the man different.

A friend who knew Roosevelt when he first entered politics described him as "brilliant, lovable, and somewhat happy-go-lucky... always amusing, always the life of the party." But serious, or focused in his beliefs? No one thought that.

Did Roosevelt's crippling disease make him a stronger, more sensitive, more serious person? There are many who believe it did.

When FDR accepted the nomination for president of the United States, he wanted everyone at the Democratic National Convention to know he would be an active candidate and president. If anyone was worried that his weak legs would slow him down, he would show

Franklin Roosevelt waves his hat as he begins a campaign train tour. Eleanor Roosevelt is on the right, partially hidden by a post. ▶

them: they would not. So he flew to Chicago, locked the braces on his legs, and stood before the delegates.

"I pledge you, I pledge myself, to a new deal for the American people," said FDR in his captivating, mellifluous voice. To a nation that had suffered three years of devastating depression, the words *new deal* sounded very good. The Republican candidate, Herbert Hoover, didn't have a chance.

Mellifluous (muh-LIFF-floous) means flowing and sweet as honey.

Whether he deserved it or not, Hoover was blamed for the Depression. Roosevelt campaigned hard, but he didn't have to. People wanted a change. The election was a landslide. Forty-two of 48 states went Democratic.

Today, because of the 20th Amendment (adopted in 1933), a candidate elected in November becomes president in January. In 1932, the delay was longer. Roosevelt did not take office until March. Between Election Day in November 1932 and Inauguration Day in March 1933, the economic situation got worse and worse.

By March, the U.S. economy seemed close to collapse. Every day more and more banks closed. Those who had gold were hoarding it. There was even a question as to whether the government had enough money to meet its payroll. Capitalism, said many experts, was too sick to recover.

▲ *The New Yorker* magazine captured the public perception of the glum outgoing president, Herbert Hoover, and the enthusiastic incoming president, Franklin Roosevelt, on Inauguration Day 1933.

A New Deal

When Roosevelt accepted the Democratic Party's nomination for president, he pledged a "new deal for the American people." A cartoonist picked up the phrase, and *New Deal* was the name soon given to President Roosevelt's domestic (home) policies. The ideas of the New Deal were based on Progressive ideas. (The Progressive Party was important at the end of the 19th and beginning of the 20th century. Theodore Roosevelt was a Progressive.) Progressive ideas that influenced FDR's New Deal thinking included: opposition to monopoly; a belief that government should help regulate the economy; and the conviction that no one wants to be poor and that most poverty is the result of social problems. The New Deal's methods were experimental; some worked, some didn't.

President Roosevelt

When former president Calvin Coolidge was asked for his ideas on how to lick the Depression, he said:

> *In other periods of depression it has always been possible to see some things which were solid and upon which you could base hope, but as I look about me I see nothing to give ground for hope—nothing of man.*

A group of prominent bankers was called to Washington to see what suggestions they had for solving the banking crisis. They had none.

President Herbert Hoover said, "We are at the end of our string. There is nothing more we can do."

That gives you an idea of the gloom and pessimism in Washington the day Hoover packed his bags and left the White House.

The next day, March 4, 1933, Franklin Roosevelt stood, bareheaded, in front of the Capitol, holding tightly to a lectern. It was his inauguration day. Some small boys perched in nearby tree limbs; dignitaries sat in special seats; but most of the crowd stood and

▲ President Roosevelt and his wife, Eleanor, on their way to the White House after his inauguration

The New Deal funded infrastructure projects, including several dams to produce electric power. In this mural, in the lobby of the Department of the Interior building in Washington, D.C., workers take on the challenges and dangers of building a large dam. ▶

shivered in the cold wind. When the new president spoke, his strong voice cut through the gloom. All across the land, people clustered around radios to hear what he had to say.

"This nation asks for action, and action now," said President Roosevelt. "We must act quickly."

And that was exactly what he did: act quickly. The first 100 days of his presidency are famous for all the things that got done. Congress was on vacation when Roosevelt took office. He called Congress back into session and quickly began to take action.

FDR was a pragmatist—someone who believes in whatever will work. Soon new programs and laws were pouring out of Washington. "It is common sense to take a method and try it," said Roosevelt. "If it fails, admit it frankly and try another. But above all, try something."

And he also said, "The only thing we have to fear is fear itself."

FDR put together a group of advisers. Newspaper reporters called them "the brain trust." Many were college professors. They were new to government, but they had ideas, intelligence, and a desire to help their country. They worked hard. Washington became an exciting place for idealistic, energetic citizen workers.

"Let me first assert my firm belief that the only thing we have to fear is fear itself," said the new president in his inaugural address. "I shall ask the Congress for...broad executive power to wage a war against the emergency, as great as the power that would be given to me if we were invaded by a foreign foe," he said, and the people cheered.

Most of Roosevelt's New Deal ideas were not really new. They were the old Progressive ideas in a new package.

Still, the New Deal changed America profoundly. Roosevelt probably saved American capitalism, even as he changed some of its habits. The New Deal made the government an active participant in citizens' lives.

Here are some things the New Deal did:

- ended most child labor
- regulated the stock market
- made bank deposits safe
- helped make employers pay fair wages to employees
- encouraged workers' unions
- limited hours of work
- helped farmers, brought electricity into rural areas
- and gave Americans an old-age pension policy called Social Security

The Tennessee Valley Authority brought electricity to rural areas throughout a large part of the southeastern United States. ▶

New Ideas for a New Deal

Here are some of the best-known New Deal programs and agencies (a star means the program still exists today):

Securities and Exchange Commission (SEC)*
Regulates the stock market.

Federal Deposit Insurance Corporation (FDIC)*
Insures bank deposits so people won't lose everything in the case of a bank failure.

Works Progress Administration (WPA)
Between 1935 and 1939, the WPA gave work to 8.5 million people. WPA workers built highways, cleared slums, and labored in rural areas. Writers were paid to write regional guidebooks and compile oral histories. Painters painted murals in public buildings; musicians organized orchestras; actors brought plays to communities that had never experienced live theater.

Civilian Conservation Corps (CCC)
Gave jobs to more than 2 million young men in the nation's parklands, building roads, trails, cabins, and campgrounds.

Tennessee Valley Authority (TVA)
Built five dams along the Tennessee River and provided cheap electric power, flood control, and irrigation water to seven states.

Public Works Administration (PWA)
Built New York's Triborough Bridge and Lincoln Tunnel; Oregon's Coastal Highway; Texas's port of Brownsville; the road between Key West and mainland Florida; and the University of New Mexico's library.

Civilian Works Administration (CWA)
Employed more than 4 million men and women. Opera singers were sent to the Ozark mountains (where none had ever sung before); teachers kept rural schools open; Native Americans restocked the Kodiak Islands with snowshoe rabbits.

Social Security Act*
Established old-age pensions, unemployment benefits, and welfare benefits for the elderly, children, and the handicapped.

◀ Civilian Conservation Corps workers built and improved parks in almost every state.

◀ A Works Progress Administration poster credits the agency with "rebuilding the self-respect of 1,500,000 American workmen."

A 1944 campaign poster, produced by the Congress of Industrial Organizations, depicts Roosevelt's wide support among many groups of Americans. ▶

OUR FRIEND

NATIONAL CITIZENS POLITICAL ACTION COMMITTEE

CCC workers prepare to plant trees in the nation's parklands. The Corps planted an estimated 3 billion trees nationwide. ▼

In order to put people to work, the New Deal sent young people out of doors and paid them to plant trees, build parks, and fight fires. It paid painters to paint murals, writers to write books, and musicians to play and create music. Needy people were given money for food and shelter.

Roosevelt did something else—something that was really new and that people in power almost never do without a battle. He shared power with those who had never held it before.

From the country's earliest days, the leaders of the United States had mostly been drawn from one group: white Protestant men of northern European descent. Franklin Roosevelt was part of that white-Protestant-male traditional aristocracy of privilege. But he opened its doors. He included in positions of government power those who had been excluded: women, blacks, eastern Europeans, southern Europeans, American Indians, Catholics, and Jews. He began a process that soon added Muslims, Buddhists, Hindus, and all who are citizens. He rejected the idea of an aristocracy of birth and replaced it with the goal of an aristocracy of talent.

For doing it, some called him "a traitor to his class." Some in the business world hated him, too. Business leaders had been the heroes of the Roaring Twenties. Calvin Coolidge had said, "The business of America is business." The Depression changed all that. Now Roosevelt was the popular hero, and the American people were demanding that business be regulated for the public good.

But the Supreme Court began vetoing New Deal legislation. FDR, fighting back, tried to add extra justices to the bench—justices who would be friendly to his New Deal policies. Roosevelt's strategy, called "court-packing," was a poor idea. It cost the New Deal support and slowed its momentum.

Before the New Deal, government had been expected to provide conditions that would help business. But government was expected to do nothing for the workers who made business profits possible. With Roosevelt, many laws were passed to help workers, farmers, and ordinary citizens. Government money was spent on the poor. Some people didn't like that idea. But others understood that, if it was done wisely, the nation would be stronger and better for it.

A Woman in the Cabinet

In 1933 President Roosevelt appointed Frances Perkins as his secretary of labor. She served for 12 years, in all his administrations, and was the first woman cabinet member.

Frances Perkins, the first woman to serve as a cabinet member ▶

The Art of the Depression

▲ William H. Johnson's *Lil Sis* is in the National Museum of American Art in Washington, D.C.

Artists were especially hard hit by the Depression. When people are having difficulty finding enough money for food, they don't have any left for the arts. Franklin Roosevelt supported a program that put writers, painters, actors, sculptors, and musicians to work. This program, run by the Works Progress Administration (WPA), may have been the most creative idea our government has ever put into practice. This wasn't welfare. The artists had to produce work that the government then owned. They weren't paid much, but they earned respect. In the eight years the program existed, 5,000 visual artists created 108,000 paintings, 18,000 pieces of sculpture, and 2,500 murals. Those works were placed in schools, libraries, post offices, and other government buildings (where you can see many of them today).

One of the WPA muralists was Aaron Douglas. He painted *Aspects of Negro Life* for the 135th Street branch of the New York Public Library.

Music and religion inform Aaron Douglas's *Aspects of Negro Life: From Slavery Through Reconstruction* (1934), part of a four-part mural. ▼

William H. Johnson also found work with the WPA. Before the Depression—back in 1918, in fact—Johnson had arrived in New York from South Carolina. Like many African Americans, he headed for Harlem, an exciting place to be, especially for writers and musicians who were creating important works during the Harlem Renaissance. Then, lured by Europe (as were

▲ Jacob Lawrence made a powerful social statement in his portrayals of black migration from South to North, as in this 1937 painting titled *Moving Day*.

"I got on the WPA. Now that gave me a certain kind of freedom.... Our great artists like Rothko, de Kooning, Franz Kline…had that moment of peace…to continue with their work. I think it's a highlight of our American history."

The WPA provided by far the most support for artists, but other government agencies also employed artists during the Depression. For example, the Farm Security Administration hired six photographers to document the effects of the Depression on farmers. Dorothea Lange was one of them. Her photographs, and many of those of her colleagues, were intended for government records, but turned out to be works of art. Lange was among the best of the "social photographers" who captured the stark reality of hard times during the Depression. Another standout was Walker Evans, whose photographs capture faces that linger and haunt long after you view them.

Dorothea Lange's 1936 photograph *Migrant Mother* depicts Florence Thompson, who was 32 years old and had 10 children. ▼

many American artists), in 1926 Johnson went to Paris. From there he moved on to Denmark, where he married a potter. They went to Africa to study African art. By this time Johnson had developed his own style of painting. It was very sophisticated although it looked simple. He was inspired by primitive art and the work of some European artists called Expressionists.

One of the greatest of the black artists who worked under WPA was Jacob Lawrence. He painted 60 small paintings that tell the story of black migration from South to North, from field to factory. They are among the most powerful social statements in American art.

Jackson Pollock, from Cody, Wyoming, was a WPA artist who later went on to develop a bold abstract style. The sculptor Louise Nevelson said,

Twentieth-Century Monsters

On the very day of Franklin Delano Roosevelt's first inauguration, the day he told America that "the only thing we have to fear is fear itself," something fearful was happening in Germany. It would change the fate of the world. The Reichstag (RIKES-tahg)—Germany's congress—was deciding to give absolute government power to the German chancellor, Adolf Hitler.

Imagine a country letting its meanest, worst people take charge. Imagine giving those kinds of people the power of life and death over the whole nation. Imagine a nation where children are taught to be tattletales and tell the secret police about anyone who protests—even their parents. Imagine a nation that burns the books of its greatest writers because it fears and hates ideas and truth. Imagine a nation that kills people because it doesn't like their religion or their ideas, or because they are handicapped. That's what happened in Germany in the 1930s.

Germany no longer even attempted to be a democracy. It willingly became a dictatorship—the most evil dictatorship in recorded history.

Adolf Hitler used dramatic staging and huge rallies to promote his own importance. ▶

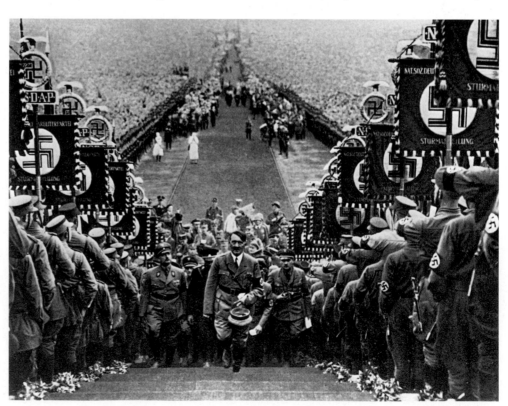

(Although the dictatorship in Soviet Russia was almost as bad.) The Germans used their intelligence and skill to create factories of death. They allowed their government to do unspeakable deeds. Some Germans did not approve, but few spoke out. To do so meant risking their lives.

But in March 1933, most people in America paid no attention to what was happening in Germany.

The Depression seemed more important. Adolf Hitler? He was a little man with a black brush mustache and dark straight hair that fell into his face. He strutted about raising his arm in a straight salute and shrieking his speeches. He didn't seem evil; he seemed silly.

The German people didn't find him silly. They were still angry about the war they had lost. Their leaders and historians had misled them about the causes of the Great War. They had been told that Germany was no more to blame for the start of the First World War than any other nation. That wasn't true. But the Germans believed it; they thought the rest of the world had picked on them. They thought the Versailles Treaty—the treaty that had ended the Great War—was unfair. They were humiliated by the terms of peace. Germany was not allowed to have a large army, navy, or air force. Germany was to make large cash payments—called "reparations" (rep-uh-RAY-shuns)—to the winners to help pay back the costs of the war. Germany was made to say that it was totally to blame for the war.

Since most Germans thought they were no more to blame for the war than others, they were furious, especially about those payments. As it turned out, we lent Germany much more than they ever paid. But most German citizens didn't know that.

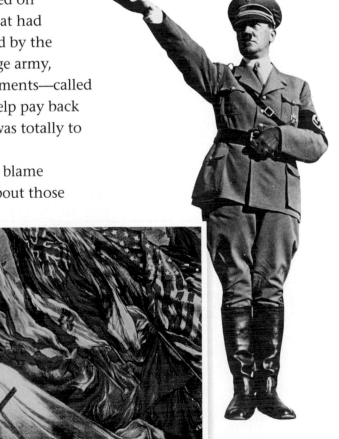

The Nazi salute became a symbol of Hitler's regime. ▼

The flags of the Allies press down on Germany's leader at the end of World War I, illustrating how the German people saw the Treaty of Versailles as a humiliating defeat at the hands of the bullying Allies. ▶

▲ In Berlin in 1930, impoverished Germans wait in a soup line.

Poverty forced whole families in Tokyo to move into slums. ▼

Germany's citizens were angry and unhappy. Their country was in awful shape economically. Soon after the war, Germany suffered a time of incredible inflation. The government began printing lots of money (partly to pay those reparations). Printing presses ran day and night. When you print a lot of currency, soon none of it is worth much. Prices in Germany rose beyond belief. In 1923, a Hershey chocolate bar cost 150,000 German marks (in the United States the same chocolate bar cost a nickel). German money was almost worthless. Buying a loaf of bread might take a bucketful of bills. People lost all their savings. They had to use up everything they had just to pay the rent. Then, after they had finally got the inflation under control, the Great Depression set in worldwide. Unemployment became a big problem.

What the German people wanted was a leader: someone who could lead them out of the economic mess, someone who could make them feel good about themselves. During this Depression era, people in other countries were looking for strong leaders, too. The Americans chose Franklin Delano Roosevelt. The Germans turned to Adolf Hitler.

They made a big mistake. That mistake would cost them and the rest of the world grief beyond imagining. Their leader was an evil genius who captured his countrymen and women in a web of words and convinced them that he could solve all their problems. He told them that others were to blame for Germany's troubles. He told them that Germany was greater than any other nation and meant to rule the world. He told them that other peoples should be their slaves. He told them that they must love their "fatherland"—Germany—before all else. He told them that they must not worry about right and wrong, because anything Germany did would be right. He told them that *might makes right*—and most believed him.

Hitler wasn't the only one who preached the gospel of nationalism—that loving your nation was more important than loving truth and right actions. Militant nationalism was a 20th-century disease.

In Japan, a military dictatorship took control of the nation and began stomping on its neighbors. The Japanese, too, were suffering from economic depression. They thought they needed more room for their growing population.

◀ The ancient Great Wall of China, built to protect China from invasion, could not keep Japanese forces from invading in 1939.

They began by attacking China with a ferocity that is still hard to believe. In a massive campaign of terror, millions of civilians were tortured and killed. Just as in Germany, the Japanese rulers told the people they were a superior race and destined to rule others.

In Spain, a strongman named Francisco Franco muscled his way to power, although many Spaniards (and other Europeans, and some Americans, too) fought against him.

In Italy, a pompous dictator named Benito Mussolini took control of the government. Mussolini was a bully, and, like all bullies, he picked on those who were weak. He sent Italian forces to Ethiopia. There, Italian tanks, machine guns, and airplanes attacked brave Ethiopians, who fought back with spears and lances.

Russia's dictator, Joseph Stalin, killed millions of his own people—anyone who he believed might threaten his rule. His kind of government, he said, would soon conquer the world.

Mussolini called his political movement *Fascism*. Hitler named his *Nazism*, for National Socialism. In Russia, the forces of evil took charge in the name of *communism*. These were all *totalitarian* forms of government. They were the opposite of

Spain's Francisco Franco ▼

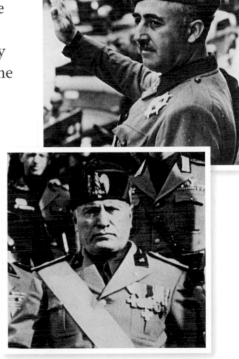

▲ Italy's Benito Mussolini

▲ A migrant family in Texas

Charles Lindbergh urged Americans not to fight Hitler. He let his antiwar feelings make him do and say things he would later regret. He allowed himself to be used by the Nazis. The America First Committee that he supported got financial aid from Nazi Germany.

democracy. In a totalitarian state, individual people don't matter—only the state is important.

Why did good people listen to these terrible leaders? Why did some modern nations become gangster nations? Those are questions that are hard to answer. It didn't happen here; it didn't happen in England. Were we just lucky, or did our democratic tradition give us the strength to resist the evil thinkers?

The Depression brought grave problems to the people of the United States. In 1933, hogs were selling for only 2½ cents a pound in the Midwest. One farmer had to sell all his hogs to pay his rent for a month. Another farmer sold a wagonload of oats to buy a pair of shoes. Hunger and malnutrition were serious problems in the '30s. Many Americans were angry and desperate. It is not surprising that some of them, too, listened to horrid voices. They needed to blame someone for their problems, so they paid attention to the Ku Klux Klan; to the German-American Bund (BOONT), which was inspired by the Nazis; to a radio preacher, Father Coughlin, who spewed out a message of hate; and to others. A few Americans no longer believed that "all men are created equal." A few wanted to throw out the Bill of Rights. But most Americans rejected the philosophies of wickedness.

Why did we escape the 20th-century virus of totalitarianism? Was it New Deal leadership? Was it our tradition of liberty and democracy? What do you think? Could it happen here?

Revolution in Russia

After the Bolshevik Revolution in 1917, the old Russian empire became a collection of republics called the Union of Soviet Socialist Republics—the U.S.S.R., or Soviet Union. The republics were not all Russian— they included Central Asian Muslim peoples such as the Uzbeks, the Tajiks, and the Azerbaijanis; Caucasian peoples such as the Georgians and Armenians; and Baltic peoples such as Latvians and Estonians. These countries were supposed to be independent, but they were not. They were controlled by Russia, the Soviet Union's largest and most powerful republic. Many in America referred to the U.S.S.R. as Russia, or Soviet Russia.

▲ The flag of the Soviet Union, adopted in 1923

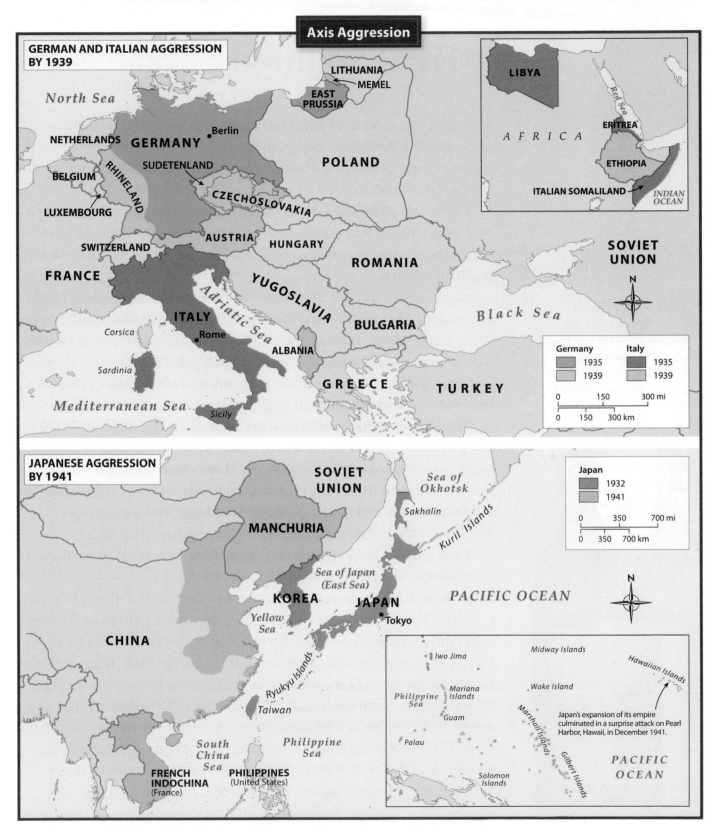

Axis Aggression

GERMAN AND ITALIAN AGGRESSION BY 1939

North Sea

LITHUANIA
MEMEL
EAST PRUSSIA

NETHERLANDS
GERMANY
• Berlin

POLAND

BELGIUM
RHINELAND
SUDETENLAND

LUXEMBOURG
CZECHOSLOVAKIA

SWITZERLAND
AUSTRIA
HUNGARY

FRANCE
ROMANIA

SOVIET UNION

YUGOSLAVIA
Adriatic Sea
ITALY
Corsica
• Rome

BULGARIA
Black Sea

Sardinia
ALBANIA

GREECE
TURKEY

Mediterranean Sea
Sicily

LIBYA
Red Sea
AFRICA
ERITREA
ETHIOPIA
ITALIAN SOMALILAND
INDIAN OCEAN

Germany
1935
1939

Italy
1935
1939

0   150   300 mi
0   150   300 km

JAPANESE AGGRESSION BY 1941

SOVIET UNION

Sea of Okhotsk

MANCHURIA

Sakhalin

Kuril Islands

Sea of Japan (East Sea)

KOREA
JAPAN
• Tokyo

PACIFIC OCEAN

Japan
1932
1941

0   350   700 mi
0   350   700 km

Yellow Sea

CHINA

Ryukyu Islands

Taiwan

South China Sea

Philippine Sea

FRENCH INDOCHINA (France)

PHILIPPINES (United States)

Iwo Jima
Midway Islands
Hawaiian Islands

Philippine Sea
Mariana Islands
Wake Island

Guam

Japan's expansion of its empire culminated in a surprise attack on Pearl Harbor, Hawaii, in December 1941.

Palau

Marshall Islands

PACIFIC OCEAN

Solomon Islands
Gilbert Islands

▲ The Axis nations of Germany, Italy, and Japan began relentless campaigns of expansion during the 1920s and 1930s. Their aggression set the stage for the death and destruction of World War II.

CHAPTER 7

A Final Solution

In Germany, as soon as the Nazis came to power, Jews were persecuted for no reason except their religion. Jews who weren't even religious were persecuted. Having a Jewish grandparent was enough to get you into trouble.

There was an evil disease in the world that had been around for a very long time. It was called "anti-Semitism." It was hatred of Jews. No one was quite sure where it came from—although the subject was studied endlessly.

No question about it, Jews have been troublesome to some kings and priests. Jews believe that every person is equal before God, which, if you think about it, means that a king is no different from a peasant. Now that is a nonconforming idea. It must have been maddening to some authorities. Imagine where it might lead if everyone thought that way. (Just where might it lead? To democracy, eventually?)

The Jews are people with a powerful book. It is a freedom document, written in Hebrew, and called a "bible." It tells stories that make people think and ask questions. It tells how, a long time ago, the Jews escaped from Egypt, where they were slaves of the pharaoh. It tells of Queen Esther and how she saved the Jews when they refused to bow to the king's agent, wicked Haman (HAY-mun).

That Bible became the starting point for a new religion, called Christianity, and for another, called Islam.

At first, Christians were persecuted. Then, in the 4th century C.E., the Roman emperor Constantine became a Christian. Before long, most Europeans were Christians. But not the Jews. The Jews stayed with their beliefs. They wouldn't change their religion even for the emperor or the pope. It was frustrating to those in charge. Others might catch their independent ideas. So some of those in power hated them and blamed them for whatever was wrong at the time. If there was a plague, it was the Jews' fault; if there was an economic disaster, it was the Jews' fault. Finally, many of Europe's Christians went on religious wars called Crusades. The crusaders' aim was to recapture Jerusalem from the Muslims; but anyone not a Christian was considered an *infidel*—a heretic—and was liable to

Pictured here is a beautiful Torah (TOHR-uh) scroll. The Torah consists of the first five books of the Hebrew Bible, including Genesis and Exodus. It contains the basic religious ideas of Judaism. ▼

▲ When Christian armies captured Jerusalem in 1099, many soldiers murdered
Jewish residents and stole their property.

be murdered. Thousands of Jews died, and Jewish property was up
for grabs among the crusaders.

In Spain, in 1492, Jews were told they had to leave the country
(Jews had already been expelled from many other parts of Europe).
They couldn't take their possessions with them. It was a windfall for
the rest of the Spaniards. Jews who converted to Christianity were
able to stay in Spain, but some were tried by a religious court called
the Inquisition, and, if they were found guilty of not being sincere
Christians, they were burned alive. That was the opposite of what real
Christianity stands for, but most people didn't question the rulers and
priests who were in command.

▲ An ancient tapestry depicts the Jewish symbols of the Menorah and the Star of David.

So anti-Semitism stayed in the air. It was still mainly about that nonconformism. Then, in 1517, Martin Luther came into conflict with the Catholic Church and things got complicated. The Catholics, and each of the new Protestant sects, seemed to believe that they alone had the only true religion; that led to centuries of religious wars. Christians were killing Christians—as well as Jews. Hatred and killing in the name of God shouldn't make sense, but it seemed to to some people (who couldn't have been thinking deeply).

There was another factor that produced anti-Semitism. It was economic. Jews were often successful and provided competition. That may have made some people jealous or annoyed.

Then, toward the end of the 18th century, things began to change. After the French Revolution (in 1789), Jews, in one nation after another, were emancipated. They entered Europe's mainstream. People who had been locked in ghettoes were suddenly let out and began a period of great achievement. Especially in Germany, Austria, and Hungary, Jews flocked to the universities, and soon many of them were doctors, lawyers, bankers, store owners, newspaper writers, musicians, teachers, and political leaders. Although Jews made up only about 1 percent of the German population, they won one-quarter of all Germany's Nobel prizes in the first third of the 20th century. Some Germans were proud of that achievement, but others saw it as a problem.

There was something else. It had to do with a science—at least some people thought it was a science. It was racism, and today we think of it as a false, or pseudo (SU-doe), science. But, in the 19th century, some thinkers (who believed in what they were doing) divided the world's peoples into races and then said that some races were better than others. They even said that race determines blood, and character, and brain size. They said that the Jews were an evil race that was polluting Aryan (white northern European) blood. They said that people of color were inferior to whites. Since this theory was supposed to be scientific, there were many who believed them.

◄ This poster depicts an idealized version of German men, members of a so-called "master race."

Hitler used that idea of racism, and bad blood, and the old anti-Semitic virus to explain Germany's problems. It was convenient. Whatever was wrong must be the fault of the Jews. Inflation? Depression? The Treaty of Versailles? It was all because of the Jews, said Hitler. He was an astonishing speaker. People were swept up by his words; they believed him. It was easier than blaming themselves.

Besides, many Jews had good jobs and nice homes. All their property was inviting. Hitler was soon giving it away.

Germany went farther down the road of wickedness than any nation in history. The Nazis used the technology of the modern world for purposes of murder. They built factories for killing. Then they hunted down the Jews of Europe, packed them in railroad cars, and sent them to be slaughtered. They didn't just kill Jews. Hitler hated Slavs (who lived in eastern Europe), gypsies, people who were crippled, and anyone who didn't agree with him. The Nazis killed as many of those people as they

Children stand behind a barbed-wire fence at the Nazi concentration camp at Auschwitz in southern Poland. ▼

Jews being arrested in 1943 ▼

▲ Jews were required to wear a Star of David patch with the word *Jew*.

▲ Abuse, starvation, and death awaited many victims of the Holocaust—the Nazi campaign of systematic mass murder of Europe's Jews and others considered to be "inferior."

could. They enslaved others. It made Hitler and his terror troops feel powerful (and it set an example for other dictators in the future). Because of what was happening to the Jews and Hitler's other victims, all of Europe shivered. People knew that after the Jews were gone it could happen to them.

Did all this have anything to do with the United States?

That is a good question.

Suppose you see someone beating up someone else. Really beating her up. She is going to end up in the hospital or maybe dead.

What do you do? This isn't your fight. If you try to break it up you almost certainly will get slugged. Should you call the police? Should you stay out of it? If someone is killed it won't be your fault. Or will it?

Are we responsible for others? Do you agree that "He who permits evil, commits evil"?

In 1939, 20,000 children—all under 14—were in danger in Germany. Hitler wished to get rid of them. He was willing to let them leave the country. Many were Jewish; some were not. Quakers, Jews, Catholics, and members of other American church groups agreed to take responsibility for them. It would not cost the government any money. Surely America would accept them.

Guests or Prisoners?

After 1943 (until war's end), no Jews entered the United States except for 874 "guests of the president" who were denied visas, sent to an internment camp in Oswego, New York, kept behind barbed wire, and told they would have to leave the country as soon as the war was over. Some had close relatives in the U.S. One refugee, whose paralyzed wife lived on Long Island, could not visit her even at holiday time.

More than 55,000 immigrant quota spots for eastern Europeans went unfilled in 1944. During the war years, about 100,000 German prisoners of war—mostly Nazi soldiers—were safe in the United States.

This is the land of promise. The land built on a spirit of generosity. The land that, from the days of the Pilgrims, has been a place of refuge for the persecuted of other nations.

Those who had founded this nation, and written its Constitution, had been clear about it. Although they were much alike—white, male, Protestant, and of English descent—the Founders didn't limit the nation to people like themselves. For they were unselfish in spirit and very wise. They believed they were creating something new on earth, a generous nation that would find strength in diversity. A nation that would take peoples from all over the world and allow them to become a new people—an American people—more varied in its roots than any before it.

The Founders offered the gift of citizenship, not just to their kinsmen, not just to the strong, or the handsome, or the rich, but fully and equally to all who came here to live.

The nation grew, and its citizens understood what was intended. Under the Statue of Liberty they carved the words *Give me your tired, your poor, your huddled masses yearning to breathe free.* Men, women, and children—from all over the world—came to this "promised land." Many were refugees—people fleeing tyranny and persecution.

▲ The United States, which has often welcomed immigrants fleeing from tyranny and oppression, has sometimes lapsed into periods of nativism and prejudice against immigrants.

Of course the children Hitler was threatening with death would be welcome in America. Or would they?

There was another tradition here. It was not the tradition of Jefferson, Washington, and Madison. It was a spirit of greed and selfishness.

It was that selfish spirit that had caused Alien and Sedition acts to be passed soon after the nation was founded. It was that spirit that had caused men to rise in Congress and say that slavery was a "positive good." It was the spirit behind the Know-Nothing Party and the nativists. It was the spirit of the Ku Klux Klan and the only-one-race-allowed country club. It was mean-spirited. It was anti-American, but it was there.

Freedom of Conscience

In Virginia's Statute for Religious Freedom, Thomas Jefferson wrote: *Be it enacted by the General Assembly, that no man shall…suffer on account of his religious opinions or belief.*

John Adams, discussing the subject of religion and government was, as usual, blunt: *Congress shall never meddle with religion other than to say their own prayers.*

And James Madison said: *Religion and government will both exist in greater purity, the less they are mixed together.*

The Founding Fathers were clear: *ours was to be a nation founded on the idea of separation of church and state. There are no religious restrictions on citizenship in the Constitution.*

The doomed children
of Auschwitz ▶

Here is what Abraham Lincoln wrote in 1855:

As a nation we began by declaring that "all men are created equal."
We now practically read it, "all men are created equal except
Negroes." When the Know-Nothings get control, it will read "all men
are created equal except Negroes and foreigners and Catholics."
When it comes to this, I shall prefer emigrating to some country
where they make no pretense of loving liberty.

The Imperial Wizard of the Ku Klux Klan, in 1923, said: *Negroes,*
Catholics, and Jews are the undesirable elements in America. The Imperial
Wizard was a bigot, but some people listened to him. They didn't
know their history. Maybe they hadn't read the famous letter George
Washington wrote the Jews of Newport, Rhode Island. In it, he said:

The government of the United States...gives to bigotry no sanction,
to persecution no assistance.

In 1924, Congress passed a racist immigration bill. Its aim was to
keep Asians, Jews, blacks, and people who can't speak English out
of America.

Anti-Semitism and xenophobia (zen-uh-FO-bee-ya—
"anti-foreignism") had infected some Americans. Some of the people
with the disease were in Congress, the State Department, and other
government offices. Did they realize they were being un-American?

Most Americans are hospitable. Eighty-five newspapers wrote editorials urging Congress to pass a bill letting in those 20,000 children from Germany. Citizens offered their homes to the young refugees. Leaders of church, labor, and social organizations spoke out. But not loudly enough.

The head of a powerful group, the American Coalition of Patriotic Societies, told Congress to "protect the youth of America from this foreign invasion." He shouted the message of the racists. There was fear in the world, and a depression, and Congress listened.

Isn't anti-Semitism just a Jewish problem? No. It is a human problem. People who hate become hateful. A nation that allows bigotry and persecution is diminished by it. In 1939, the U.S. government gave sanction to bigotry and assistance to persecution. Those children were not allowed into the United States.

Hitler now knew that no one would rescue the children. He felt free to build death camps. That is where most of those 20,000 children—and a girl named Anne Frank—ended their lives.

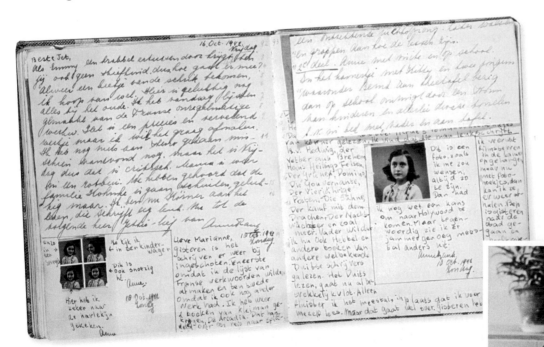

Anne Frank writes at her desk before her family was forced into hiding. ▼

▲ Anne Frank and her family fled Germany when the Nazis began to persecute Jews. They went into hiding in Amsterdam, in the Netherlands. While in hiding, Anne kept a diary (pictured above). Anne and her family were betrayed and arrested. She died in March 1945 at the Bergen-Belsen concentration camp in Germany. She was 15 years old. Her diary, with its hopeful message, was found and was published in 1947.

War and the Scientists

There were some people who felt they had to see Roosevelt. But the president couldn't see everyone who wanted to see him—especially with a war on.

It was a group of scientists. They had something very important to tell the president. How could they get to him? If they had gone to Mrs. Roosevelt they might have had no problem. But they didn't think of that. They met and planned and worried.

Then someone got a bright idea. There was one scientist whom Roosevelt would listen to. Almost anyone in the world would listen to him. He was Albert Einstein, and he was the greatest scientist of the 20th century and one of the greatest scientists of all time. He had discovered the theory of relativity. That theory changed the way science looks at the world.

Einstein was born in Germany. Because he was Jewish he had to escape from that country, and he did. He became a fellow of the Institute for Advanced Study in Princeton, New Jersey, and an American citizen. Other scientists fled the evil regimes in Germany and Italy, too. Hitler lost their fine minds and talents. Britain and the United States gained them.

Some of those scientists knew that the Germans were working on a secret weapon. It was more powerful than anything the world had ever known. If the Germans developed it, they would probably win the war and rule the world. Roosevelt had to be told.

But scientists who talked of secret weapons sounded like dreamers. Roosevelt was busy with important practical matters. He needed to strengthen the army and navy. He needed warships and carriers and tanks and planes. He had a depression to fight, too. Secret weapons? Super bombs? Wasn't that the stuff of science fiction?

Einstein's friend Leo Szilard (SILL-ard) urged him to write a letter to the president. Then Szilard convinced Alexander Sachs, a businessman and New Deal adviser, to deliver the letter. Sachs told FDR about the Germans' secret weapon. The president didn't seem to be paying attention. He must have had all those other things on his mind. Sachs was desperate. How could he get the president to pay attention?

Albert Einstein was a theoretical physicist who ranks with Galileo and Newton as one of the great thinkers who have helped us understand the universe. He published his theories of relativity in 1905 and 1916. In 1921 he won a Nobel Prize. In 1933 he wrote *Why War?* with Sigmund Freud (the father of psychoanalysis, and also a Jew).

$E = mc^2$

▲ Albert Einstein—his revolutionary theories changed the modern world.

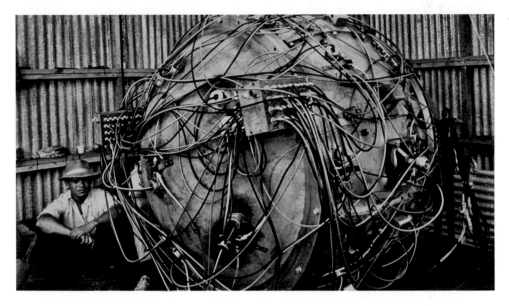

Finally Sachs remembered that Roosevelt loved history. He used that knowledge. He told Roosevelt that the French emperor Napoleon was fighting the British when he was told about an American inventor, Robert Fulton, who had built a ship powered by steam. It could carry troops. Napoleon didn't pay attention. Steam power? All he knew about was sails. Roosevelt realized that if Napoleon had listened he might have been able to invade England and win his war.

Roosevelt didn't want to make the mistake Napoleon had made. He was ready to listen to Sachs. He was ready to read Einstein's letter. He decided that the United States should work on the secret weapon and try to develop it before the Germans did.

It was an enormous decision. It would be very costly. It was a race against time. The scientists told Roosevelt that they intended to split tiny particles of matter—the nuclei of atoms—and that would release vast amounts of energy.

They could use that energy to make the most powerful weapon the world had ever seen. Roosevelt was convinced. The president made the decision to let the scientists go ahead with their plans. The project was top secret. Not even the vice president knew about it.

The Manhattan Project

The top secret project to make the world's most powerful weapon was called the Manhattan Project. Much of the work was done at a base on an isolated mesa in New Mexico. J. Robert Oppenheimer led the Manhattan Project. Leo Szilard, a Hungarian-born physicist, figured out that when a nucleus breaks apart it can start a chain reaction splitting other nuclei and setting off an enormous explosion. That's called nuclear fission.

In a squash court under a grandstand at the University of Chicago, Leo Szilard, Enrico Fermi, and some other physicists layered uranium and graphite into a 24-foot-high sandwich. There, in 1942, the world's first planned nuclear reaction took place under tight controls.

Fighting Wolves

You are probably wondering how three nations—Germany, Italy, and Japan—could be a threat to the whole world. Have you ever thought about how a wolf terrorizes a flock of sheep? A lone wolf doesn't attack a big flock. He picks them off one by one. Give him enough time and he can kill them all.

Germany, Italy, and Japan were wolves. They were powerful. They thought they could devour the world's nations, one by one. They believed most other countries—especially the democracies—were weaklings.

They had good reason to believe that. In a democracy, everyone's ideas are heard. Sometimes democracies have a hard time acting quickly, because so many individuals and groups are debating each other. In the 1930s there were strong *isolationist* voices in America. They said that the oceans—the Pacific and the Atlantic—protected us from danger. They said we didn't need to pay attention to what was going on in the rest of the world. Some of the isolationists were selfish. They didn't even want to help victims of the war.

Others who were *pacifists* didn't think it right to fight any war. They believed that if we behaved peacefully others might do the same.

Still others—in the military—were attached to old ways of thinking. They thought that battleships could protect us. Our battleships were huge. Some were 800 feet long. Imagine three football fields. (A football field is 300 feet long, so chop off a bit.) Float that picture, and add a crew of about 2,800 men, and guns that fire shells 20 miles or more, which was farther than any other weapon of the time. Battleships were much feared.

A few voices disagreed. They said that air power had changed all the rules of war. The oceans were no longer enough protection. Colonel William ("Billy") Mitchell of the U.S. Army said we needed to build up our air force. He said we needed to build aircraft carriers for our navy. An aircraft carrier is a floating airfield

Isolate means "to separate from others." Isolationists believe a nation should stay out of world affairs. Some of the World War II isolationists were the same people who prevented the United States from joining the League of Nations after the Great War.

Isolationists wanted to keep the United States out of World War II. ▼

KEEP U.S. OUT OF WAR BE NEUTRAL

that carries its own airplanes. It is really big. (A bit longer than a battleship, and much wider.)

Mitchell pestered everyone: congressmen, army officers, naval officers, newspapermen. They got annoyed. Only a few people thought air power was important. Because he criticized his superiors in public, Mitchell was finally court-martialed and thrown out of the army. Some people said his ideas were laughable.

The official program of the Army–Navy football game, in November of 1941, showed a picture of the battleship *Arizona* with this caption: *Despite the claims of air enthusiasts no battleship has yet been sunk by bombs*. (That was meant as a slap at Billy Mitchell and those who agreed with him.)

The USS *New Jersey* was a 45,000-ton, super-modern battleship. Some in the military believed battleships could protect the United States in any war; others argued that the nation must develop air power as well. ▼

▲ President Roosevelt had to fight both the Great Depression and Congress to build the nation's military. When the country finally turned to war production, the results were astonishing.

The United States had become weak militarily. We listened to the isolationists. It was partly for a good reason: we hated war. In 1941, our military force ranked 19th in the world, smaller than that of Belgium. At the same time, the armies and navies of Germany, Italy, and Japan had become strong.

Once its economy had recovered from the terrible effects of the Great War, Germany ignored the Versailles Treaty. It built a powerful army and air force. It turned out hundreds of submarines. Japan's naval fleet was awesome. Only a few people seemed concerned. "War could have been prevented," said a British statesman named Winston Churchill. "The malice of the wicked was reinforced by the weakness of the virtuous."

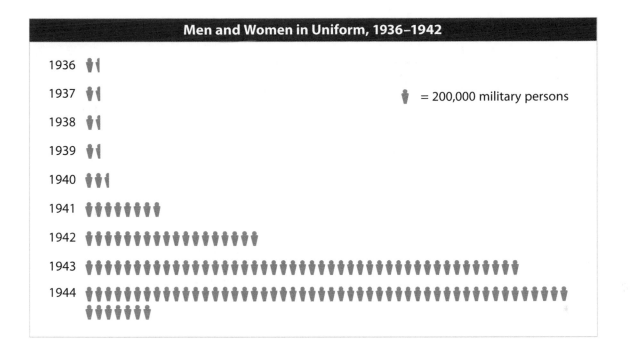

Men and Women in Uniform, 1936–1942

1936

1937   = 200,000 military persons

1938

1939

1940

1941

1942

1943

1944

Roosevelt understood that the totalitarian powers were dangerous. He knew they hoped to rule the world. He took them seriously. The president wanted to build up our armed forces. It wasn't easy to fight the isolationists in Congress. He began by sending war supplies to England. That got our factories going. But we were still behind most other nations and way behind Germany, Italy, and Japan, who were making plans to divide the world among themselves, and were known collectively as the Axis.

Militarily, we were weaklings. However, we had an advantage that the Axis powers didn't consider. It was the very thing they thought gave us a disadvantage. We were a democracy—a nation of free people. When free people set their minds to something, they become a powerful force. It took some time, but we became astonishingly strong.

Whether we wanted it or not, war was coming. We would win this war in our science laboratories and factories as well as on battlefields. The American people had been through a testing period that toughened them for a fight. The testing period was the Depression. We were used to tightening our belts and working hard. All of that, and more, was going to be necessary to win this war. It would be the most awful war in all of history.

Pearl Harbor

It is Sunday, December 7, 1941, and the sun is shining in Washington, D.C. To the morning churchgoers it seems just another bright winter day. At the White House, 31 guests are expected for lunch. There will be guests for dinner, too. None of that is unusual. The White House has become an informal, busy place since the Roosevelts moved in. That was more than eight years ago. FDR was reelected in 1936 and again in 1940. No other president has served more than two terms.

The American people (or most of them, anyway) have great faith in their president. These are dangerous times, and alarming things are happening all around the world. It is important to have a leader who can be trusted.

Hitler has steamrollered his way to some astounding victories. He has taken Austria, and Czechoslovakia, and Poland, and Denmark, and Norway, and Holland, and Belgium. One by one he picked off all those countries. The democracies let him do it. The democratic nations are so sick of war that they are willing to do anything to try to avoid it. What they have actually done is to make the war much worse than it would have been if they had stopped Hitler earlier.

It was when the Nazis marched into Poland that Britain and France finally responded. (Both nations had pledged their help to Poland if it was attacked.) Britain and France went to war.

Nazi troops enter Poland in September 1939. ▶

What they faced was something called *blitzkrieg*. That was the German word for "lightning war," which was a good description. The Germans sped their troops, tanks, and artillery across nations, obliterating them almost before they knew what was happening.

When superbly trained, well-equipped German forces raced into France, the country was overwhelmed. A large British–French army was trapped at Dunkirk, on the English Channel. It looked as if the soldiers were doomed. Then the British government sent out an appeal for boats. Soon fishermen, dentists, grocers, tugboat captains—anyone with a boat that could make it across the Channel—were sailing, back and forth, back and forth, ferrying soldiers to England. They saved an army, but they couldn't save France. On June 14, 1940, German tanks rolled into Paris.

Now almost the only European democracy left is Britain. And Britain is under attack. German bombers are pounding that small island. It looks as if it will go next. Everyone knows that the Nazis plan to invade England. Hitler's goal is world conquest. Americans have plenty of reason to worry.

In Asia, Japan has earlier occupied Manchuria (in 1931) and other parts of China (in 1937) and has just invaded French Indochina

▲ German planes conducted relentless attacks in an attempt to destroy England's cities and morale in preparation for an invasion of Great Britain.

▲ General Hideki Tojo led the military government of Japan.

Nationalist China's old walled capital city, Nanking, was captured by the Japanese in December 1937. The unspeakable horrors of the conquest of the city have come to be known as "the Rape of Nanking."

(now Vietnam, Laos, and Kampuchea) in July 1941. Japan is also threatening Thailand, the Philippines, and other Pacific nations. The United States sends letters to Japan objecting to this aggressive behavior and finally imposes a total trade embargo and freezes Japanese funds in U.S. banks. Inside Japan there is a power struggle between civilian and military leaders.

In the summer, Prime Minister Prince Fumimaro Konoe offers to meet with Roosevelt. The president doesn't understand the importance of the request. He refuses the meeting. Konoe resigns and is replaced by army minister General Hideki Tojo. In Japan, the military is now supreme.

This very day, December 7, Secretary of State Cordell Hull receives a call from two Japanese diplomats. They ask for an emergency meeting. Hull expects to be given the Japanese government's answer to an American peace letter. At the White House, after lunch, the president works on his stamp collection (he began collecting stamps as a boy). His good friend Harry Hopkins is with him; so is his Scottie dog, Fala. They are relaxing. The phone rings. It is close to 2 p.m. Eastern time.

Secretary of the Navy Frank Knox is on the line. His voice is quivering. A message has just been received from Hawaii. This is what it says: AIR RAID ON PEARL HARBOR—THIS IS NOT A DRILL.

Pearl Harbor, in the Hawaiian Islands, is where the Pacific Fleet is headquartered! On Sunday morning ships were lined up in the harbor; their crews were having breakfast, or relaxing, or sleeping. At 7:02 a.m. Hawaiian time, a radar operator saw some blips on his screen. The operator didn't pay attention to them. He thought they were bombers he was expecting from the West Coast.

By 7:55 a.m. he knew better. That was when the first dive bombers—with the red Japanese sun painted on their sides—let their bombs loose on Battleship Row. The battleship *Arizona* gave off a tremendous roar, split in two, and slipped to the bottom of the harbor. That was just the beginning. Almost all the American planes on the island were damaged or destroyed. Most of the warships were crippled or sunk. And about 2,400 soldiers, sailors, and civilians were killed.

At 2:05 p.m. Washington time (which is 8:05 a.m. Hawaiian time), the Japanese envoys arrive at Secretary of State Cordell Hull's door. They are part of an elaborate Japanese plan of deception, but their timing is off. Before the secretary can see them, his phone rings.

It is the president, with the awful news of the Japanese attack. Now Hull is from Tennessee, and he claims he has a Tennessee temper. The stories of what he says to those envoys will differ, but it is known that they leave quickly, with their heads down.

Hull is soon at the White House. So are many government and military officials. Newspaper reporters begin arriving. At 2:25 p.m. the story goes out on newswires to the American people. The reports from Pearl Harbor are humiliating, but that isn't the only bad news. This same day, the Japanese have attacked American and British bases at Midway, Wake Island, Guam, Hong Kong, Singapore, and the Philippines.

It is an astonishing act of aggression. But this president is at his best in a crisis. His advisers are angry, fearful, and frustrated. The president remains calm. He came into office during the nation's worst economic crisis. This is worse: the free world is fighting for survival.

Pearl Harbor is a disaster, but it may also be a lucky break. It unites the nation. There are no more isolationists. Everyone joins the war effort. Pearl Harbor shows the damage that air power can do. It changes people's thinking on that subject.

▲ The USS *Shaw* was one of about 20 ships attacked by the Japanese at Pearl Harbor. The majority of the ships, including the *Shaw*, were repaired and went on to sail again.

A small boat rescues a seaman from the USS *West Virginia*. About 2,400 people were killed in the attack on Pearl Harbor. ▼

The next day the president goes before Congress. The Japanese have launched an "unprovoked and dastardly attack," he says. December 7 is "a date which will live in infamy." He asks Congress to declare war on Japan. Three days later, Japan's allies—Germany and Italy—declare war on the United States. It is World War II. It will make the awful First World War seem like a fire drill. The United States will fight this war against the wolves, maintain its democracy (as it did during the terrible Depression), and remain, as Abraham Lincoln said, the last best hope of Earth.

Two Great Leaders Speak and Inspire

Winston Churchill was an orator who could, and did, inspire a nation. This is part of what he said to the British people on June 4, 1940:

Prime Minister Winston Churchill makes the victory sign. ▼

"We shall go on to the end...we shall fight on the beaches, we shall fight on the landing grounds, we shall fight in the fields and in the streets, we shall fight in the hills; we shall never surrender...until in God's good time, the new world, with all its power and might, steps forth to the rescue and the liberation of the old."

▲ President Franklin Roosevelt used his popular fireside chats to communicate with the American people.

In radio broadcasts called "fireside chats," Franklin Delano Roosevelt liked to talk to the American people as if he were a friend sitting in their living rooms. Usually those chats were filled with humor, but on February 9, 1942, he didn't have anything funny to say:

*"We are now in this war. We are all in it—all the way. Every single man, woman, and child is a partner in the most tremendous undertaking of our American history....
On the road ahead there lies hard work—grueling work—day and night, every hour and every minute. I was about to add that ahead there lies sacrifice for all of us. But it is not correct to use that word. The United States does not consider it a sacrifice to do all one can, to give one's best to our nation, when the nation is fighting for its existence and its future life...."*

"We are now in the midst of a war, not for conquest, not for vengeance, but for a world in which this nation, and all that this nation represents, will be safe for our children.... We are going to win the war and we are going to win the peace that follows."

Taking Sides

This is how the war was fought:

On one side was the Berlin–Rome–Tokyo Axis led by Adolf Hitler, Benito Mussolini, and Japan's premier, General Hideki Tojo.

On the other side were three major Allied forces. Who were they? Who were their leaders?

President Franklin Delano Roosevelt represented the United States. His was already a voice of freedom respected all over the world.

Britain, the second Allied power, was led by Winston Churchill. Like Roosevelt, Churchill had a powerful voice and was inspiring when he spoke. Churchill had an American mother and a father who was a British lord. When he was young he was a poor student, but he got better. He went to Sandhurst—the British West Point—and became an army officer, a good one. He got medals for bravery. Then he became a newspaper reporter, learned to pilot a plane, wrote history books, entered politics, and became a member of Britain's

> Berlin, Rome, and Tokyo are the capitals of which nations?

> President Roosevelt said Four Freedoms were essential for world peace:
>
> - Freedom of speech
> - Freedom of religion
> - Freedom from want
> - Freedom from fear

U.S. Office of War Information posters promoted the need for a united effort by the Allied nations. ▼

▲ Although the Soviet Union's Joseph Stalin was a ruthless dictator, the U.S.S.R. was a valuable ally against Hitler.

Parliament. He was one of the first Englishmen to see the danger of Hitler's Nazi Party and to speak against it. That was when most people in England and America were acting like ostriches. They buried their heads in the sand, closed their ears, and didn't want to hear anything about war.

The third Allied power? Was it France? No. France was under German control. (However, as you know, a free French army was saved at Dunkirk. It was led by General Charles de Gaulle, and it did fight with the Allies.) How about China? Was China the third power? No. China was fighting Japan. And China was in turmoil. Civil war between the Communists and the Nationalists had broken out in China in the 1930s. (That war wouldn't be finally decided until 1949: the Communists would win.)

You may have a hard time believing what the third Allied power was, but here it is: Soviet Russia (the U.S.S.R.). Russia's leader, in 1941, was the dictator Joseph Stalin. He was head of the Soviet Communist Party. He ruled Russia using secret police and terror. Many of his own people hated him. But others were fooled by Stalin. Roosevelt may have been one of them. Dictators often have charm, and Joe Stalin had a lot of charm—when he wanted. But what mattered was that he was fighting Hitler and so were we. As Winston Churchill said, "If Hitler invaded Hell I would make at least a favorable reference to the Devil in the House of Commons."

Russia, however, didn't start out on the Allied team. Here is some background.

In 1939, Hitler and Stalin signed a friendship pact. They said they would not fight each other. They made plans together to march into Poland—one from the east, the other from the west—and to gobble up that nation. They did it. Poland was squashed and divided.

Before the Nazi army marched into Poland, Hitler told his generals:

The victor will not be asked afterward whether or not he told the truth.

In starting and waging war it is not right that matters but victory.

Close your hearts to pity! Act brutally!… The stronger is in the right.

His generals did as they were told.

▲ London's Tower Bridge stands out against a background of smoke and fire during the first mass air raid on the city in September 1940.

That was when France and England finally realized that they couldn't avoid war—although now it would be a difficult one. They had let Germany build a huge military force. At the same time, the free nations had cut their armies and navies. There wasn't a lot anyone could do when Germany marched armies into Belgium, Holland, Luxembourg, and France. The Nazis were winning everywhere.

The German air force—the Luftwaffe (LOOFT-vah-fuh)—soon began dropping bombs on England—tons and tons of bombs.

Then Hitler made some stupid moves. First, he went into Greece and Yugoslavia, where his forces faced some heroic fighters. That stopped Germany for a while. Then Hitler double-crossed Stalin. He decided to invade Russia. That had been his plan all along. He had even written a book, called *Mein Kampf* (it means "my struggle" in German), that told all about his goal of world domination. "No human being has ever declared or recorded what he wanted to do more often than me," he said.

The Nazi blitzkrieg, or lightning war, smashed through Belgium in May 1940. ▼

Anyone who read Hitler's writings knew what he had planned. He said that Germans were the "master race," and that they needed more room and other nations to serve them as slaves. Churchill and Roosevelt paid attention. They knew Hitler was capable and effective, as well as evil. For a long time, most other politicians just didn't take him seriously.

But Hitler didn't intend to share power. The Russians were a threat to his goal of world domination. So, when some of his generals told him not to go into Russia, he didn't listen. He needed oil and wheat and other resources from Russia. Besides, he thought Russia would be an easy victim. So did experts everywhere. The American secretary of war predicted that it would take Germany three months to conquer Russia.

The Germans prepared the most massive army ever assembled. Their forces stretched from Finland to the Black Sea. They attacked with the latest in military equipment: tanks, bombs, and artillery.

At first, the Germans had an easy time of it. The Russians weren't prepared; much of their military equipment was out of date. Hitler instructed the German army to turn Russia into a slave nation. The Nazis murdered millions of Russians.

But check a map and notice the size of Russia. Look at Moscow and Leningrad (which today is called by its old name, St. Petersburg). Those cities are very far north. They are cold places. Winter came early in the fall of 1941. The first snow fell in Moscow on October 2. The Germans weren't prepared for the cold. They got stuck in a Russian winter. It happened to be the coldest winter in 30 years. The temperature dropped to 60° below zero. The German army was far from home and having a hard time getting supplies and food. German soldiers froze. German soldiers starved. So did Russians. It

Back in 1812, Russia's winter had stopped Napoleon. Hitler should have remembered that.

Thousands of German soldiers fell victim to the Russian winter. They faced sub-zero temperatures without winter uniforms, gloves, or boots. ▼

◀ Russian soldiers fought relentlessly against the Nazi invasion. The U.S.S.R. lost more soldiers and civilians in World War II than any other nation.

was a disaster for both sides. But the Russians were at home and able to outlast the hungry, discouraged German army.

FDR sent his friend Harry Hopkins to Russia. "Give us anti-aircraft guns and aluminum and we can fight for three or four years," said Stalin. He was right. We sent guns, aluminum, food, tanks, planes, and more. The Russians gave their lives.

The Russians went all out in their fight against Nazi Germany. No nation fought harder.

No one knows how many Russians died in World War II. Some say 15 million. Some say more. No other country has ever suffered such war losses. Russia was our ally and friend during the world war. But Russia under Soviet communism was a dreadful place. Stalin was a vicious dictator. Stalin expected something for fighting Hitler. What he expected, and got, was domination over the other countries of Eastern Europe. Could Hitler have been destroyed without Stalin's help? Perhaps not. Certainly it would have taken many, many more American and British lives.

World War

Billy Mitchell was right: air power changed war. In World War II more people were killed by bombs or pieces of shells (called "shrapnel") than by bullets. In World War II cities were bombed; huge civilian populations were massacred.

There was something else about air war: it made killing a mechanical act. Imagine being in the infantry. You see the enemy eye to eye; it makes you realize the enemy is just like you—human. Officers know that some soldiers are never able to pull their triggers. They are never able to murder—even to save themselves. But a bomber pilot doesn't see his victims. A bomb can't tell the difference between an enemy soldier and a child on her way to school. It will kill them both.

An enormous number of bombs were dropped—by both sides—during World War II. Billy Mitchell thought air power would eliminate the need for foot soldiers. He was wrong about that. There was still plenty of old-fashioned infantry fighting.

World War II was truly a world war. Here are just a few of the places where American troops fought; see if you can find them in an atlas.

France, Germany, Tunisia, Sicily, Italy, Morocco, Burma, Guam, Malaysia, Philippine Islands, Wake Island

In World War II, bombs that were dropped from airplanes (like these German bombers over London) killed more people and destroyed more property than all the ground fighting. ▼

Now imagine you are a general and you are planning a battle on a Pacific island. Suppose you want to get 15,000 men onto the island and surprise the enemy. How are you going to do it?

A parachute drop?

Maybe, but remember, parachutes make great targets. You'd be better off bringing them in by boat. Many of those islands don't have deep harbors, though. Big ships can't come in close.

Can the soldiers swim in?

Not with their guns and artillery and trucks and tanks and food and ammunition and medical supplies.

We're going to have to invent and develop new kinds of landing equipment and war gear. And we're going to have to do it very fast. We'll design huge landing craft that have big rooms—called "holds"—that can be flooded to form miniature lakes so that boats can zoom out. We'll design other landing ships that will carry tanks and trucks as well as men. We'll design *amphibious* (am-FIB-ee-us) vehicles that will go on land or water. One of the most useful—a truck that swims—will be called a "duck." Another new, tough vehicle—which can handle rough roads, mountain passes, and rutted fields—we'll call a "jeep."

We'll design superb submarines that can stay under water for months at a time. Then we'll design torpedoes and depth charges to destroy submarines. The Axis nations will be doing the same thing. Submarine warfare will be very important in this war. German subs are called "U-boats," and the Atlantic Ocean is full of them.

We're going to do amazing things in medical science so that disease and infection will no longer be the major causes of wartime deaths. The lives of many badly wounded men will be saved.

A *torpedo* is like a giant bullet with a propeller that travels through water and can sink a ship. *U-boat* is the abbreviation for the German word *Unterseeboot*—"undersea boat."

◄ German U-boats in the Atlantic threatened supply and troop ships throughout the war.

German scientists were ahead of the Allies in developing rockets, including the V-2 rocket, which was put into action against the Allies in September 1944. ▼

A gunner in an American B-17 bomber known as the Flying Fortress ▶

All through the war we will keep improving our weapons, planes, tanks, and armored vehicles. The Germans and Japanese have a head start on us. They have fine scientists and technicians. This war will become a race to see who can produce the best weapons fastest. The Germans are working on rockets—called V-1s and V-2s—that are devastating. Luckily, it will take most of the war to get them perfected. When they start shooting rockets at England there will be many, many deaths. (The V-2 rockets are being designed to hit the United States.) We are behind on rocket development. After the war, German rocket engineers will tell us they got many of their ideas by studying the work of our rocket expert Robert Goddard.

We know something that they don't suspect we know. They think they are smarter than we are. They are wrong. We have learned to read their most difficult codes. That will prove more valuable than almost anything else we do.

Have you ever tried writing in code? It's easy. Just put numbers in place of letters and you have a code. Armies have always needed codes. Suppose a general wants to tell a faraway commander to attack. He sends a messenger. But he wants his orders in code in case the messenger is caught. He certainly doesn't want the enemy to know his plans.

In George Washington's day, a screen was sometimes put over a piece of paper. There were holes in the screen. The secret message was the words that showed through the holes. Everything else was there to fool you.

During World War II, both sides moved huge armies and navies and tried to do it secretly. Most orders were sent by telegraph. Anyone could listen. So codes were vital. They became very complicated. The Germans and Japanese thought no one could possibly figure out their complex codes.

We cracked the Japanese secret code even before the war began. Solving the German military code was much harder. German coded messages were sent and received on special machines. Then a German tank was captured in Poland. It had a code machine inside. The machine was smuggled out of Poland to England. When it got

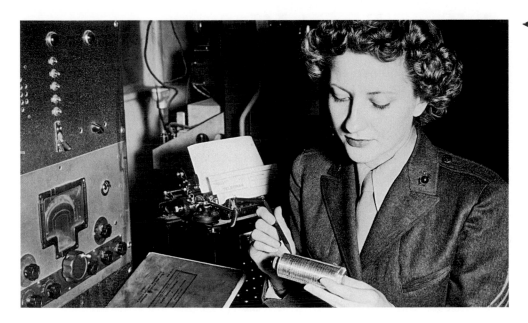

◀ Many women in the U.S. Marine Corps worked in the science of cryptography, finding ways to code and decode information.

to England no one could figure out how to work it. The English called the code machine Enigma. An *enigma* is a puzzle. They put some of their best scientific and mathematical minds on the job of solving the puzzle. It was incredibly difficult. How they did it is a fascinating story. Several books have been written about it. You can find them in the library.

Once the code was broken, we knew almost everything the Axis powers were planning to do. Now we Allies had to pretend that we didn't know some things. We didn't want the codes to be changed.

Cryptography Means Code Making

In World War II, code makers (who all seemed to be geniuses) created extraordinary code machines in order to write secret languages that would baffle the enemy. But code breakers were, if anything, even smarter than the code makers. Just about all the codes did get broken—except for one that stumped all the geniuses. No one could figure it out. Maybe that's because it happened to be a real language, spoken by real people, who were faster than any of the fancy machines.

The language was Navajo, and it was spoken by 420 marines who called themselves Dineh—the People. In western movies, Indians are usually known for their silence. These Native Americans did plenty of talking. They made up their own code using their own words: Hitler was Daghailchiih (mustache smeller), bombers were jaysho (buzzards), and bombs, ayeshi (eggs). Navajos landed on every major island in the Pacific. Major Howard Conner said, "Without the Navajos the marines would never have taken Iwo Jima." They were a secret weapon in the Pacific.

▲ Hundreds of Navajo-speaking marines served as radio operators in the Pacific. The code they developed using their native language was never broken.

A Two-Front War

During World War II the United States had to look in two directions at the same time. We were fighting a two-ocean war. That was a terrible problem for our generals and admirals. How do you divide your forces? How do you protect two huge coasts from attack?

Looking west (to East Asia), the view was frightening. In the Pacific Theater the Japanese moved like lightning. (Military officers call a war region a "theater." Strange, but that's the way it is.) Their forces were well trained and well equipped. At the start, Japan's aggressive strategy seemed to work. Remember, on December 7 they didn't just bomb Pearl Harbor—they attacked a whole string of strategic spots, almost simultaneously! In just a few months, the Japanese captured Thailand, the Philippine Islands, the Malay Peninsula, Java, Burma, Guam, Wake Island, the Gilbert Islands, Singapore, and Hong Kong. Check those places on a map and you'll see: the Japanese controlled East Asia. People in India and Australia were trembling. They thought they were next.

The European Theater wasn't any better. As you know, the Nazis controlled most of Europe. They even had troops in North Africa; the Mediterranean was a kind of Nazi sea.

So was the Atlantic Ocean. That was because of the German U-boats. England and Russia were desperate for help. The United States

Western Europe and the Far East (East Asia) were named by people who considered Jerusalem to be the center of the world. Western Europe is indeed west of Israel, and East Asia east of Israel—but to us they are the opposite. That is because the earth is a ball—which does make things confusing.

Simultaneously (sy-mul-TAY-nee-us-lee) means "at the same time."

In the first four months of 1942, German U-boats sank almost 200 Allied ships. ▶

had to ship weapons, tanks, oil, and men across the Atlantic to Europe. But the U-boats seemed to be everywhere. In the first four months of 1942, almost 200 of our ships were sunk. One summer day, people in Virginia Beach, Virginia, watched in horror as a ship was torpedoed and sunk in sight of the beach. Ships were being sunk faster than they could be built. Each time a ship was torpedoed, American men drowned.

▲ American general Dwight Eisenhower was appointed to lead the Supreme Headquarters Allied Expeditionary Force.

Somehow, people in this country didn't get discouraged. We were convinced we could win this war and we set about doing it. FDR became a great war president. No matter how gloomy things seemed, President Roosevelt remained confident and optimistic. He gave courage to the nation.

He had good people to work with. General George C. Marshall, his chief of staff, was a superb general and modest. Someone said he had the wisdom of George Washington and the strategic sense of Robert E. Lee.

Tough and experienced Admiral Ernest J. King, chief of naval operations, did his job well. So did Admiral Chester W. Nimitz and generals Dwight D. Eisenhower, H. H. "Hap" Arnold, Douglas MacArthur, and others. Remember all the trouble Abraham Lincoln had with his generals? Roosevelt was lucky; the nation was lucky, too.

The American aircraft carrier USS *Yorktown* is hit by a bomb during the Battle of Midway in June 1942. ▼

But the first battles were grim. Admiral King warned, "The way to victory is long; the going will be hard." He was right. We started out as losers. Then things began to change. Maybe it was because the Japanese got greedy. They didn't know when to stop. They thought they were invincible, which means "unbeatable." Nobody is unbeatable. We had been taking a pounding in the Pacific. But when we won three big victories, the Japanese learned to respect our fighting ability. The victories were in the Coral Sea, at Midway Island, and at Guadalcanal (all in 1942).

The Coral Sea battle wasn't exactly a victory. There was a series of mistakes

▲ American navy torpedo bombers fly over a burning Japanese ship during the Battle of Midway.

on both sides—big mistakes. Our losses were heavier than the enemy's. But we prevented them from capturing a strategic base in New Guinea, and that may have saved Australia from invasion.

The Japanese expected an easy win at tiny Midway Island. If they controlled that island they would control the air over Hawaii. Then, perhaps, they could attack our West Coast. In addition, they intended to destroy the ships in our fleet that had escaped Pearl Harbor—especially our aircraft carriers. Their plan was to lure us into a trap and surprise us. What they didn't know was that we could decode their secret messages. We knew of their plans. Still, they almost won. The battle over Midway was ferocious.

At first, things were awful for us. Forty-one of our torpedo bombers took off after the Japanese ships, and most were shot down. Then our dive bombers arrived and destroyed four massive Japanese aircraft carriers. It was the first defeat the Japanese navy had suffered. And it was a battle that proved that air power would be the key to this war.

The battle for Guadalcanal was something else. If you hold on for a chapter, I'll tell you about it. But before that, you need to learn about something going on at home.

Black and White Blood

Charles R. Drew was uncommonly gifted. He was a star athlete (in football, basketball, baseball, and track!); a brilliant student at Amherst College; an outstanding doctor (he was a professor of medicine at Howard University); and the man who developed the idea of a blood bank for storing blood plasma (during World War II).

In 1942, he organized the blood-bank programs for both the U.S. and Britain, and supervised the Red Cross's blood-donor program. Besides all that, he had an amiable personality—people liked him. But he was enraged that black blood and white blood were segregated in blood banks, and he spoke out against that absurdity. He was killed in a car accident. A myth has grown that because of his color, he was refused treatment at an all-white hospital. That is not true. What is true is that his talents were often frustrated by the idiocy of prejudice.

Dr. Charles R. Drew ▶

Forgetting the Constitution

Haruko Obata lived in a house in lovely, tree-shaded Berkeley, California. Her father was a professor at the University of California. Haruko was an American citizen. Like most Japanese Americans, she was proud of her Asian heritage, but she didn't approve of the ways of the warlords who ruled the Japanese empire. In school she studied the Constitution and its guarantees. She was happy to live in the land of liberty.

Then, one day, Haruko's world changed. Her father came home and told the family they were moving. They had just a few days to get ready. They could take only as much as they could carry. They might never again see the things they would leave behind. They were going to live—against their wishes—in a prisonlike camp.

The Japanese internment camps on the West Coast and the internment camp for Jews in Oswego, New York, were run by the same government agency. Even the food was the same.

◀ Families sent to relocation centers could take only what they could carry.

▲ Americans of Japanese ancestry arrive at the Santa Anita Assembly Center in California.

Hysteria is a state of violent emotional agitation and uncontrollable fear.

What had they done? Just a minute, and I'll get to that. But first, imagine that you are Haruko. You have some hard decisions to make, and you need to make them quickly. What will you choose to take with you? Sorry, your dog can't go. You'll have to give her away. Books? Games? Toys? Not if they are heavy. No one knows exactly where this camp is. It may be very cold. Or hot. You won't be able to take much besides clothes. Your parents must sell the car, the house, and almost all their possessions; because they do it so quickly, they will get hardly anything for them.

You and your family are going to a camp that is surrounded by a barbed-wire fence. Armed guards stand in watchtowers. If someone tries to walk out into the desert, he will be shot. What have you done that is so terrible? Why are you and your family in this prison camp?

You have not done anything wrong. Yes, you read that right. The Obatas have done nothing at all. They have been fine citizens.

But they are of Japanese descent, and the United States is at war with Japan. There is anti-Japanese hysteria in America, especially in California. Some of it is understandable. War is terrible. The Japanese government is horrible. But the Japanese in America have nothing to do with that. Some people don't understand that. Many authorities expect the Japanese to attack the West Coast. A Japanese submarine fires shells that land—harmlessly—near Los Angeles. People are terrified. There are rumors that Japanese American fishermen are sending signals to Japanese ships and planes. There is no evidence for this, but in wartime how can anyone be sure?

Reports of Japanese atrocities in Nanking, China, and elsewhere are horrible (and turn out to be true). But Japanese Americans have nothing to do with that, just as German Americans have nothing to do with the savagery in Nazi Germany.

Most Japanese Americans feel anguish. They love the United States, its opportunities, and its inspiring vision. But they also take pride in their ancient Japanese heritage. For them, World War II is like a civil war.

In addition, the Japanese in America face an old problem—racism. A racist law prevents Japanese immigrants from becoming citizens. However, anyone born here is automatically an American citizen. Two-thirds of the Japanese Americans are *Nisei*—the Japanese word for those born in America—and they are citizens.

The war brings very real fear, and the racists use that against the Japanese. There is something else here, too. It is greed. Japanese Americans have been industrious; their property is valuable. If they are put behind barbed wire, their property will have to be sold, and quickly, for much less than it is worth. Some people will profit mightily.

The first calls for internment (putting the Japanese in camps) come from newspaper columnists. Then a group of West Coast

Racism has been part of America's history from the time of the first contact of Europeans and Native Americans. But so has the fight against racism. That clash—between bigotry and decency—is found in the human drama in every culture (and perhaps in every human heart).

Internees gather behind the barbed-wire fence at a relocation center. ▼

politicians join in. They include Earl Warren, who will later become chief justice of the Supreme Court.

The attorney general reminds the secretary of war that the Fourth Amendment protects citizens from "unreasonable searches and seizures." The 14th Amendment says, "nor shall any State deprive any person of life, liberty or property without the due process of law." But we are at war, and the War Department is worried about "national security." The right of habeas corpus has been shelved in wartime before.

President Roosevelt issues Executive Order 9102. One hundred and twenty thousand Japanese Americans have a few days to get ready. They will be sent to 10 different internment camps.

There is much more to this story—much, much more. Mostly it is of a people who—as soon as they got settled—didn't cry. They did their best in a bad situation. They planted seeds and grew crops. They raised farm animals. They fed themselves and sent their surplus to support the war effort. They fixed up their sleeping quarters. They established schools, churches, recreational centers, newspapers, scout troops, baseball teams, and their own camp governments.

Some were let out of the camps to work in war factories. Many became soldiers. A Nisei regiment fighting in Europe won more commendations than any other regiment in the whole United States Army. Infantryman Harry Takagi explained:

> *We were fighting for the rights of all Japanese-Americans. We set out to break every record in the army. If we failed, it would reflect discredit on all Japanese-Americans. We could not let that happen.*

More than 16,000 Nisei served in the Pacific, most in military intelligence work as interpreters. Some went behind enemy lines as American spies. Japanese American women volunteered and served in the Woman's Army Corps, as army nurses, and in the Red Cross.

In the course of the war, 10 people were convicted of spying for Japan. All were white. Only one Japanese American was convicted of treason; she was Iva Ikuda Toguri, a graduate of UCLA, who was in Tokyo when the war began and couldn't get home. Toguri, known as Tokyo Rose, agreed to do propaganda broadcasting to avoid work in a munitions factory. She was paid $6.60 a month.

At first, people in the War Department objected to the idea of Nisei serving in the army. But, finally, President Roosevelt spoke up. He said:

The principle on which this country was founded and by which it has always been governed is that Americanism is a matter of the mind and heart; Americanism is not, and never was, a matter of race or ancestry.

Eventually, the camps were closed and people went out and did their best to build new lives. It wasn't easy; they had lost all their possessions. Many still faced racism when they tried to find jobs and new homes.

Forty years after the end of the war, the American government officially apologized to the Japanese Americans for the terrible injustice done to them during World War II. Those who had been in the camps were given money in partial payment for their suffering. Today, when we Americans think back on the internment camps, we feel shame.

Thousands of interned Japanese Americans volunteered to serve in war factories and in U.S. military forces. The 442nd Regimental Combat Team became the most decorated regiment in United States military history. ▼

A Hot Island

General Eisenhower, who was a likable fellow, wrote in his diary in March 1942: "One thing that might help win this war is to get someone to shoot King."

He was kidding. The King he was talking about was Admiral King. They disagreed on strategy. Do you think wars are easy to plan? Do you think the leaders all agree on how to go about it? Not often.

Most of our military leaders believed we should fight the war in Europe first and then the war in the Pacific. That made sense. Splitting your fighting forces is never a good idea. Besides, we didn't yet have enough supplies for two regions. But Admiral King said we couldn't just sit back and let the Japanese take over the Pacific. If we did, they would become so powerful that it would be almost impossible to win the war against them.

When the Japanese started building an airfield on an obscure island in the Solomon Island chain, Admiral King said that the United States needed to go on the offensive. So far—in Europe and the Pacific—we had been defensive fighters. King insisted that we take that island from the Japanese. It was an important decision. Not everyone agreed with it. It would cost many lives—American and Japanese. It turned out to be a decision that helped win the war.

The obscure island was named Guadalcanal, and it was such an out-of-the-way place that no one even had a map of it. But it was the right spot for a war base.

A B-17 Flying Fortress flies over the remote but strategic island of Guadalcanal. ▶

Find Australia on a map. Then look north, to New Guinea. To the east of New Guinea are the Solomon Islands. Guadalcanal is one of the southernmost of the Solomons. Anyone who has an air base on Guadalcanal can make big trouble for ships and airplanes going to Australia, New Zealand, or even Japan (which was where the American military planned to go eventually). We couldn't let the Japanese put planes on that island.

From the air, Guadalcanal looks like a heavenly place: very green, with high mountains, thick forests, sandy beaches, and coconut palms. But Guadalcanal is intensely hot (note the nearness of the equator). Its jungles are filled with monster leeches, huge scorpions, poisonous centipedes, giant ants, writhing snakes, skulking rats, snapping crocodiles, and hungry anopheles (uh-NOF-fuh-lees) mosquitoes (whose bites bring malaria).

Most of Guadalcanal is tropical rainforest—steamy, thick, muddy jungle. Where there isn't rainforest there is kunai (KOON-i) grass, with stiff, saw-toothed blades, often seven feet high, that can leave your arms and legs a mess of cuts. On Guadalcanal, you can't even see the enemy hiding in the grass or behind those jungle trees.

The 1st Marine Division landed in August 1942. Marines are trained to fight on land or sea. The 1st Marine Division was

During the Spanish-American War, Walter Reed, an American doctor, discovered that quinine (KWY-nine) cures malaria. Quinine comes from a plant found in Java. The Japanese had captured Java. Doctors were working on synthetic quinine, but not fast enough for the troops who fought on Guadalcanal.

U.S. Marines charge up the beach at Guadalcanal. ▼

▲ American army soldiers had to make their way through Guadalcanal's dense, dangerous jungle.

specially trained and tough. They needed that toughness. Guadalcanal was one of the hardest-fought battles in history. It went on for six months. It combined jungle fighting with terrible sea and air battles.

At first, things seemed easy. The marines surprised the Japanese on the island, who were mostly construction crews building an airfield. The marines captured the airfield. They named it Henderson Field, after a pilot who had been killed at Midway Island.

To tell the story of what happened next would take a whole book. Here is some of it:

Let's begin with the military word for a mistake. It is SNAFU, a combination of letters for *Situation Normal, All Fouled Up*. It means that someone goofed.

Who goofed on Guadalcanal? Both sides. The pressure and fear of battle often lead to mistakes. One captain, unloading marines onto the beach, didn't want to risk a Japanese attack on his ships. So he pulled out before the loading was finished, taking supplies and U.S. Marines with him. He stranded the marines already on the island. That was just one of the goofs.

The Japanese officers matched our snafus. They were too sure of themselves. They kept sending small forces to Guadalcanal. They thought Japanese fighters were unbeatable. They thought Americans were not good fighters. They were wrong.

In six months, the marines, and the army units that came to fight with them, lost 1,598 men on Guadalcanal. Japanese war records show an incredible 23,800 deaths. Many Japanese deaths came in suicidal charges. Surrender was considered shameful. The Japanese also suffered many deaths from tropical disease. Our medical care was much better.

Most of the battle for Guadalcanal was fought at sea. Each side lost 24 big ships and many smaller ones. About 20,000 American and Japanese sailors went down there with their ships.

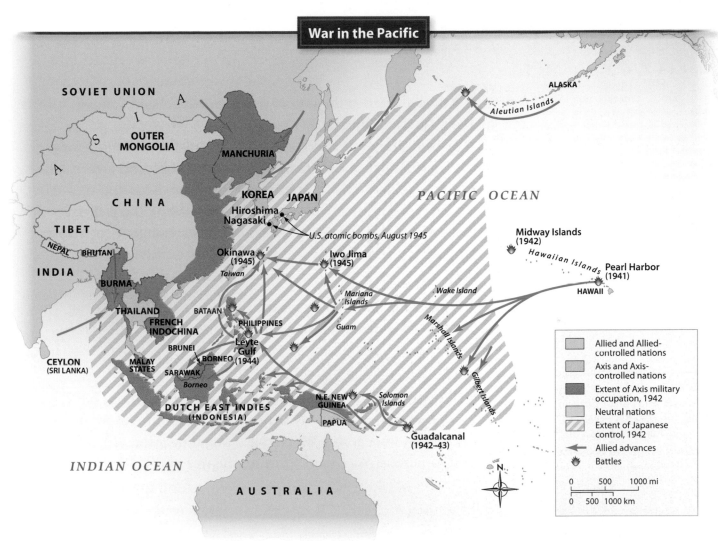

War in the Pacific

SOVIET UNION

OUTER MONGOLIA

MANCHURIA

CHINA

TIBET

NEPAL   BHUTAN

INDIA

BURMA

THAILAND

FRENCH INDOCHINA

CEYLON (SRI LANKA)

MALAY STATES

BATAAN

BRUNEI

SARAWAK

BORNEO

Borneo

KOREA   JAPAN

Hiroshima
Nagasaki
U.S. atomic bombs, August 1945

Okinawa (1945)

Taiwan

PHILIPPINES

Leyte Gulf (1944)

Iwo Jima (1945)

Mariana Islands

Guam

DUTCH EAST INDIES (INDONESIA)

PAPUA

N.E. NEW GUINEA

Solomon Islands

Guadalcanal (1942–43)

PACIFIC OCEAN

ALASKA

Aleutian Islands

Midway Islands (1942)

Hawaiian Islands

Wake Island

Marshall Islands

Gilbert Islands

Pearl Harbor (1941)

HAWAII

INDIAN OCEAN

AUSTRALIA

N

	Allied and Allied-controlled nations
	Axis and Axis-controlled nations
	Extent of Axis military occupation, 1942
	Neutral nations
	Extent of Japanese control, 1942
→	Allied advances
	Battles

0   500   1000 mi
0   500 1000 km

▲ After Japan's unprovoked attack on Pearl Harbor in 1941, the United States pursued a strategy of island-hopping, taking one island at a time in the drive toward Japan.

The first of the sea fights—off nearby Savo Island—was the worst disaster in United States naval history. We were whipped. After that, it was a seesaw of a conflict.

The battles on the island were ferocious. The Japanese were a brave foe. They had not lost a war in 400 years. But the marines outfought them. They held Guadalcanal. The marines ended the myth that the Japanese were invincible.

Guadalcanal was a turning point in the war. We went from defense to offense. The Japanese went from offense to defense. A captured Japanese document said, "Guadalcanal Island…is the fork in the road which leads to victory for them or us." We took the right road. It would lead to Japan.

Axing the Axis

"We have reached the end of the beginning," said Churchill, early in 1943. He was right.

The beginning was horrible. The Germans had perfected their blitzkrieg (that lightning attack with planes, tanks, and armies all charging together). The Japanese used the same tactic and mowed down everyone in their way. The Allies were losing the war. The Axis seemed invincible. Then things began to change. This is what happened:

- In February 1943, Japan pulled out of Guadalcanal.

- That same month, we cracked the Nazi naval code, Triton. Now we knew where their submarines were. The Atlantic was full of U-boats, but we began sinking them. The German U-boat admiral couldn't figure out what was happening.

- We realized that the Germans must have broken our naval code. That would explain why they always seemed to know where our convoys were going. We changed our code. More ships made it to Europe. We began winning the war of the Atlantic.

The term *convoy* can refer to a group of ships. Ships carrying troops or supplies traveled together with destroyers for protection against submarines.

▲ German U-boats patrolled the Atlantic.

Soviet soldiers battle a German army in the ruins of Stalingrad. ▶

- The Russians trapped a German army at Stalingrad. Then they laid siege to that army. They starved them. Finally, the German army surrendered. Then the Russians went on the offensive. They headed for Germany. Hitler hadn't planned on that.

- America's factories reached high gear. We began turning out guns, ships, tanks, planes, and other military equipment at an incredible rate—faster than anyone had believed possible. Picture this: a flat, sandy, empty field at a place called Willow Run (in Michigan). Now picture the same field, six months after Pearl Harbor. What you see is a vast building, half a mile long and a quarter of a mile wide. Steel, rubber, and other raw materials are fed into one end of the room; airplanes emerge from the other end—almost 9,000 airplanes the first year. It is not surprising that many historians say the Second World War was won in America's factories and laboratories.

▲ Workers construct a Boeing B-17 Flying Fortress bomber. During World War II, the American aerospace industry became the largest single industry in the world, producing more than 9,000 planes in one month in 1944.

Allied tanks played a major role in the desert warfare of North Africa. ▶

A *front* is a battle line. Stalin's front was in Russia and eastern Europe. He wanted the Allies to launch a western front so that the Germans would have to fight on two sides at once.

• In 1943, the Russians were fighting the Axis alone on the European continent. Stalin was crying for help. He asked his allies to land forces in Europe and take some pressure off his troops. He asked for a second front. American and British leaders agreed, and made plans for a joint landing. Its code name was Operation Torch.

But when the landing came, it was in North Africa, not Europe. That wasn't exactly what Stalin wanted, but it did help. North Africa was a good place to begin our offensive. It had been 23 years since we fought in World War I, and our troops needed combat experience. North Africa became a war school for us, with General Dwight D. Eisenhower in charge.

The Nazi forces there were led by General Erwin Rommel, who was known as the "desert fox." Rommel was intelligent, wily, and tough. His Afrika Korps had been destroying British troops. Then the British went on the offensive, heading west from Egypt. (Massive supplies helped.) Combined Allied forces headed east from Morocco and Algiers. A small French force came north from Chad. Rommel was caught in a pincer. We had managed to outfox the fox. We drove the Axis from North Africa. The Germans no longer controlled the Mediterranean Sea.

- We were now bombing Germany from the air day and night, but we needed to do more than that. We had to invade and help destroy Hitler's forces. Should we land in France and push east to Germany? Should we land in Italy and move north? Should we go through Greece? Finally, it was decided. We would start on the Mediterranean island of Sicily and go on to Italy. Check a map and you'll see why Sicily was important.

- The invasion of Sicily was given the code name Husky. We landed by sea and air and captured the island. Amphibious ducks were used for the first time. But there was a snafu: we let an Axis army escape to Italy.

- The Italian people were now fed up with war. Our bombs were blasting Rome. Things hadn't worked out as some Italians thought they would. Their morale collapsed. They kicked Mussolini out of power. Their army went home. They got out of the war. Because of that, we thought Italy would be easy to capture. It wasn't. More snafus. The German army moved into the mountainous Italian peninsula and captured the mountaintops. Picture the enemy shooting down at you as you attempt to climb. That's what happened. The Germans were on the heights. Our soldiers faced ferocious fire. Italy was a bloody standoff.

- Planning began for Operation Overlord—code name for the invasion of France. It was to be the largest amphibious invasion in all of history. The Nazis knew it was coming, so they began planning to defeat it. We assembled men and materials in England. The Germans readied their defenses. They laid explosive mines all along the coast, layers and layers of mines. Then they put steel and concrete barriers in the water and on the beaches. They added barbed wire, huge steel spikes, and more mines on the beaches. They built rooms of thick concrete—called "bunkers"—and filled them with heavy antitank guns, versatile medium-size guns, deadly flamethrowers, and machine guns. They called all this the Atlantic Wall.

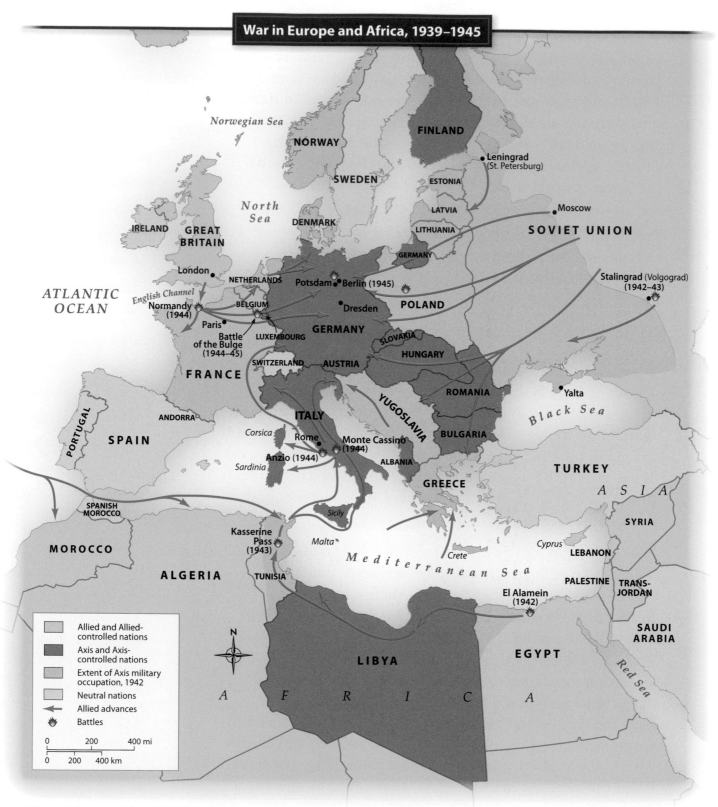

War in Europe and Africa, 1939–1945

Norwegian Sea

FINLAND

NORWAY

SWEDEN

• Leningrad
(St. Petersburg)

ESTONIA

*North
Sea*

LATVIA

• Moscow

DENMARK

LITHUANIA

SOVIET UNION

IRELAND

GREAT
BRITAIN

GERMANY

Stalingrad (Volgograd)
(1942–43)

London •

NETHERLANDS

Potsdam • • Berlin (1945)

*ATLANTIC
OCEAN*

English Channel

Normandy
(1944)

BELGIUM

• Dresden

POLAND

Paris •

Battle
of the Bulge
(1944–45)

LUXEMBOURG

GERMANY

SLOVAKIA

SWITZERLAND

AUSTRIA

HUNGARY

FRANCE

YUGOSLAVIA

ROMANIA

• Yalta

Black Sea

ITALY

PORTUGAL

ANDORRA

Corsica

Rome •

Monte Cassino
(1944)

BULGARIA

SPAIN

Anzio (1944)

ALBANIA

TURKEY

Sardinia

GREECE

A S I A

SPANISH
MOROCCO

Sicily

SYRIA

Crete

Cyprus

LEBANON

Kasserine
Pass
(1943)

Malta

M e d i t e r r a n e a n   S e a

MOROCCO

ALGERIA

PALESTINE

TRANS-
JORDAN

TUNISIA

El Alamein
(1942)

SAUDI
ARABIA

EGYPT

LIBYA

Red Sea

A   F   R   I   C   A

	Allied and Allied-controlled nations
	Axis and Axis-controlled nations
	Extent of Axis military occupation, 1942
	Neutral nations
←	Allied advances
	Battles

N

0   200   400 mi

0   200   400 km

▲ After initial successful assaults deep into the heart of western Europe, Russia, and
North Africa, the Axis powers were forced onto the defensive as the Allies struck back.

They fortified the whole coastline—from the Netherlands to the west coast of France—although they were sure they knew the exact spot where the landing would be made. Everyone knew.

The best route is obvious: from Dover, England, to the Pas de Calais (pah-duh-KAL-ay) in France. It is the shortest distance across the treacherous English Channel, it has gentle beaches, and it is the best place to land if you are heading for Germany's heartland. German intelligence officers decoded Allied messages that told of invasion plans for Calais. German pilots bombing England brought back photographs of tanks and trucks lined up near Dover. Spies reported on plans for a second invasion, on the same day, into Norway.

The messages were all fakes. The tanks and trucks were big balloons, designed to look real from aerial photographs. We weren't going to land at Pas de Calais. We weren't planning a Norway invasion. The German spies were double agents working secretly for us.

Women at Work

The image of a strong woman popularly known as "Rosie the Riveter" became part of a campaign to encourage women to work in war-related industries. American women threw themselves into the war effort. They worked on production lines in factories and shipyards. Women also did many other nonmilitary jobs usually held by men in peacetime—delivering mail, driving buses, and so on. Many worked as volunteers for the Red Cross or other organizations that supported servicemen.

During World War II, thousands of American women entered male-dominated industries such as aircraft construction. ▶

▲ Rosie the Riveter became the symbol of American women's contributions to the war effort.

Going for D-Day

General Erwin Rommel, Germany's brilliant desert warrior, looked at the skies and decided to take a two-day trip home to Germany. It was his wife Lucie's 50th birthday (he had bought her a gift—shoes from Paris); he also wanted to see the Führer and ask for more troops. The weather was too rough for an invasion, he said.

General Eisenhower looked at the same skies and decided to go for it. The English Channel was in turmoil, but the moon was full and the tides were low.

> Hitler was known in Germany as *Der Führer* (FEW-rur), which means "the leader" in German.

The invasion began at night, when paratroopers dropped behind enemy lines. They captured bridges and lit flares to guide the gliders that followed. With all the sophisticated equipment available, it was a tiny child's toy—a snapper that made a sound like a cricket—that the paratroopers used as a signal during the night so they could find each other.

Then, at daybreak, the sky filled with airplanes—wingtip to wingtip—9,000 of them. Two submarines raised flags to mark a landing area. The largest armada ever assembled appeared off the French coast: landing vehicles, minesweepers, attack transports, tankers, cruisers, battleships, ocean liners, yachts, hospital ships, and puffing tugs—all the boats and ships that could be found. They made an awesome fleet 20 miles wide. Giant military barrage balloons floated above to interfere with enemy planes.

It was June 6, 1944, and forever it would be known as D-Day. The Allies were heading for the treacherous, mine-strewn beaches of Normandy in France, 100 miles from the nearest English port across the turbulent Channel. Enemy soldiers, in bunkers on top of the Normandy cliffs, some of them 150 feet high, waited behind formidable heavy guns. But most were asleep. No one was expecting an attack in this weather. Rommel wasn't the only officer on vacation. Most of the German leaders had taken the weekend off.

General Dwight Eisenhower, Supreme Allied Commander, meets with the troops 24 hours before D-Day. ▼

▲ On June 6, 1944, landing ships offloaded tanks, trucks, supplies, and personnel at Omaha Beach as the invasion of Normandy began.

What happened next? The landing had been planned with the precision of a ballet. Everyone had a place and time in the drama. And, at four of the five landing beaches, things went more or less on schedule. But on Omaha Beach (one of two beaches where Americans landed), everything seemed snafued. The first men ashore couldn't secure the beach. What was supposed to take minutes took hours. Of 32 tanks, with collars that were supposed to keep them afloat, 27 sank in the choppy water with men inside. Allied planes, sent to bomb the enemy's gun-filled bunkers, went too far, missed the guns, and dropped their bombs on French cows. Immense traffic jams of men and supplies backed up in the water and on the beaches. Mines and shells were exploding everywhere. Gliders dropped men and supplies behind the beaches into swampland, where many sank.

Facing heavy machine-gun fire, American soldiers leave their landing craft and wade to shore on the Normandy coast. ▶

▲ In World War II, many soldiers suffered from combat fatigue. Most returned to combat after receiving care behind the front lines.

Emplacements are the areas where heavy artillery (guns) are positioned.

Flailing means moving wildly.

General Omar Bradley, on the command ship *Augusta*, thought about calling off the landing. Then a destroyer came up into the shallow water and lobbed a shell right inside a main bunker. When other ships added their firepower, the Nazi gunners in the concrete emplacements were in big trouble. The navy had opened a crack in the German defenses and the Yanks were on their way.

Slowly at first, but then steadily, soldiers and medical personnel began to land and head inland, into the fierce guns on top of the bluffs. No word is big enough to describe their effort. *Heroic* will have to do.

The operation had been brilliantly planned. Troops and officers had trained for a year; it paid off. Equipment specially designed for this invasion worked superbly. Tanks unrolled reels of steel matting that made roadways across the sand. Other tanks, with flailing chain arms, detonated mines and began to make the beach safe. Some tanks carried small bridges. Naval engineers had built huge floating harbors; they were towed into place.

In the midst of the fighting, over the noise of battle, a British major shouted out words from Shakespeare's play *Henry V*, about another invasion of France.

We few, we happy few, we band of brothers;
For he today that sheds his blood with me
Shall be my brother; be he ne'er so vile,
This day shall gentle his condition.
And gentlemen in England now a-bed,
Shall think themselves accursed they were not here;
And hold their manhoods cheap whiles any speaks
That fought with us upon Saint Crispin's day.

It was D-Day, not St. Crispin's, but poets would write of this day, too: of heroism, of achievement, and of the waste of war. It was there to see on the beaches. They were littered with tanks and bodies and the leftovers of men's lives: socks, Bibles, toothbrushes, diaries, mirrors, letters, first-aid kits, photographs, and food rations.

By nightfall, Allied troops—American, British, Canadian, Free French, Polish—were holding French soil. We had made it. We were on our way to Berlin.

For the Axis, it was the beginning of the end.

A bomber crew returns from a mission to support the D-Day landings in Normandy. ▼

A Wartime Diary

You are a newspaper writer, a war correspondent, covering this world war. When it ends you will write a book about the times you have lived through, so you have been keeping a diary to record events. It is 1945. Here are some excerpts from your journal and some notes from this author:

January 1: Allied forces are beginning to turn back a powerful German army in Belgium. Soldiers are calling this the Battle of the Bulge. *A strong German offensive created a bulge in the Allied defensive line.* Whatever you want to call this battle, it is fierce. Still, it looks as if this will be a good year for the Allies. Germany's armies are being battered on the ground, its cities pounded from the air.

January 20: FDR is inaugurated for a fourth term as president. No other president has served more than twice.

January 24: Russian soldiers have crossed the Oder River and, for the first time, are on German soil.

January 27: Today, in Poland, Soviet forces liberated a German concentration camp. It is named Auschwitz. People in the camp were used as slaves by a German industrial chemical company. The company has left charts of the costs and profits of slave labor. But the camp was built primarily for another purpose. It was built to kill people. The horror and evil of it all are more than anyone wants to believe. *Three million people were murdered at Auschwitz, most of them Jews.*

February 1: The sky is thick with planes—an incredible sight! One thousand airplanes are flying over Europe on their way to bomb Berlin.

February 4–11: President Roosevelt has flown to Yalta, in the Crimea, to meet with England's Winston Churchill and Russia's Joseph Stalin. They are said to be planning for the final battles

▲ Russian soldiers march toward Germany.

◀ An American tank moves along an icy road in the Ardennes Forest during the Battle of the Bulge, the last major German offensive of WWII.

▲ Douglas MacArthur returns to the Philippines in 1945.

of the war. They agree to call a meeting of the world's nations in San Francisco in April, to form a peacekeeping organization called the United Nations.

February 14: John D. Rockefeller, Jr., donates $8.5 million to buy land in New York City as a permanent home for the United Nations. Woodrow Wilson's idea of a league of nations may finally be achieved.

February 19: American marines have landed on Iwo Jima, an island in the Pacific. Reports tell of incredibly hard fighting and great losses on both sides.

February 24: General Douglas MacArthur promised to return to the Philippines—and he has done it.

March 7: The U.S. 1st Army has crossed the river Rhine and is inside Germany. All German armies have been pushed back into the Fatherland.

March 9: Today, 325 low-flying bombers dropped incendiary bombs on Tokyo. The bombs are filled with jellied gasoline meant to set fires. The Japanese capital became so hot that the water in its canals boiled. Still the Japanese refuse to surrender. *Later reports list 267,000 Tokyo buildings burned to the ground; 89,000 persons dead.*

March 21: Today we watched an enormous air armada fly overhead on its way to Germany. *There were 7,000 Allied planes.* Until now, most bombing raids have been at night, to make it difficult for the antiaircraft guns and fighter planes to see the bombers. Now Germany has little firepower left; the bombers fly at will. Bomb damage there is said to be devastating.

The Axis powers now have no hope of winning and yet neither Germany nor Japan will give up. Those who began this insane engine of war have cut out the brakes. They can't seem to stop. It is their own people who are suffering most. Do the warlords care?

◄ Despite intense resistance and terrible losses, American marines raise the flag on the island of Iwo Jima.

April in Georgia

Where is Tokyo? Where is Dresden?

The madmen who run Japan and Germany refuse to give up. They talk of leading their nations in a fight to the death. Terrible firebombs are dropping on Tokyo and Dresden. Hundreds of thousands of people are dying. Just as a fist squeezes its contents, so British, American, and Russian troops are squeezing Germany. In the Pacific Theater we are making plans to invade Japan. Everyone expects that invasion to be bloodier than the one in Normandy.

The Allies will win this war—that now seems clear--but the German and Japanese leaders are making it very difficult. Like ancient rulers who had their followers killed and buried in their tombs, these leaders seem determined to kill their own people.

The president knows of something that might end the war quickly. It is that secret weapon that almost no one else knows about. Partly because of this, he feels he can relax and catch up on some paperwork. He is exhausted. He has just turned 63, but he looks much older.

The desolate ruins of Dresden, Germany, after the Allied firebombing in February 1945 ▼

The war has been a terrible strain: he has traveled around the world, he has run for a fourth term as president, he has been active as commander in chief of the armed services, he has been an inspiring leader. He needs to take it easy for a few days. He makes plans to go to Warm Springs, Georgia. He first visited Warm Springs years earlier, when he was recovering from polio. The waters are healing. He has been back many times and has grown to love the slow-paced gentleness of the South.

In Georgia, wild violets are blooming; so are purple-blue wisteria and sweet-smelling honeysuckle. It is springtime—April 12, 1945—and, at Warm Springs, cooks are preparing a picnic. The smells of barbecued beef and chicken fill the air. As the president works, an artist sits nearby, making sketches for a watercolor portrait.

▲ A cartoon depicts Roosevelt, Stalin, and Churchill at the Yalta Conference, treating the world as a jigsaw puzzle.

Almost exactly 80 years earlier, another American president had decided to relax and go to the theater, knowing that a terrible war was coming to an end.

Like that other president, Roosevelt is concerned about the peace that is to come. He wants this war to have meaning. Soon after the war began, he met with Winston Churchill and signed a document called the Atlantic Charter. It says that after the war, nations will be free to choose their own forms of government. That is called "self-determination." Roosevelt wants to end the old, before-the-war imperialist ways. Then, a few European nations ruled much of the world. Sometimes they ruled well; sometimes not well. To Roosevelt, that doesn't matter now. People should be free to govern themselves. Great Britain still controls India and Burma. France expects to regain control of Indochina (which includes Vietnam). Japan has attempted to become an empire. The United States rules the Philippine Islands.

Roosevelt thinks imperialism—even well-meaning imperialism—is wrong. He will show the world: America has no desire for other lands. We will begin by granting independence to the Philippines. He is planning to go to the independence ceremonies himself.

Russia is a worry. The Russian people have fought magnificently. They have been brave allies. But they aren't a free people. Stalin is a dictator. Winston Churchill believes that Stalin cannot be trusted.

Roosevelt is beginning to have worries about Stalin, too.

At Warm Springs he works on a speech to be given at a dinner to honor Jefferson's memory. This is part of what Roosevelt writes:

The once powerful, malignant Nazi state is crumbling. The Japanese war lords are receiving, in their own homeland, the retribution for which they asked when they attacked Pearl Harbor.

But the mere conquest of our enemies is not enough.

We must go on to do all in our power to conquer the doubts and the fears, the ignorance and the greed, which made this horror possible.... If civilization is to survive, we must cultivate the science of human relationships—the ability of all peoples, of all kinds, to live together and work together, in the same world, at peace....

The work, my friends, is peace. More than an end of this war—an end to the beginnings of all wars. Yes, an end, forever, to this impractical, unrealistic settlement of the differences between governments by the mass killing of peoples.

The president is sitting in a leather armchair; he turns to the artist. "We've got just 15 minutes more," he says. Some cousins of his and a friend are in the room. They are quiet. The president is studying papers. The 15 minutes are almost up when he raises a hand to his temple. "I have a terrific headache," he says. They are the last words he will ever speak.

◀ This portrait of FDR remained unfinished after the president died suddenly at Warm Springs, Georgia.

President HST

The solidly built, gray-haired man with metal-rimmed glasses sat at a high desk facing the Senate floor. A gold-bordered blue velvet drape hung behind him and made a frame for his chair. Vice President Harry S. Truman was presiding over the Senate. At least that was what he seemed to be doing. Actually, he was bored and was writing a letter to his mother and sister, who were back in his hometown of Independence, Missouri. This is part of what he wrote:

> *Dear Mama & Mary: I am trying to write you a letter today from the desk of the President of the Senate while a windy Senator...is making a speech on a subject with which he is in no way familiar.... Turn on your radio tomorrow night at 9:30 your time.... I think I'll be on all the networks.... I'll be followed by the President, whom I'll introduce.*

It had amazed almost everyone—including Truman—when he was asked to be vice president. He hardly knew FDR. Some said it was the Democratic National Committee that selected Harry Truman; that the other candidates considered were all controversial.

Truman didn't seem to have any enemies. But he didn't have many enthusiasts, either. He had become a senator at age 50. He'd fought in the Great War and had tried a number of jobs—he'd been a farmer and a men's store owner—but the store failed, and he wasn't very successful at anything until he got into politics, first as a postmaster and then as a county official. He was a bookish sort, with an astounding knowledge of history: quiet, honest, likable, and fair-minded, although he sometimes lost his temper. It was as head of a Senate committee investigating military contracts that he had impressed people—including Roosevelt. His committee probably saved the government billions of dollars.

Harry Truman was a likable, honest, and hardworking senator from Missouri when he was nominated as FDR's running mate in 1944. ▼

When the windy senator finally finished, Truman went to visit his old friend, the speaker of the House of Representatives, Texan Sam Rayburn. Rayburn's office was a gathering place where congressmen relaxed and gossiped. It was called—in jest—the Board of Education. It was there that Truman got a call from the president's press secretary, Steve Early. He was to come to the White House at once. Early's voice had an urgent tone.

Truman headed through the underground passage to the Senate Office Building—there his Secret Service agents lost track of him. But his car and driver were waiting. As he drove the 15 long blocks to the White House, he guessed that the president had flown in from Georgia and wanted him for something ceremonial.

Upstairs at the White House, he learned differently. Eleanor Roosevelt put her hand on his shoulder and said softly, "Harry, the president is dead." For a moment he could say nothing. Then he asked if there was anything he could do for her.

"Is there anything we can do for you?" she answered. "You are the one in trouble now."

Two hours after receiving word that FDR had died, Harry Truman was sworn in as president of the United States, with his wife and daughter looking on. ▶

A Final Journey

It was as if a member of the family had died. He had been a world-dominating figure for 12 years—strong, witty, compassionate, able. Young people could remember no other president. The nation was in a state of shock.

Those who had felt left out by government before—the poor and disadvantaged—were especially grieved. This was a president who had done more than talk about fairness and opportunity; he had acted to begin to make them reality. And, while he had broken precedent by running for office four times, he had not forgotten that as president he was the servant of the people. He had never assumed kingly trappings. He had never lost his sense of humor or his easy informality.

In Warm Springs, the flag-draped coffin began its long, sad train journey—to Washington first, and then to Hyde Park, where the president was to be buried. Sitting inside the train, Eleanor Roosevelt kept remembering a poem about Lincoln's death. It wouldn't leave her mind:

> *A lonesome train on a lonesome track*
> *Seven coaches painted black,*
> *A slow train, a quiet train*
> *Carrying Lincoln home again.*

The poem Eleanor Roosevelt remembered was written by Millard Lampell.

◀ Navy Chief Petty Officer Graham Jackson weeps as he plays "Goin' Home" while President Roosevelt's body is carried from the Warm Springs Foundation, a hospital FDR founded for polio patients.

At night, unable to sleep, she said:

I lay in my berth…with the window shade up, looking out at the countryside he had loved and watching the faces of the people at stations, and even at the crossroads, who had come to pay their last tribute all through the night…. I was truly surprised by the people along the way; not only at the stops but at every crossing.

In the train's press car, reporters looking out the window saw black sharecroppers on their knees, hands outstretched in prayer. As the train slowed in a South Carolina city, members of a Boy Scout troop began singing "Onward, Christian Soldiers"; then others joined in, and soon, according to one who was there, "eight or ten thousand voices were singing like an organ." Everywhere people cried. The sobs continued as the coffin was carried, by horse-drawn caisson, through Washington to the White House. Then, during the memorial service, the whole grieving nation came to a halt and paid its respects.

Airplanes sat on runways; radios were silent; telephone service was cut off—there was not even a dial tone; news-service teletypes typed the word *silence* and went dead; movie theaters closed; cars and

Thousands of people stood in silence to pay their respects as the horse-drawn carriage carrying Franklin Delano Roosevelt's casket made its way toward the Capitol. ▶

buses pulled to the curb; 505 New York subway trains stopped; stores shut their doors; and everywhere—in other countries, too—people put hands on hearts, or fell to their knees, or just stayed quiet. That day newspapers carried no advertisements.

Clearly he had been a great president. But how great? What would history say of him?

A poll of 50 leading historians soon ranked him just behind Lincoln and Washington as one of the three greatest presidents. Winston Churchill said that in world importance, Roosevelt was first.

And yet, as much as some loved and respected him, others hated and vilified him.

Later historians would look at him through two lenses. As an effective president, they agreed, he was like a magnificent symphony conductor who knows all the notes and just what to do with them. No question about it, they still agreed, he was a great president. But there was something that bothered many. As a human being, he was sometimes less than great. His personality was flawed. It was too bad to have to acknowledge it, but he could be devious. He could tell a person something and not mean it. He could tell a story that made him look good but wasn't quite true.

▲ Franklin Roosevelt changed the presidency and the nation.

Perhaps it was that tendency to always act as if everything was fine, even when it wasn't, that some found disturbing. He was used to pretending. It was both a strength and a weakness.

Eleanor (who was more partner than wife) said:

Because he disliked being disagreeable, he made an effort to give each person who came in contact with him the feeling that he understood what his particular interest was.... Often people have told me that they were misled by Franklin.... This misunderstanding not only arose from his dislike of being disagreeable, but from the interest that he always had in somebody else's point of view and his willingness to listen to it.

He listened intently, and that was flattering. People thought it meant that he agreed with them. He didn't tell them differently.

So some felt he couldn't be trusted.

But no one could take his achievements as president from him. They changed the nation. Here are the most important of them:

- He led the nation through two of its worst times—a depression and a world war—with gusto, courage, and an unfailing confidence.

    The only thing we have to fear is fear itself.

- He was inspiring. He made people believe in their country and want to do their best for it. Perhaps only during that time when the Constitution was written were more brilliant thinkers attracted to government service.

    This generation has a rendezvous with destiny.

- He believed in government for the people. During the Roosevelt administrations, Social Security, farm programs, aid for home buyers, aid for dependent children, and other caring programs were begun. He paid attention to laboring people and their needs. Some called it a "revolution." Perhaps it was. It was in line with a tradition of revolution that could be traced to the ideas of Thomas Jefferson, Andrew Jackson, the Populists, and the Progressives.

    As we have recaptured and rekindled our pioneering spirit, we have insisted that it shall always be a spirit of justice, a spirit of teamwork, a spirit of sacrifice, and, above all, a spirit of neighborliness.

- He strengthened the two-party system. Since before the Civil War, only two Democrats—Grover Cleveland and Woodrow Wilson—had been elected president. (And Woodrow Wilson made it because the Republican Party was split.) After Roosevelt there was a better balance between the parties.

    Here in the United States we have been a long time at the business of self-government. The longer we are at it the more certain we become that we can continue to govern ourselves; that progress is on the side of majority rule; that if mistakes are to be made we prefer to make them ourselves and to do our own correcting.

The WPA built housing for low-income families. ▼

CLEVELAND METROP

Over 8 million people worked for the WPA over the course of the Depression. ▶

- He brought new people into government. He named a woman, Frances Perkins, to his cabinet. He began the process to "include the excluded." (Wartime America was a land that accepted much discrimination.)

  We are going to make a country where no one is left out.

- He cared about the environment. He sent young people from the inner cities out to plant trees, and he worked to protect our nation's natural heritage.

  The conservation of our natural resources and their proper use constitute the fundamental problem which underlies almost every other problem of our national life.... The government has been endeavoring to get our people to look ahead and to substitute a planned and orderly development of our resources in place of a haphazard striving for immediate profit.... We are prone to think of the resources of this country as inexhaustible; this is not so.

- By his personal example he showed that—for people with energy and intelligence—there need not be any such thing as a handicap.

  If you have spent two years in bed trying to wiggle your big toe, everything else seems easy.

- He won the war and set the stage for the prosperity that was to follow. It might not have happened with another leader.

  In the future days, which we seek to make secure, we look forward to a world founded upon four essential freedoms.

  The first is freedom of speech and expression—everywhere in the world.

  The second is freedom of every person to worship God in his own way—everywhere in the world.

  The third is freedom from want.... The fourth is freedom from fear.

▲ Franklin Roosevelt remained committed to protecting basic freedoms, including freedom of speech (as illustrated in this painting by the American artist Norman Rockwell).

Day by Day

*M*ore from the diary that you, the newspaper reporter, are keeping. (And a few more comments from this author.)

April 12, 1945: American soldiers enter the Nazi concentration camp at Buchenwald and find death everywhere. Germans interviewed say they didn't know anything about the concentration camps. *As camp after camp is discovered, the Allies react with cold fury. More than 10 million human beings have died in the concentration camps. In one camp American soldiers discover bins with thousands of pairs of babies' shoes.*

April 13: Everywhere there is shock and disbelief. The president is dead! It is hard to imagine the United States without FDR. The bombing of Germany continues—day and night. Germany's cities are in ruins. Mostly the bombs kill civilians. Are they to blame for this war? *This bombing of cities is called "strategic bombing." There is something about it that is strange. The tougher the bombing, the more it makes people want to work hard and fight back. When the German Luftwaffe was bombing England, it seemed to inspire the English to fight and produce. All selfishness was forgotten. Military production went up. The same thing happened in Germany and Japan. After last year's fierce raids on Germany, there was a short lull and then aircraft production greatly increased. The military experts don't want to believe it, but it seems to be true. The military experts say the purpose of the bombing is to destroy morale.*

April 14: The British liberate the Bergen-Belsen concentration camp. *On March 12, in this camp, a 14-year-old Dutch girl died. Her name was Anne Frank. After the war her diary is found and published.*

April 20: Hitler is 56 today. Is there anyone left who wishes him a happy birthday? *Probably. His strongman ideas had wide appeal. Democracy is difficult; it asks people to think and take part in their government. The totalitarian governments treat people like sheep—or is it dogs?*

April 21: Russian troops have entered the suburbs of Berlin, Germany's capital. The fighting is said to be fierce, although the Nazis have no hope of victory. *In less than one month, between April 16 and May 8, the Russians lose 304,887 men—killed, wounded, and*

◄ Former prisoners of the Nazi concentration camp at Buchenwald stare out from the wooden bunks in which they slept three to a bed.

▲ Soviet tanks and planes after the fall of Berlin in May 1945

missing—capturing Berlin. The total number of American deaths in the whole war, in Europe and the Pacific, is about 325,000.

April 24: If only there were a way to end this war quickly. The deaths now seem so unnecessary. *On this day President Truman gets his first detailed briefing on the top-secret superweapon.*

April 26: Italy's dictator, Benito Mussolini, has been hanged by Italians fighting on the side of the Allies.

April 30: Hitler is dead. He has killed himself. He was living like a mole underground in a concrete bunker in Berlin. *Hitler boasted that his creation—the German Third Reich—would live forever. Many believed him. It lasted 12 years.*

May 7: German military leaders have surrendered to General Dwight D. Eisenhower at a school in Rheims, France. It is unconditional surrender. The war in Europe is over. It is hard to believe.

▲ Celebrations erupted in London (pictured here), New York, and cities around the world when news arrived of the Allied victory in Europe.

May 8: President Harry Truman proclaims this VE (Victory in Europe) Day. It is his 61st birthday. People are cheering and hugging and crying and partying. *Maybe they should wait—the war isn't over in the Pacific.*

May 11: A Japanese pilot, trained for a suicide mission, crashes into the aircraft carrier *Bunker Hill;* 373 Americans are killed.

June: The cities of Nagoya, Kobe, Osaka, Yokohama, and Kawasaki have been firebombed. The destruction in Japan is said to be staggering. Japan's cities are built of wood. They burn quickly. Two million buildings have been destroyed; perhaps 10 million people made homeless; hundreds of thousands are dead or injured. The Japanese warlords still won't surrender.

July: Japan's 60 largest cities have been burned. There is almost no food in Japan; people are starving. Four hundred Japanese have been arrested because they talked of surrender. *In the New Mexican desert, scientists prepare to test an atomic device. No one knows if it will work. No one knows how powerful it is. They learn on July 16:*

it is more powerful than anything ever before devised by humans. It was "as though the earth had opened and the skies had split," said one who was there. You, and America's other citizens, are not told of the test.

July 26: Truman, Churchill, and China's leader, Chiang Kai-shek, broadcasting from a peace conference at Potsdam, Germany, demand the unconditional surrender of Japan but assure the Japanese of a "new order of peace, security, and justice." Otherwise, they warn, there will be "prompt and utter destruction of the Japanese homeland." The Japanese premier Baron Suzuki says the proposal is "unworthy of public notice." *At Potsdam, Harry Truman tells Joseph Stalin that the United States has a new and powerful weapon. The Soviet leader shows little interest. Plans for the secret weapon, stolen by spies, sit inside the Kremlin, Russia's government center. Stalin, a dictator admired by Hitler, knows all about the bomb.*

President Harry Truman (center) met with Winston Churchill (left), Joseph Stalin, and other leaders at Potsdam, Germany. They demanded Japan's surrender, but the Japanese leaders refused. ▼

A Little Boy

The men of the 509th Composite Group of the 313th Wing of the 21st Bombing Command of the 20th Air Force have been carefully chosen from a group of ace pilots. All have volunteered for a special mission. No one tells them what the mission will be. But whatever it is, they know they will be flying B-29s, the big workhorse bombers that are known as superfortresses.

Right away, there is something strange about the training they get at an airfield in Utah. Instead of flying planes loaded with huge bombs, they train with a single bomb of moderate size. And they are trained to worry about storms, especially electrical storms. Then, when they are sent to the Pacific, to the island of Tinian in the Marianas group of islands, they just sit around. It is frustrating. From Tinian it is an easy flight to Japan. The other airmen on the island are flying B-29s and dropping big bomb loads on Japan's cities. The 509th is sent on training flights—over and over again.

◀ A B-29 bomber flies over Japan.

▲ After weighing the advice of experts, President Truman made the momentous decision to use the atomic bomb to end the war.

Meanwhile, in Washington, President Truman has come to a decision. He has called on two teams of experts: a team of scientists and a team of civilians and soldiers. They are to help him decide about the new superweapon. Will it be used? Can anything be used in its place? Both teams agree: the weapon should be used. They believe it will bring the war to an end. Without it, the war could continue for 10 or more years. Military chiefs, who don't know about the secret weapon, are pressing Truman to let them invade Japan. If that happens, America can expect a million casualties; Japan might have 10 times that number.

Colonel Paul W. Tibbets, Jr., is commander of the 509th. He has named his plane the Enola Gay, after his mother. In early August, a single bomb 28 inches in diameter and 10 feet long is loaded onto the Enola Gay. The bomb weighs four metric tons and is nicknamed "Little Boy." A similar device was exploded in the New Mexican desert, but no one knows exactly what will happen when one is dropped from an airplane. Colonel Tibbets and the others now realize that this is dangerous stuff they are about to handle. If the Enola Gay crashes on takeoff, as some B-29s have done, Tinian could disappear.

The plan is to drop Little Boy on the Japanese city of Hiroshima. Hiroshima has been selected because of its war-making industries and because it is the headquarters of the 2nd Japanese Army. On August 4, more than 700,000 leaflets are dropped on Hiroshima warning that the city will be demolished. The warning is not taken seriously.

Captain William S. Parsons, of the U.S. Navy, is a surprise passenger on the Enola Gay. He has decided he will put the detonating parts of the bomb together after the plane is in the air. It will be safer. He doesn't know how to do that, but he has a day to learn. He learns.

At 1:45 a.m. on August 6, 1945, three B-29s take off for Japan. They will check on weather and on aircraft in the target area. The Enola Gay and two other B-29s follow an hour later.

A replica of the bomb known as Little Boy ▶

The night is perfect, with shining stars and a picture-book moon. As they fly, Captain Robert A. Lewis, co-pilot on the Enola Gay, writes a letter to his mother and father.

I think everyone will feel relieved when we have left our bomb,

he writes. Later, he adds:

It is 5:52 and we are only a few miles from Iwo Jima. We are beginning to climb to a new altitude.

When they are over Honshu, Japan's central island, he writes,

Captain Parsons has put the final touches on this assembly job. We are now loaded. The bomb is alive. It is a funny feeling knowing it is right in back of you.

For most people in Hiroshima the workday begins at 8 a.m. By 8:10, factories and shops are beginning to buzz. On August 6, the entire 2nd Japanese Army is on a parade field doing calisthenics. It is a bright, sunny morning and some children can be seen outdoors playing. (Many of Hiroshima's children have been evacuated to the suburbs.) A group of middle-school students has gotten up early and already put in more than an hour's work on a fire-control project. As clocks near 8:15 a.m., the Chuo Broadcasting Station reports that three B-29s have been spotted heading for Hiroshima.

At 8:15 the bomb bay opens; Little Boy is on his way. *There will be a short intermission while we bomb our target,* Captain Lewis writes. Then he adds, in letters that scrawl wildly on the page, *My God!*

Einstein's Regret

Albert Einstein regretted his part in the atom bomb's development. "I made one great mistake in my life," he said, "when I signed the letter to President Roosevelt recommending that atom bombs be made...but there was some justification—the danger that the Germans would make them."

Einstein at Princeton ▶

He has not been prepared for what happens. The size and fury of the explosion are greater than anything ever before created by humans. The airmen are still able to see the inferno clearly when they have put 270 miles between themselves and the target. It is a sight they will never forget.

The atomic bomb (for that is what it is) has created a fireball whose center reaches 4,000° Celsius. (Iron melts at 1,550° Celsius.) The fireball gives birth to a shock wave and then a high-speed wind. Buildings are smashed by wave and wind and burned by fire. Dust from destroyed buildings makes the city night-dark within minutes of the bombing. The wind tosses people about. Thermal rays burn their bodies. As the fireball fades, a vacuum at the blast's center pulls up dust, air, and bomb debris, creating an enormous mushroom cloud that rises into the atmosphere. Liquid rain alternates with downpours of sparks and fire. The rain is ink-black and oily. Within minutes, the 2nd Japanese Army no longer exists. Seventy-eight thousand people are dead. One hundred thousand are injured.

The atomic age has begun.

The explosion of a single atomic bomb left Hiroshima in ruins. ▼

Peace

The Americans demand surrender—otherwise, they tell the Japanese, "they may expect a rain of ruin from the air." The Japanese do not respond.

On August 8 Russia enters the war against Japan. Russian forces attack Japanese armies in Manchuria and Korea. For some Japanese leaders this is more threatening than the bomb.

On August 9 a second atomic bomb is dropped. This one hits the port of Nagasaki. The nightmare of fire, wind, rain, and radiation is repeated. Has this war driven sane people to act insanely?

In Japan, the warlords and government ministers meet in stormy sessions to decide the fate of their people. They are split down the middle; most of the warriors vote to continue the fight, although everyone knows that may mean the destruction of the Japanese people. As Emperor Hirohito described it:

> *There was no prospect of agreement no matter how many discussions they had.... I was given the opportunity to express my own free will for the first time.*

The emperor decides for his people.

From Tokyo, cables are sent to Washington, London, Moscow, and Chungking. Japan will accept the terms of the Potsdam Declaration, with one request: that the emperor remain as head of state.

As soon as Harry Truman hears the news he calls Eleanor Roosevelt. Mrs. Roosevelt is now America's ambassador to the United Nations. President Truman tells her that he wishes her husband were alive to accept the peace proposal.

A mushroom cloud rises over Nagasaki after a second atomic bomb exploded on August 9, 1945. ▶

Allied officers and crew crowd the decks of the U.S. battleship *Missouri* as senior Japanese delegate Mamoru Shigemitsu signs the official surrender documents ending World War II. ▶

When news arrived of the Japanese surrender, jubilation and spontaneous kissing broke out at Times Square in New York City and indeed throughout the nation. ▼

In Japan, some army officers break into the imperial palace, set fire to the home of the prime minister, and attempt to stop a broadcast of the emperor's words. They fail, and, along with the war minister, commit suicide in the public square.

The emperor, who wants to be sure that his words are exactly right, has recorded them in advance. The actual broadcast is taking place elsewhere.

It is August 15, 1945, and Hirohito's voice is heard in the first public speech an emperor has ever made. He asks the Japanese people to accept the coming of peace.

PART 2

POSTWAR AMERICA

About Democracy and Struggles

For more than a century, western Europe's nations had dominated the globe. Now, in 1945, they were exhausted. Two awful wars had been fought on their territory. Their peoples had suffered horribly. After World War II, it was as if there were a vacuum. We filled the vacuum. We became the world's most powerful nation.

Our economy had been changed, and strengthened, by the war. We had acted quickly and with imagination. Using something we called "know-how," we had built tanks, ships, airplanes, and bombs better and faster than anyone thought possible. Women, blacks, and others—who were not always treated according to America's creed of fairness—worked as hard as anyone else. Many fought and died for their nation. Then, when the black soldiers came home, they were often not allowed to vote. Women workers were paid less than men for doing the same job. Was that fair?

Those citizens began to demand equal rights, which was their right as Americans. Anyone who read the Declaration of Independence knew *all men are created equal*. Elizabeth Cady Stanton had changed that to *all men and women are created equal*. Did all really mean all? Did it mean all people of every color and description? Most Americans thought so.

But some people said those words in the Declaration without really listening to them. The U.S. government often did the same thing. Our nation wasn't guaranteeing basic human rights to all its citizens. Habit and selfishness were standing in the way of fairness—and no one did much about it. That was going to change. It would take a struggle to overcome the demons of bigotry—a struggle that continues today.

This poster from 1943 reminded Americans of the brave service of men like Dobie Miller, who was awarded the Navy Cross for his heroic actions aboard the USS *West Virginia* during the attack on Pearl Harbor. ▼

"above and beyond the call of duty"

DORIE MILLER
*Received the Navy Cross
at Pearl Harbor, May 27, 1942*

After World War II, our nation engaged in another struggle: America versus the Soviet Union. The Soviet Union was the second most powerful nation in the world. We had been allies and friends during the war. But there was something about the Soviet Union that made us nervous. It was a communist nation with a totalitarian government.

Totalitarianism is a political idea; *communism* is an economic idea. In a totalitarian government, the leaders have total control. They tell people what they can do and say and punish them if they do otherwise. Totalitarianism is the opposite of free government.

Communism is a method for controlling work and distributing a nation's farm produce, manufactured goods, and services. Under communism, the government owns almost everything—land and business and industry. Citizens work for the government, not for themselves.

Under *capitalism*, citizens do work for themselves. Businesses are mostly owned by individuals or corporations. If you check Article 1, Section 8, of the Constitution, you will see the responsibilities of Congress in our capitalistic nation.

▲ A Soviet poster encourages the people of the U.S.S.R. to work hard for the good of the state.

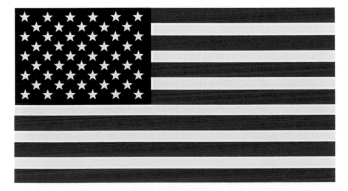 

▲ The Cold War pitted capitalism against communism, the West against the East.
(At left, the flag of the U.S.; at right, the flag of the U.S.S.R.)

Totalitarianism and democracy are enemies. Communism and capitalism are rivals. After two world wars, we were fearful of rivals. Soviet Russia wasn't the only communist dictatorship. China and Cuba would soon become two others. Could we all live together on the same planet? Or would there be a World War III? In 1945, we were about to begin a war of nerves with the communist nations.

All the People

America is a nation built on ideas instead of on a sameness of birth and background. One of our national ideas is that what you believe is no business of the president or the government. The Founders called that *freedom of conscience,* or *freedom of religion.*

Another great idea is that *we, the people,* can be responsible for ourselves. We can run our own government. We can pick our own leaders. That is called *democracy.*

It may seem surprising to you that freedom and self-government are unusual. But they are. America's founders understood that a fair government is a process and not an easy one. It doesn't happen all at once. Improving that government is a process without end.

One thing is clear: if citizens don't get involved in their government, they can lose their precious rights. In a democracy, if you want to change things, you have to be part of the process. You have to be willing to help make our democracy what it was meant to be: a government for *all the people.*

Americans all—we the people—all the people ▼

A (Very Short) History of Russia

In order to understand American history in the 20th century, you need to know some Russian history. Does that sound strange? Well, things were happening in Russia that would decide much that happened in the United States. Partly it was because we were obsessed with Russia, which means we couldn't get that country out of our minds. Partly it was because there were real dangers to the world from communist Russia's dictatorship.

After World War II we were determined to be mightier than the Soviet Union. Because of that, we spent vast sums of money on our military forces. We built huge stockpiles of expensive weapons—more than enough to blow up the world. We persecuted some of our own citizens because of fear of communist ideas. Sometimes we even seemed to lose faith in our way of life because we mistakenly thought Russian communism was more powerful.

Now for that Russian history. In 1917, during World War I, Russia had a revolution. For centuries, Russia had been a feudal society controlled by tsars—who were like emperors. The word *tsar* (ZAR) comes from *caesar*, which was the title of ancient Rome's great leaders.

Many of Russia's tsars were selfish tyrants with absolute control over their people. The Russian people wanted something better: they wanted the things that all people want—peace, opportunities, and freedom. Alexander Kerensky led a revolution in 1917. When Vladimir Ilyich Lenin heard that

Russian revolutionaries storm the Winter Palace, a symbol of the tsar's power and lavish way of life. ▶

news in Switzerland, where he had been exiled by the tsar, he headed home to Russia. Lenin—who was the head of a radical political party called the Bolsheviks—ousted Kerensky in a second revolution a few months after the first.

Lenin formed a communist government. It was an experiment. Communism had never been tried in a whole nation before. Lenin had to use force to make it work. He soon created a vicious, unfree, totalitarian government.

When Lenin died, Joseph Stalin took over. He was worse than Lenin, and worse than any of the tsars. He killed millions of his own people. Russians who protested were murdered or sent to prison camps in Siberia. Most never came home again. Meanwhile, Stalin and his followers were telling the rest of the world that the Soviet Union was turning into a wonderful, perfect society. It was

A political cartoon depicts a giant Joseph Stalin trampling on Russia and Eastern Europe. ▼

▲ In 1918, Vladimir Lenin established the world's first communist government in Russia.

▲ Thousands who opposed Stalin were sentenced to hard labor at camps in frigid Siberia.

hard for outsiders to find out the truth. There was no free press; the government controlled all the media. Many people believed the experiment was working.

Communism, to those who hadn't tried it, seemed like a fine economic plan. Most of the ideas for modern communism came from a 19th-century thinker named Karl Marx. Marx wanted to make the world better. He looked at capitalism and saw that, without regulation, wealth soon piled up in a few hands and left many people miserable. There was something even more disturbing: money power usually led to political power. So the poor had double troubles. They had no money and no political power. Marx said capitalism was doomed. And, during the worldwide Depression of the 1930s, it seemed as if he was right.

The official name for Lenin's nation was the Union of Soviet Socialist Republics, or the U.S.S.R. The U.S.S.R. was also known as the Soviet Union or Soviet Russia, or, often, just Russia. Russia was the largest of a group of states, or republics. None were free, independent republics. The union lasted until 1991.

Under Marx's economic system, people are supposed to work hard and give their products to the government, which is then expected to distribute things fairly to everyone as needed. People don't get paid according to how much they work, but rather according to how much they need. Unfortunately, Karl Marx didn't know a lot about human nature. Most people need a reason to work hard.

Russia, China, and several other nations tried communism. There was neither economic nor political freedom in any of them. Work and pay were decided by the government. And there was no leaving if you didn't like the system. The communist nations were huge police states.

Things didn't turn out the way Marx had predicted. In communist countries, productivity was low and government distribution was not fair. In Russia, the government became terribly inefficient and wasteful. Perhaps communism didn't get a good test, as some said, but, mostly, the experts who had hoped for great things from Karl Marx's ideas were disappointed.

There was something else that surprised a lot of experts: capitalism wasn't doomed. If Karl Marx could have risen from his 19th-century grave he would have been astonished to find that in the United States, in the second half of the 20th century, capitalism helped a great many people pursue happiness. Free markets brought cars, washing machines, nice clothes, and TV sets to most Americans.

But none of that was clear in 1945. We didn't understand ourselves, and we certainly didn't understand the Soviet Union. Some 40 years after World War II, Russian communism collapsed because the system proved unworkable. But in 1945, some people thought Russia was the hope of the future. Some were terrified of communism without really knowing why. Others feared that communists were about to take over the United States. It was very confusing.

◀ Soviet propaganda portrayed the experiment in communist economics as a grand success. In fact, it was a failure.

The Making of a President

Vice President Harry S. Truman became president near the end of World War II, after President Franklin Roosevelt died. It was, as he said, an accidental presidency. He had been a senator—a quiet, hardworking senator—who seemed an ordinary, likable man. Then, to his surprise, Roosevelt asked him to be vice president. He was just getting settled in that job when, suddenly, he was president. He felt, he said, as if a bull had fallen on top of him.

To most Americans, Harry Truman seemed more like a next-door neighbor than a president. Except for a year in France as an army captain in World War I, he'd hardly been anywhere. He'd been a farmer, a bank clerk, a shopkeeper, and a county administrator—all in Missouri. When he arrived in Washington, at age 50, you could almost see the rough edges. Sometimes he lost his temper and didn't think much about what he was saying. But he was never mean, or dishonest.

In fact, his honesty was legendary. When he wrote letters home to his mother and sister, as he did almost every day, he paid for the stamps himself. The franking privilege—which allows senators and presidents to send their mail free—was meant for government business, he said. He never used it for his personal letters. He lived modestly on his salary, and he didn't use his position to earn extra money. When a Republican who was a political rival left his briefcase at the White House, some of Truman's Democratic aides wanted to go through it and see what it held. President Truman would not do a sneaky thing like that.

When he was president, some people made jokes about him, but others noticed that he was very good at making decisions. Later, a historian wrote of him, "With more fateful decisions than almost any president in our time, he made the fewest mistakes." A senator said he was usually wrong about all the little things, but right about all the big ones.

Harry Truman was president during clamorous times. An army of men was returning from military to civilian life; they needed jobs and homes. People were

After World War II, hundreds of thousands of American soldiers and sailors were welcomed home. ▼

moving from farms to cities faster than ever before. Could those cities become good places for everyone living in them? Europe and Japan were devastated. How would they rebuild? People of color were being treated unfairly. Would that continue? How would we change from making tanks and bombs to making dishwashers and automobiles? And what about Russia? The Russian leader, Joseph Stalin, had made promises he wasn't keeping. Truman the president had to answer those and many other questions. He said that knowing history helped him do the job.

Harry Truman could have been a history teacher; he knew a whole lot about the subject. His interest began when he was a boy and his father read a book to him about the ancient Greeks and Romans. He found he loved stories about people, especially real people. So, as soon as he could read himself, he started on biographies. Andrew Jackson became a special hero of his. Jackson was a man of action who represented the common people. A man who was independent, free-thinking, and not at all stuck up.

Truman was born on a farm in Jackson County, Missouri (which was named after Andrew Jackson). When Harry was six, the family moved to nearby Independence. There, Harry discovered the public library and started reading all kinds of books.

Reading gave him information; it allowed him to think for himself. He was soon forming his own opinions, and he didn't always agree with those around him. There was one president whom everyone in Truman's family hated. Really hated. They could hardly talk about him without getting angry. But the more Harry Truman read about that president, the more he admired him.

This photograph shows the town square in Independence, Missouri, as it appeared when Harry Truman was a boy there. ▶

It was the Civil War president, Abraham Lincoln. People hated Abraham Lincoln? They certainly did. You see, Harry Truman was a boy at the end of the 19th century, when many men and women could remember the Civil War as if it had just happened.

Truman's grandparents, both sets of them, had come to Independence, Missouri, in the 1840s, during the early pioneer days, when Missouri was a border state—and a slave state. They came from Kentucky by steamboat, newly married, bringing slaves they got as wedding presents. They weren't unusual; most of their neighbors were slave owners, too.

The Kansas–Missouri region was one of the hottest and meanest regions before and during the Civil War. Some terrible things were done there—on both sides.

One morning in 1861, while one of Truman's grandfathers, Solomon Young, was away, his grandmother was working on her farm. Suddenly a band of Union raiders galloped into the yard, ordered her to cook a big meal for them, killed all her chickens and 400 hogs, set fire to the barns, and then rode off with the freshly butchered meat, 13 mules, 15 horses, and the family silver. While all this was going on, 11-year-old Martha hid under the kitchen table.

Two years later, Martha and the rest of the family were marched to a Yankee fort where they were kept prisoners. Their home—a white-pillared plantation house—was burned to the ground by Union soldiers. Are you surprised that Martha Young hated Yankees and President Lincoln?

Martha was Harry Truman's mother. She grew up to be a strong woman who played the piano well, had a good education, and said what she thought—a trait that she passed on to her son. (He was a good piano player, too.) Once, when she came to visit the White House, the only empty bed was Lincoln's famous one. Now, most White House guests feel very privileged if they can sleep in the very bed where Abraham Lincoln slept, but not Martha Truman. She said if that was the only bed, why, she'd just sleep on the floor. She was well known for her sense of humor, but this time her son knew she wasn't kidding. He found another bed for her.

▲ Harry Truman, age 13

Truman enjoyed playing the piano throughout his life. ▼

A Curtain of Iron

Britain's great wartime leader, Winston Churchill, had something to say, but no one was listening. So, in 1946, when President Truman asked the former prime minister to speak at tiny Westminster College in Fulton, Missouri, Churchill didn't hesitate. He said yes.

Churchill wanted to talk about Russian communism. Many people did not know what to think about Stalin and Soviet Russia. During World War II (which ended in 1945), Russia was the ally of Britain and the United States. No people fought harder against the Nazis than the Russians. No nation suffered war losses as enormous as Russia's. When the war ended, everyone hoped for friendship between the new superpowers: Russia and America. Around the world, many people believed that Russian communism was an acceptable form of government.

Ominous means "threatening."

Winston Churchill thought differently. Churchill had warned of Adolf Hitler and Nazism long before most Britons or Americans took them seriously. Once again, he wanted to tell the world of a dangerous dictator and an ominous form of government. "A shadow has fallen upon the scenes so lately lighted by the Allied victory," he said at that small Missouri college. The shadow he was talking about was vicious totalitarian rule. "From Stettin in the Baltic to Trieste in the Adriatic an *iron curtain* has descended across the Continent," Churchill continued. (The continent Churchill was referring to was Europe.)

The curtain of iron was blocking out truth and freedom. Nations behind that curtain were prisoners of Russia.

When World War II ended, the armies of the winning Allied powers—the U.S., the U.S.S.R., and Great Britain—moved through Europe, freeing the nations that had been conquered by Hitler's Nazis. The Allies promised to help the liberated nations. They promised to help them hold open elections and form free governments. After that, the Allied armies were supposed to leave (which was what we did).

Winston Churchill spoke his mind about the dangers of communism. As one newspaper said, "When Mr. Churchill speaks, the world listens." ▼

Russia wouldn't go. Soviet armies stayed in control in Poland, Romania, Bulgaria, Czechoslovakia, Hungary, Yugoslavia, Latvia, Lithuania, Estonia, and East Germany. There were no free elections there. Elsewhere—in nations like Italy and France—the communist parties were growing strong. Joseph Stalin bragged that the whole world would eventually go over to communism.

But most people didn't stay behind the iron curtain willingly. Armed guards stood at every Soviet border. Iron curtains would soon extend over several Asian countries. Some east European countries, like Hungary and Yugoslavia, attempted

▲ Soviet tanks roll into Budapest, Hungary.

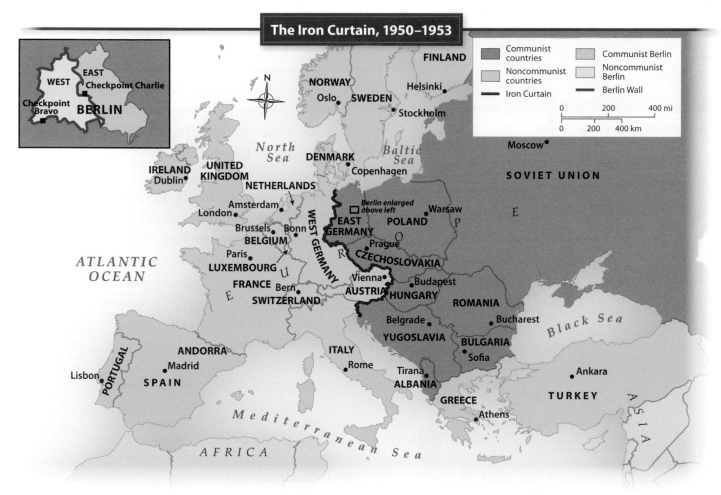
▲ Winston Churchill called the division between the communist nations of Eastern Europe and the democratic nations of Western Europe an "iron curtain."

▲ President Harry Truman (seated, second from left) meets with his military advisers.

to rebel and become independent. The Hungarians were crushed and their leaders killed. The president of Yugoslavia, Marshal Tito (TEE-toe), was as crafty as Stalin himself, and he managed to keep the Soviet Union at arm's length. But even Yugoslavia was not really a free country. It had only one political party, and that was communist.

In an address to Congress, President Truman said, "I believe that it must be the policy of the United States to support free peoples who are resisting attempted subjugation by armed minorities or by outside pressure." (To *subjugate* is to conquer or bring under control.) Truman decided the United States would come to the aid of any nation endangered by communism. We would not let Soviet Russia expand further.

We began by sending $400 million in emergency aid to Greece and Turkey. That program of assistance was called the Truman Doctrine. The idea behind the Truman Doctrine was to keep communism from spreading. That policy was known as "containment." It was the beginning of a *cold war* against Russia. The Cold War lasted more than 40 years.

Why a "Cold" War?

Because the United States and the Soviet Union did not directly engage each other in a "hot" war—a war with shooting and bloodshed—the tense 40-year standoff between the superpowers is known as the Cold War. Although the Soviet Union and the United States never directly fought each other, battles did take place in countries where people allied themselves with one superpower or the other.

Germany Divided

At the end of World War II, the Soviets occupied eastern Germany while Britain, France, and the United States occupied the western portion of the country. Just as Germany was divided, so was Berlin, its capital city.

The city of Berlin was located more than 100 miles inside the Soviet-dominated part of Germany. Stalin wanted to drive the Americans and their allies out of the western half of the city. In June 1948, he ordered a blockade of West Berlin. Without supplies, West Berlin's people would soon face starvation. Stalin hoped his blockade would bring the entire city under Soviet control.

In response to the Soviet blockade, the British and Americans organized a massive airlift of food and other supplies. In the Berlin Airlift, as the rescue operation is known, more than 277,000 flights delivered 2.3 million tons of supplies to West Berlin. Because of the difficult flying conditions, 73 Allied airmen lost their lives in the course of the Berlin Airlift.

▲ A sentry on the western side of the Berlin Wall looks across at his counterpart in the eastern sector.

In May 1949, Stalin lifted the blockade. In that same year, Germany was divided into two countries. The western part became a separate, democratic nation, the Federal Republic of Germany, often called West Germany. The eastern part of Germany became the German Democratic Republic, often called East Germany, with East Berlin as its capital. Despite its name, East Germany was far from democratic. The Communist Party controlled the government and took its directions from the Soviet Union.

In 1961, the Russians built a concrete wall in the middle of the city of Berlin and topped it with barbed wire to keep people in the eastern half from fleeing to West Berlin and freedom.

Children in West Berlin cheer an American cargo plane loaded with supplies for the beleaguered city. ▼

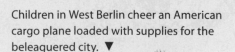

CHAPTER 27

The Marshall Plan

Two signs sat on President Truman's desk. The first sign quoted a man from Truman's home state of Missouri. It said, ALWAYS DO RIGHT. THIS WILL GRATIFY SOME PEOPLE & ASTONISH THE REST. They were the words of Mark Twain.

The second sign said, THE BUCK STOPS HERE.

Which means: the president has the final word and can't blame anyone else for his decisions.

Harry Truman had some big decisions to make. Those decisions would profoundly affect Americans and people around the world. In one of the most important of his decisions, he persuaded the American people to act generously to the defeated nations. What Harry Truman had in mind had never been done before in the history of the world.

Truman knew how defeated people feel after a war. He knew that his Confederate ancestors carried hate in their hearts all their lives. He knew that Germany's anger after World War I had helped bring about a second world war.

So he supported a plan that would send billions of dollars in aid and assistance to our allies and to our former enemies. It was

The rebuilding of Germany began with aid from the Marshall Plan. ▼

called the Marshall Plan (named for Secretary of State George C. Marshall, who introduced the idea in a speech at Harvard College), but it reflected President Truman's thoughts. After a terrible war, he was asking the winning nation to help everyone recover—including the losers. The president said, "You can't be vindictive after a war. You have to be generous. You have to help people get back on their feet." (*Vindictive* means you're out for revenge.)

Marshall Plan aid was very concrete (that's a pun). U.S. money rebuilt steel mills in Belgium, ceramics factories in France, railroads in Germany, and bridges and buildings in a whole lot of places.

Marshall Plan aid was offered to all of Europe's nations—including the Soviet Union and those countries under Soviet control. The Soviet nations refused the aid. Sixteen nations accepted with enthusiasm. It was very expensive. It was very unselfish. The plan encouraged

Europeans to use American aid and add their own brains and know-how. It worked. Prosperity began returning to the free nations of Europe. It also helped us. Those newly prosperous European nations now had money to buy American goods. And they did.

In East Asia, General Douglas MacArthur was sent to defeated Japan as head of an occupation army. The U.S. was determined to rid Japan of its war leaders and bring democracy, freedom, and prosperity to that nation. The Japanese wrote a new constitution; it made Japan a democracy. Land was redistributed so that more people could have it. (Before, there had been a few huge landowners and many poor farmers; now there was a better balance. Soon there would be great prosperity.) Women were allowed to vote. (Thirty-nine women were elected to Japan's congress, called the Diet.) Secret political societies were prohibited. And religious discrimination was ended. The United States poured aid into Japan—food, clothing, medicines, and other supplies. Ancient temples and museums were restored. We were very generous. No nation had ever done that kind of thing for a defeated foe.

▲ General Douglas MacArthur poses with Emperor Hirohito of Japan.

Another Truman plan, called Point Four, gave aid to developing nations. Developing nations are also called Third World nations. These countries are less wealthy and less modern than the industrial nations. Many developing nations are in Africa, Asia, and Latin America.

Did everyone approve of these generous policies? Not at all. Some people in Europe and Asia said they didn't want to take aid from America. They thought we wanted something in return. Some people in Congress yelled about all the money it was costing. "Why should we help others?" they asked. "Why should we help our former enemies?" they screamed.

In January 1946, the first General Assembly of the United Nations met in London, England. Secretary of State James F. Byrnes headed the U.S. delegation, which included Eleanor Roosevelt, widow of the former president. In October, the General Assembly accepted a gift from John D. Rockefeller, Jr., to pay for a UN headquarters site in New York City.

The United Nations headquarters in New York City ▶

In 1948, President Truman issued an executive order integrating the U.S. armed services. Integrated units fought together for the first time during the Korean War. ▶

A *lynching* is an outside-the-law execution.

People also screamed when President Truman decided to do something to help people in the United States. He decided it was time to do something about civil rights, especially about lynchings and segregation. The army, navy, and air force were all segregated. Blacks and whites served in separate units. Blacks got the worst jobs. That wasn't fair. Like other Americans, they were willing to fight for their country. Why should they be treated differently?

In Mississippi, when some black soldiers returned home, they were dumped from army trucks and then beaten. In Georgia, a black man was shot and killed because he had voted. When Truman heard of those outrages he was horrified.

He sent proposals to Congress to stop lynchings and to outlaw the poll tax that kept some people (mostly blacks) from voting. He ordered an end to segregation in the armed services, and he created a commission on civil rights.

People infected with prejudice and hate began to howl. A Florida county commission said the president's program was "obnoxious, repugnant, odious, detestable, loathsome, repulsive, revolting and humiliating." A Mississippi congressman said Truman had "run a political dagger into our backs and now he is trying to drink our blood."

Israel and an American Peacemaker

On May 14, 1948, the state of Israel came into being. It was a hard birth, coming after almost 2,000 years of Jewish longing to return to their homeland, and after promises of a Jewish state by the victors of World War I. But the Jews weren't the only people who laid claim to that hauntingly beautiful land. The Arabs, who lived there, claimed it, too—and didn't want to share it. The story is complicated. Here is some of it.

About 4,000 years ago, in the time of Abraham and Moses, Israel (or Palestine, as it came to be called) became the home of the Jews. Two thousand years later, in the year 70 C.E., the Romans drove many of the Jews from their country.

They settled throughout the Roman Empire, living in a diaspora (die-ASS-por-uh), or exile. Jews prayed for a return to the holy city of Jerusalem.

At the end of the 19th century, in response to fierce European anti-Semitism, the Zionist movement emerged. Its aim was to re-create a Jewish nation in Israel. Zionist Jews began moving to Palestine. By the time of the First World War (1914), 90,000 Jews were living in Palestine, which was part of the southern region of Syria, under the control of Turkey.

Turkey sided with Germany in that first World War and lost its empire. The Allies (who won) gave Great Britain the job of ruling Palestine.

A view of the city of Jerusalem ▼

In 1917, the British Foreign Office issued the Balfour Declaration (written by the foreign secretary, Arthur James Balfour), which said: "His Majesty's government views with favour the establishment in Palestine of a National Home for the Jewish People." President Woodrow Wilson cabled his support of the declaration.

Many Jews set out for their ancient homeland. They drained and irrigated land, planted trees, built the new city of Tel Aviv, and made schools and homes. Some Arabs protested their presence. Some attacked and killed Jews.

By 1939, more than 30 percent of Palestine's population was Jewish. But that year, the British, bowing to Arab pressure, limited immigration into Palestine to 1,500 Jews a month. Jews were desperate to escape from Europe. The alternative was Hitler's death camps. But they had nowhere to go. The U.S. had immigration quotas that kept most Jews out. So did many other nations. Six million European Jews were murdered.

After World War II, about 250,000 survivors of the camps remained in Europe. Their homes had been taken, their families killed. President Truman urged that 100,000 be allowed to enter Palestine. But the British stuck to their monthly quotas. When boatloads of survivors arrived on their shores, they were turned away.

In 1947, when the British announced their intention to leave the region in May of the following year, the United Nations got involved. The UN recommended that the land be divided into separate Jewish and Arab states, largely determined by population. This division was called "partition." Jerusalem, a city sacred to three religions, would be held under international control. Jewish leaders agreed to the UN's partition. Arab organizations were all against it.

Jews and Arabs were soon fighting a civil war. At first the Arabs seemed to be winning, but the Jews fought back and stunned everyone with their victories. The day before the British left Palestine, the Jews announced the birth of a new nation. They called it Israel. It was founded on democratic principles. The Arabs kept fighting.

Most Americans were sympathetic to Jewish hopes for a homeland, but the U.S. State Department was not. Arabs controlled vast quantities of oil. There were fears of Russian influence. The president was advised not to recognize a Jewish nation.

◀ Jewish immigrants aboard a refugee ship in 1948

▲ Young Jews in Tel Aviv celebrate the proclamation of the new state of Israel.

◄ Ralph Bunche

In the months that followed, thousands of Jews and Arabs died. Neither side won, but the Jews controlled most major cities, and the Arab forces realized they faced real fighters.

The UN got involved again. An American peacemaker took over as the UN mediator. He was a man who had known prejudice himself. His name was Ralph Bunche. The grandson of a slave, Bunche was the first black to earn a Ph.D. in political science from Harvard. He had been a professor at Howard University in Washington, D.C. He set the boundaries of today's Israeli state. It took incredible determination and patience. At first the Israelis and Arabs wouldn't talk to each other. He vowed, "I'll never adjourn this meeting. I'll stay for 10 years if necessary." It took him only 81 days. Ralph Bunche was awarded the Nobel Peace Prize in 1950.

In the following decades, there would be more fighting between Israelis and Arabs, and more peace talks. The region remains troubled, and peace still elusive.

But Truman, urged by an old friend, agreed to meet with Chaim Weizmann, a scientist who was Israel's first president. After the United States recognized Israel on May 14, 1948, the Soviet Union did, too. But on May 15, Lebanon, Syria, Transjordan, Iraq, and Egypt joined together to send armies to crush the young nation. Most of the Arabs in Israel fled, for reasons that would be disputed in years to come. The war created two refugee populations—equal numbers of Arabs from Israel and Jews from Arab lands.

Palestinian refugees trek across the scorching heat of Jordan near the shores of the Dead Sea. ▶

A "Lost" Election

In the presidential election of 1948, Democrats could count on winning in the South. No Southern state had voted for a Republican for president since before the Civil War. The South was known as "the solid South." It was solidly Democratic.

Now, because of Truman's civil rights proposals, many Southern politicians were furious with their party. They weren't quite ready to turn Republican, but they were certainly against Harry. So some formed another party. It was called the Dixiecrat Party.

Other Democrats were unhappy with the president for different reasons. Some thought Truman was too hard on communism. They wanted the United States to try to get along with Joseph Stalin and the Soviet-controlled countries. Some wanted more domestic reforms. Those people formed another party. It was a new Progressive Party.

When a candidate splits his own party in three—well, he is in trouble. In 1948, Harry Truman and the Democrats were in trouble. Besides, the Democratic Party had been in power since 1932, so most people said they were ready for a change.

Truman was nice enough. But after that giant of the war years, Franklin Roosevelt, Harry Truman seemed almost embarrassing. Sometimes he just popped off and said whatever was on his mind. He wasn't dignified. He wasn't meant to be president, some people said.

So everyone knew that Harry Truman didn't have a chance to get elected in 1948. Some Democrats tried to dump him. They wanted someone else as their candidate. But Harry S. Truman was stubborn. He was head of the party and he was going to run for election.

The Republicans chose Thomas E. Dewey as their candidate for president. Dewey was governor of New York. He was much younger than Truman, but he acted old and wise. He had a trim, compact build, dark hair, and a small dark mustache. He was dignified. He didn't say much. He didn't campaign hard. He just began to act as if he were president, because everyone knew he would be soon.

Franklin Roosevelt had used radio to talk to the American people. Truman wasn't a good speaker on the radio. But he was pretty good in person, especially when he spoke without a prepared speech and

President Truman casts his vote in the 1948 Democratic primary. ▼

just said what he thought. So Harry Truman got on a train and began his campaign. (In those days most people traveled long distances by train. There weren't many big highways, and air travel was still a novelty and expensive.)

The president's train had bedrooms, a dining room, a car for newspaper reporters, a car for presidential aides, office space, and a wood-paneled sitting room for the president and his family—16 cars in all. The train crossed the nation—twice. When it pulled into a city, or town, or hamlet, the president stood on the back platform and spoke to anyone who came to the railroad station to hear him. Lots of people came. Wouldn't you go to hear a president?

Truman liked to introduce his wife, Bess, and his daughter, Margaret, to those who appeared at the whistle stops. "Would you like to meet the Boss?" he'd say before Bess appeared. (Bess told her husband that if he called her "the Boss" one more time, she'd get off the train.)

Sometimes Harry Truman gave his first speech before six in the morning. He was a farm boy and used to getting up early. He gave speeches all day long—10 or 15 a day. Sometimes he got off the train for an outdoor rally. Usually there were flags and bunting and local politicians to share the platform.

Sometimes high school bands played and marched, and the president gave a luncheon or dinner speech in a big city hall. It was exhausting to everyone except Harry Truman, who seemed to get

▲ First Lady Bess Truman, whom the president affectionately called "the Boss"

Presidential candidate Harry Truman, his daughter, Margaret, and wife, Bess, campaign from the rear platform of a train in Bridgeport, Pennsylvania. ▼

Harry Truman had a hard time with Congress. That body approved his foreign-aid plans but turned down many of his domestic (home) proposals. Some of those proposals—for civil rights, national health insurance, and urban planning—were farsighted. But Congress did pass some important bills. One was called the G.I. Bill of Rights. It gave military veterans a chance for a free college education. It educated a generation of Americans (mostly men), and that helped create a broader and stronger middle class.

▲ Thomas E. Dewey accepts the Republican Party's nomination for the presidency.

more energetic and feisty as the campaign continued. His speeches were fighting speeches. He lashed out at the Republican Congress (which wasn't passing the laws he wanted), and he attacked those who asked for special government favors: he called them "power lobbies" and "high hats." People cheered his spirit (even if they didn't seem impressed with him otherwise). "Give 'em hell, Harry," they said. Tom Dewey had a train, too. But he didn't get up early, and he didn't give many speeches. He didn't need to. It was clear that he was going to win. *Everyone* said so.

Newsweek magazine asked 50 leading journalists—people whose business it is to know politics—who would win. *All 50 said that Truman would lose.* One of Truman's aides bought *Newsweek* and read it on the train. Not even one reporter gave the president a chance to win. The aide tried to hide the magazine, but Truman spotted it and read the article. "Don't worry," he said, "I know every one of those 50 fellows, and not one of them has enough sense to pound sand into a rat hole."

The sensible *New York Times* conducted a survey. It sent reporters around the country for a whole month. The reporters concluded that 29 states would go to Dewey, 11 to Truman, and four to the Dixiecrats. The others were undecided.

Every leading poll showed a Dewey landslide.

On November 2, 1948, the American people voted.

That evening, Dewey's supporters crowded into the ballroom of a New York hotel. They were there to celebrate. Men wore black tuxedos and women wore evening gowns. Each Republican woman was presented with an orchid as a victory corsage. Waiters carried trays of elegant food.

In Washington, the Democrats hadn't even rented their usual hotel ballroom. They were short of money and there was no point in wasting it—they had nothing to celebrate.

Newspaper reporters wrote articles congratulating the new president on his victory—that way they could go to bed as soon as the returns came in. At the *Chicago Tribune*, the morning's headline announcing Dewey's victory was set in type.

As night arrived, the counting began. (In this time before computers, vote counting was slower than it is today.) Maybe it was habit, but many people stayed up to listen to their radios. They

◀ In one of the greatest gaffes in newspaper history, the *Chicago Tribune* went to press before the election results were in.

expected a quick decision. Election results were being broadcast on television, for the first time. But most people didn't have television sets. Harry Truman didn't have one. He was staying at a small hotel. He ate a ham sandwich, drank a glass of buttermilk, and went to bed early. When it was announced that he had won in Massachusetts, one of his Secret Service men woke him with the news. "Stop worrying," said Truman, and went back to sleep.

At midnight he woke up, turned on the radio, and listened as a deep-voiced radio commentator announced that although Truman was a million votes ahead, they were just early votes: Dewey was sure to win.

At 1:30 a.m. the Republican national chairman said that it looked as if Dewey would win in New York state and would soon be president of the United States. The guests cheered.

At 4 a.m. the Secret Service agents received a call from Democratic headquarters. Illinois had been put in Truman's win column. They couldn't resist waking their boss. "That's it," he said. "Now, let's get back to sleep."

At dawn, Truman got up. The deep-voiced radio announcer was saying that it was a very close election—but Dewey would win. By mid-morning it was clear: all the experts were wrong! Truman was no accidental president. He had won the job on his own.

A Major Leaguer

In 1945, we were a Jim Crow nation. It was nothing to be proud of, but that's the way it was. In the South, everything was segregated: schools, buses, restaurants, hotels, even phone booths. The rest of the country wasn't as blatant about it, but there was plenty of separation and prejudice.

Those who approved of Jim Crow segregation said that things were "separate but equal." They were separate all right. But they were rarely equal. And they certainly were not on the ball field.

When it came to the national pastime—which is what baseball is called—there were the major leagues, the minor leagues, and there were the negro leagues (for ballplayers of color).

The major leaguers played in fine ballparks, traveled first class, and slept in decent hotels. The negro leaguers? Well, they put up with a lot: shoddy conditions, no ballparks of their own (they rented what they could find), travel any way they could make it, and—usually—lower pay (except for the incredible Satchel Paige, who in 1942 managed to make more money than anyone in any league).

One thing the negro leagues did have in abundance was talent. When black players played all-star games against white teams they usually won. Just think about it, and you can see how insane the system was. All those good ballplayers and no one letting them play

Baseball greats like first baseman Leonard Buck played in the negro leagues but could not play major league baseball. ▼

in the majors! There were plenty of whites who understood that, and there were plenty of whites without prejudice.

One of them was the general manager of the Brooklyn Dodgers, Branch Rickey. Rickey decided he was going to change baseball. He was going to make it the national pastime for all Americans.

But he knew it wouldn't be easy. Fighting prejudice never is. Rickey was the right man for this job. He had founded baseball's system of farm teams back in the 1920s. That means he came up with the idea of taking over minor league teams (which had been independently owned, just like the major league clubs) and using them to develop ballplayers for the major leagues. Branch Rickey was used to scouting good players. He knew how to pick them. He was also a shrewd businessman. Black ballplayers (then) were a pool of inexpensive talent. They played an exciting, hustling kind of baseball. And they would bring a huge new black audience to the majors.

If Rickey was going to change baseball and some of the nation's attitudes by integrating the Brooklyn Dodgers, he knew he would have to find a ballplayer who was not only a great athlete, but, even more important, a great person. When he found Jack Roosevelt Robinson he had just the man he was looking for.

Jackie Robinson was a spectacular athlete. He had earned letters and trophies in four sports at the University of California at Los Angeles (UCLA). He was very smart and did well in school. And he had the strength to fight for his beliefs. As an officer in the army, Robinson refused to move when a bus driver asked him to sit in the back of the bus (where blacks were expected to sit). That got Jackie in trouble, but he wouldn't back down. He faced a court martial (a military court) for disobedience. But the young lieutenant had acted within his rights; the army dropped the charges against him.

▲ Public facilities throughout the South were segregated by race.

Brooklyn Dodgers general manager Branch Rickey watches as Jack Roosevelt (Jackie) Robinson becomes the first African American to sign with a major league baseball team. ▼

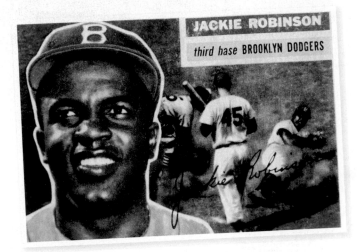

▲ Jackie Robinson's rookie baseball card

Some people thought him a troublemaker, but Branch Rickey was impressed. Here was a man of courage, he believed.

Rickey asked Robinson to come to New York. He said he wanted to talk about a new negro team. Then, in his office, Branch Rickey told Jackie the truth: he wanted him to break baseball's color line. Both men knew the first black ballplayer in the major leagues wouldn't have it easy. Rickey told Robinson that if he wanted the job—no matter what happened to him—he had to promise not to fight back. He would have to take abuse and hold his tongue. At all times he would have to be a gentleman.

"Mr. Rickey, do you want a ballplayer who's afraid to fight back?"

"I want a player with guts enough not to fight back," said Rickey.

Robinson had never backed away from a fight. He knew that if someone insulted him it would be very difficult to do what Rickey asked: to "turn the other cheek." But he agreed; he gave his word. He was going to do something bigger than anything he'd done before; it was more important than his feelings. It was for his people and for all people.

The two men talked for three hours. Still, neither of them realized how much courage Jackie Robinson would actually need. He had tough times ahead of him. He was going to be spiked, spat on, sent death threats, hit with pitches, and called awful names. How would you have responded?

Branch Rickey began by sending Jackie Robinson to Brooklyn's leading farm team, the Montreal Royals. The Royals' manager, Clay Hopper, had grown up with prejudice. He had never had a black friend. He begged Branch Rickey not to make him coach Jackie Robinson. Rickey knew he was a good coach; he told him to do his job. By the end of the season Hopper had learned a lesson: most prejudice comes from ignorance. He told Robinson, "You're a real ballplayer and a gentleman. It's been wonderful having you on the team."

On April 15, 1947, Jackie Robinson, up from Montreal, batted in Brooklyn for the first time as a major leaguer. He was put out four

When some Dodgers said they wouldn't play on the team with a black man, Rickey traded them away.

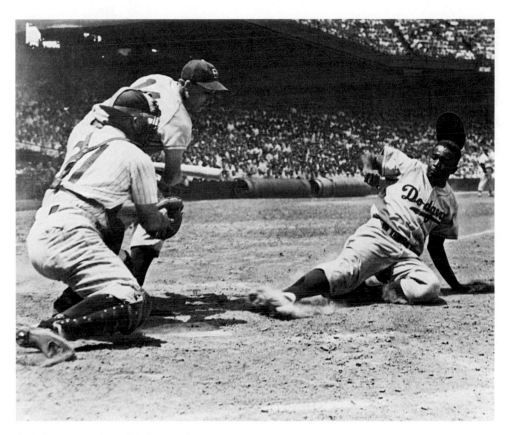

▲ Robinson steals and slides into home.

times that day. He didn't do much better the rest of the week. Had Rickey made a mistake?

Then, when the Dodgers went to Philadelphia to play the Phillies, even Rickey was stunned by what happened. The Phillies' manager, Ben Chapman, spewed hate language and encouraged his players to do the same. "At no time in my life have I heard racial venom and dugout abuse to match the abuse that Ben sprayed on Robinson that night," said one of Branch Rickey's aides. "I could scarcely believe my ears," said Robinson.

Jackie Robinson took a deep breath and kept his word. The abuse wasn't all verbal. Runners were sliding and cutting him with their spikes, pitchers were throwing at his head. It was too much for his teammates—even those who hadn't wanted a black player on the club.

Sometimes actions bring unexpected results. The poor sportsmanship of some other teams brought the Dodgers together. They were behind their new teammate now.

Jackie Robinson, here seen signing autographs, won fans across the nation. ▶

Soon Robinson was swinging—and connecting. And when it came to base running? Hardly anyone has ever done it the way Jackie Robinson did. He gave pitchers the jitters. And when he stole home? Well, have you ever seen anyone steal home? There isn't much in baseball that is more exciting. Robinson was a fantastic base stealer.

In his rookie season, Jackie Robinson finished first in the league in stolen bases and second in runs scored. He tied for the team lead in home runs. Dodgers fans began cheering and cheering. The nation's most important sports paper, the *Sporting News* (which had said that Rickey was unwise to bring a black to the majors), named him rookie of the year. In September, the Brooklyn Dodgers won the National League pennant. And, at the end of the season, Branch Rickey told his star, "Jackie, you're on your own now. You can be yourself." Robinson no longer had to keep quiet, and he didn't.

Jackie Robinson had won the affection and respect of his fellow ballplayers and of the nation. He was the first; he took the punishment; he made it easy for those who followed. Baseball was now the national pastime for all the people.

Spies

The times were prosperous but not content. There was fear in the air.

Some Americans were afraid there might be a communist revolution in the United States. They believed that our nation was filled with communists.

Some thought that President Roosevelt's New Deal laws were inspired by communists. That legislation had changed America with strong child labor regulations, minimum wage standards, Social Security, and new taxes. All that had put some limits on capitalism. More people shared the wealth. The gap between rich and poor had been narrowed. There was a newly prosperous middle class (as there was when the nation was founded). That strong new middle class was challenging the old guard and its ways. Now Harry Truman wanted to change society even more, with his civil rights ideas and with a program of liberal reform called the Fair Deal. "Suppose he gets his national health insurance—who will pay for it?" some people asked. "Those who have the most money will pay most of the bills," they said. To many, it sounded like communism.

Then communist spies were discovered in the United States. They had stolen atom-bomb secrets and sold them to Russia.

As if that weren't bad enough, shocking news came from England—some top British intelligence officials turned out to be Soviet spies. And that wasn't all: in a case that filled newspaper headlines day after day, a former State Department adviser and president of an international peace organization—a man named Alger Hiss, whom everyone trusted—was convicted of lying about his involvement with an admitted communist. A young congressman, Richard Nixon, captured the attention of the whole nation with his hard questioning of Alger Hiss. When Hiss was found guilty of *perjury* (lying under oath) Americans were dismayed. It really did seem that the State Department might be full of spies and traitors. Alger Hiss spent four years in jail. (Hiss was guilty of lying, but was he a spy? People still argue about that.)

Former State Department official Alger Hiss takes the stand under oath in congressional hearings. Hiss denied the charges but was convicted of perjury. He spent the rest of his life trying to clear his name. ▼

▲ Mao Zedong, China's communist dictator

Of course, everyone knew that Russia had spies in the United States and that we had spies in Russia. Nations spied on each other then. They still do.

No question about it, these were confusing and frightening times. The United States had believed it was alone in having atomic power. Then, soon after the war's end, Russia tested an atom bomb. The thought of Joseph Stalin, a cold-blooded tyrant, with an atom bomb was terrifying. (It became still more terrifying when both nations developed hydrogen bombs.)

And there was China. For centuries, China was under the rule of an emperor. In 1911 he was overthrown. So, even before World War II, the Chinese people looked to new leaders. That led to a civil war, with two groups fighting for control of the huge country. One group, led by Chiang Kai-shek, was known as the Nationalists. The others were the communists, led by Mao Zedong.

During the Second World War, most Chinese fought together against their common enemy—Japan. But as soon as the war was over, they were fighting among themselves again. Finally, the communists won. But things didn't work out as most people

Hoover of the FBI

J. Edgar Hoover was head of the Federal Bureau of Investigation (the FBI) from the time of Woodrow Wilson until Richard Nixon was president. Almost no one else in Washington could say he had worked under 10 presidents. And almost no one in Washington was as powerful as the FBI chief.

Hoover hated communism and immigrants and anyone who disagreed with him, and he was in a position to scare and influence others. In a speech he said that in America there were half

▲ J. Edgar Hoover kept detailed files on everyone he didn't trust.

a million "fellow travelers and sympathizers ready to do the communist bidding." He had no proof of that, but he believed it. So did many who heard him.

expected. China's communists brought land reform and some stability to the country, but they also brought unfree totalitarian government. In America, people with loud voices said that Harry Truman was to blame for China's new communist government. (This may not seem to make sense now. Well, it didn't then, either, but some people listened.) Newspapers carried angry letters about China and how "we" lost it.

We had had some unusually well-trained China experts attached to our State Department. When those experts predicted that China would fall to the communists, the anticommunists in America didn't want to hear that news. America's China experts were accused of being communists themselves. They were fired, and replaced by others who were strangers to the region. That left us with almost no experts in the difficult years that were to come. Because of poor advice, we would make some bad mistakes in East Asia, especially in a place called Vietnam.

In 1950, however, we acted boldly. Most people think we did the right thing when the ruler of North Korea sent a powerful army into South Korea. Look at the maps and you'll see Korea, the big peninsula that juts out into the sea between China and Japan. Korea was an ancient, independent country. It was divided in two at the end of World War II. It was divided at latitude 38° north, also known as the *38th parallel*. Korea was supposed to be brought back together with free elections. The communists—who controlled the north—never allowed those elections.

The Russian-educated North Korean leader, Kim Il Sung, intended to make all of Korea communist. His army had the latest Russian tanks and equipment.

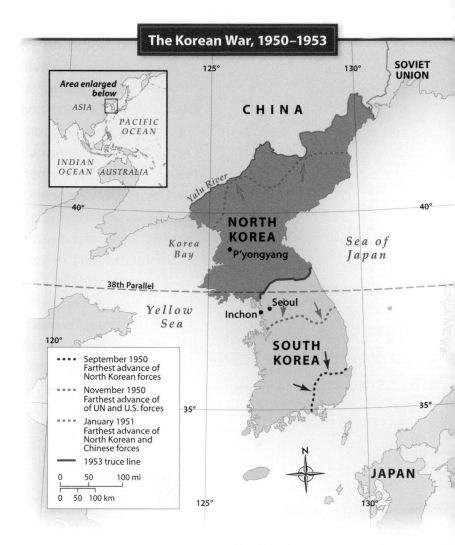

▲ Hostilities between communist and noncommunist forces in Korea escalated when China and the United States entered the conflict. The armistice line of 1953 still divides North Korea and South Korea.

The leader of South Korea, Syngman Rhee, had been educated in America. His army was poorly trained and badly equipped.

When North Korea's army entered South Korea, it was a test for the world community and for Truman and his policy of *containing* communism—of keeping it from expanding into new regions. Led by the United States, the United Nations acted quickly and sent troops. Russia could have vetoed the action but they were boycotting the UN. With the Korean War, the Cold War turned hot. The Truman administration termed it "police action" and a "conflict" rather than a war, setting a precedent that got around the constitutional requirement that Congress authorize war. The president gave himself power unintended in the Constitution. Future presidents would use that power again and again.

To the general public, and those who fought, it was a war, and not an easy one. At first the North Korean army drove the combined forces (South Korean, United Nations, U.S.) all the way to the

U.S. troops emerge from a helicopter onto an open field during the Korean War. Helicopters were used on a large scale for the first time during the Korean conflict. ▼

134

southern tip of the peninsula. Then General MacArthur's army made a daring landing at Inchon Harbor and the North Koreans were driven back to the North. MacArthur then convinced Truman, who had his doubts, that the UN troops should advance into North Korea, but when the soldiers drove almost to the northern border of North Korea and China, that brought communist China into the war.

The Chinese sent highly trained, well-equipped troops. The war turned again. It was a terrible situation. We were no longer just at war with North Korea. Truman and his advisers feared that this might be the start of World War III. The fighting kept zigzagging back and forth. Everyone had expected a quick war, but now it seemed as if the Korean War would never end.

The American people were jittery and worried. We were fearful that communism would dominate the world. Because of those fears, we did some foolish things at home. We lost faith in ourselves. Some people thought that communists were about to take over the United States. There was no good reason to believe that, but fear often isn't reasonable. So we Americans took part in (or kept quiet during) a communist hunt in the United States. We persecuted some of our own citizens. It was a time of panic—as bad as, or maybe worse than, the "red scare" of 1919 and 1920.

In 1949, the United States and 10 European nations formed the North Atlantic Treaty Organization (NATO). It was to be an instrument of defense against the threat that they felt the Soviet Union and its eastern European satellite countries posed to the West.

Tail Gunner Joe

He was a liar. Not your ordinary small-time fibber. No, Senator Joseph McCarthy was an enormous, outrageous, beyond-belief liar. Trouble was, some people believed him. After all, no one thought a United States senator would lie.

Of course, most people didn't realize he had lied to become a senator. He said he was a big war hero, a tail gunner who had shot down lots of enemy planes. Actually, he had spent most of the war at a desk job. And he made up stories about his opponent, Wisconsin senator Robert M. La Follette, Jr. Those stories helped him beat La Follette.

Joseph McCarthy was a man who liked attention. He wanted people to notice him; he needed an issue. What was an issue that would capture headlines? Communism. Some people were afraid that America might become a communist nation. Joe McCarthy would tell them the danger was real. He would scare them. At a speech in Wheeling, West Virginia, he waved a piece of paper and said it contained the names of 205 communists who worked in the U.S. State Department.

McCarthy's list was a fake, but many Americans believed him. That was the beginning of McCarthy's witch hunt. Before he was finished, he had accused hundreds of people of communist activity.

Senator Joe McCarthy's actions gave rise to a term, *McCarthyism,* which one dictionary defines as "public accusation of disloyalty…unsupported by proof." ▶

◀ In the 1950s, posters like the one pictured here fueled fear of communism.

He never proved a single case against even one person. But it didn't seem to matter. He was a master of publicity. McCarthy was an exciting speaker. His accusations captured people's attention. Whatever he said got printed in bold headlines. And he knew how to use that new medium—television.

Many of the people McCarthy accused lost their jobs. Some lost their homes. Often their friends deserted them. Their lives were ruined.

The nation was infected with a bad case of anticommunist hysteria. It was sick. What about free speech and the guarantees of the First Amendment? Those rights were in trouble. During the McCarthy era, most people were afraid to speak out. It was a time of great fear.

Hysteria is an exaggerated emotional reaction to fear, horror, or disgust.

McCarthy wasn't the only one who ignored the Bill of Rights and its protections. The House of Representatives had a committee called the House Un-American Activities Committee. It ruined lives, too. HUAC decided to investigate the movie industry; many people had the idea that artists and actors were likely to be communist sympathizers.

Anyone questioned by the committee might be put on a list, called a "blacklist." People on the blacklist—actors, producers, writers, cameramen—were unable to get jobs in the film industry. Some filmmakers had been members of the Communist Party; some had attended communist meetings, often out of curiosity or out of Depression-time fear that capitalism was doomed. People called before the congressional committee were asked to name others who had

▲ Senator McCarthy swears in Dashiell Hammett at a Senate hearing on suspected communist activity. Hammett, an author of detective novels, was suspected of being a communist.

Detest means loathe or hate.

attended those meetings. Anyone named would probably be put on the blacklist. Some writers and actors refused to answer HUAC's questions; many were sent to jail.

To repeat: it was a time of great fear. Ordinary people in America were afraid to buy books, subscribe to magazines, or join organizations that might have the slightest left-wing leanings. Lots of people believed McCarthy's baseless lies. Fear of communism muddied their thinking. But in a free country it is not a crime to hold any kind of belief—and that includes communist beliefs.

The anticommunist extremists wanted to prevent people from reading about communism. They wanted to make it a crime to be a communist. McCarthy made a list of 418 American authors who he said had disloyal ideas. His list included great writers like Ernest Hemingway, John Dos Passos, and Henry David Thoreau. The State Department removed their books from overseas libraries (which were the only libraries it controlled).

Thirty-nine states passed anticommunist laws. Texas made membership in the Communist Party a crime punishable by 20 years in prison. A Connecticut law made it illegal to criticize the U.S. government or flag. Loyalty oaths were demanded of government workers, including many teachers! The oaths varied—generally the jobholders had to say that they supported the government or were not communists.

If HUAC's members had read the Bill of Rights, they had forgotten what it says. They didn't seem to understand that our Founders had challenged us to do something very difficult: to provide free speech to all, including those whose ideas we detest. Thomas Jefferson and James Madison and the other Founders thought America's citizens should be free to examine any idea, including ideas most people find loathsome. Now that isn't easy at all. You can only do that if you really believe in Jefferson's words that "truth is great and will prevail if left to herself."

Many of our government officials turned cowardly during this time of great fear. But some had courage. Senator Margaret Chase Smith of Maine spoke out in Congress.

I think it is high time that we remembered that the Constitution speaks not only of the freedom of speech but also of trial by jury instead of trial by accusation…. I am not proud of the way we smear outsiders from the floor of the Senate and…place ourselves beyond criticism.

Edward R. Murrow, a television newsman (who had broadcast on the radio to America every night from London when it was being bombed during the Second World War), showed courage and integrity, too. He decided to give the American people a clear picture of Joe McCarthy. Murrow made a TV film that showed the senator yelling at witnesses, belching, picking his nose, and making contradictory statements. Murrow knew he might get blacklisted himself, but that didn't stop him. He said, "This is no time for men who oppose Senator McCarthy's methods to keep silent." Then he added, "We must always remember that accusation is not proof."

McCarthy kept attacking. He accused the U.S. Army and many of its officers and soldiers of being communist sympathizers. But he produced only an army dentist who may, at one time, have been a communist sympathizer. Television (which was a new addition in many American homes) let people see the Army–McCarthy hearings and the senator's shouting, sneering manners.

Most people were disturbed by what they saw. But that didn't stop Joe McCarthy. He went on smearing innocent people.

Then a quiet, elderly man, who was well respected in his home state of Vermont but little known elsewhere, spoke out in the Senate. His name was Ralph Flanders, and he asked the Senate to vote to censure (condemn) Joseph McCarthy. One senator

A political cartoon depicts how, during the time of the McCarthy hearings, thousands of Americans were smeared by (usually unjust) accusations of being communists. ▼

immediately said that Flanders must be on the same side as the communists.

But by this time most Americans had had enough of Joe McCarthy. Murrow's film had shocked them. Senators began hearing from the voters; most of them were tired of the witch hunts. The Senate voted on Ralph Flanders's measure: Joseph McCarthy was censured for outrageous behavior. The man who had ruined lives and terrorized much of the nation was disgraced. However, he remained in the Senate. (McCarthy died a few years later from a liver ailment caused by too much drinking.)

Neither the executive branch, nor the legislative branch, nor the judicial branch of our government acted boldly during the time of the communist fear. Later, most Americans were ashamed of the McCarthy witch hunts. Joseph McCarthy and HUAC made us aware of the preciousness and fragility of our right to free speech.

Freedom of speech is guaranteed by the Bill of Rights. It is your constitutional right as an American citizen. But that freedom to speak out is easy to attack in times of crisis. It takes citizens who appreciate its importance to make sure we keep it as a basic right. And don't forget, the right of free speech also belongs to those whose ideas you hate.

A Letter to HUAC

Playwright Lillian Hellman was called before the House Un-American Activities Committee. It was 1952, and she sent this letter to the committee chairman:

Dear Mr. Wood:

…I am most willing to answer all questions about myself. I have nothing to hide from your Committee and there is nothing in my life of which I am ashamed…. But…I am not willing, now or in the future, to bring bad trouble to people who, in my past association with them, were completely innocent of any talk or any action that was disloyal….

I was raised in an old-fashioned American tradition and there were certain homely things that were taught to me: to try to tell the truth, not to bear false witness, not to harm my neighbor, to be loyal to my country, and so on…. I am prepared…to tell you everything you wish to know about my views or actions if your Committee will agree to refrain from asking me to name other people….

Sincerely yours,
Lillian Hellman

▲ American playwright Lillian Hellman

Liking Ike

Some people called them "the nifty fifties" and said it was a glorious time. After all, there was a singer named Elvis Presley, the beginning of rock and roll, two new states (Hawaii and Alaska), hula hoops, a movie star named Marilyn Monroe, the Salk vaccine (which prevented polio), and television. TV wasn't new. It had been invented in the '30s. Back then, a Harvard expert said it would never make an impact like radio, because "it must take place in a semi-darkened room, and it demands constant attention."

By 1946, a few people were willing to pay attention. That year, 7,000 small, black-and-white TV sets were sold in the United States, and regular programming was under way. By the mid-'50s, more than 5 million TV sets were sold each year. In 1956, videotape was developed. That meant shows could be taped, edited, and rerun. Before videotape, all TV was "live." If an actor made a mistake, everyone saw and heard it.

In 1950, 90 percent of America's homes did not have TV. By 1960, 90 percent of America's homes did have it. That magic box brought the whole world into living rooms from Honolulu to St. Paul to Miami. TV wasn't just a luxury for the rich; it was very democratic. Everyone had TV: rich and poor, city folks and country cousins. Everyone saw the same events and laughed at the same comedians.

▲ Hula hoops were all the rage in the 1950s.

The King

Elvis Presley was called the King of Rock 'n' Roll, and that is exactly what he was. He was a white boy who sang black music with tremendous natural talent and energy. He made it acceptable to white listeners. In terms of popular success, no American musician could touch him. Elvis was polite and he didn't smoke or drink, but many adults found his performances dangerous. It was the way he danced that upset them most—they'd never seen anything like it. But America's youth fell in love with him.

Elvis Presley performs for adoring fans. ▶

By the mid-1950s, many Americans owned televisions. TV changed the way Americans got their news, spent their leisure time, and ate their meals. ▶

It gave us a common culture. But some people asked: what kind of culture is it?

About a third of the children's programs featured crime and violence (although 1950s violence seems tame today). TV became a babysitter—it kept the kids quiet—and fewer parents took time to read to their children. Families ate their dinners in front of the TV set and talked to each other less. Television changed the way politicians campaigned: there were no more Harry Truman whistle-stop train trips. Before long, the candidates—packaged by makeup artists and TV coaches—were coming right into the living room.

But all that was just beginning in 1952, when we elected a new president, our 34th. His name was Dwight D. Eisenhower, and he was immensely popular. People called him "Ike." Eisenhower, an army general, had been Supreme Allied Commander (which means he was head man) in Europe during World War II. He had light blue eyes, a balding head, a grandfatherly manner, and the friendliest grin you can imagine. His campaign buttons said I LIKE IKE—and most people did.

Former General Dwight David Eisenhower, a hero of World War II, became the Republican presidential nominee in 1952. ▼

He was so popular that Democrat Harry Truman asked him to run for president. But Eisenhower was a Republican, so he ran against Truman's party. After 20 years of Democratic leadership, Americans were ready for a change. The Democrats had been the party of active government. Franklin Delano Roosevelt was a strong, dynamic president who gathered idea people around him; he brought college professors into government. Harry Truman was naturally combative; he liked to confront problems and make decisions.

Eisenhower's style was very different. He was a conservative, and most of his advisers were businessmen. He believed the president should be a strong moral leader. But he didn't think he should take sides.

Ike believed in persuasion and patience. He thought the president should act quietly. Eisenhower put a sign on his desk. It was in Latin but, translated, it said *gentle in manner, strong in deed*. Which was exactly how he tried to be. Eisenhower promised stability and as little government action as possible. He played golf and always seemed relaxed. His critics called him the "stand-still" president. They thought he was lazy. They were wrong.

Eisenhower worked hard and held the reins of the presidency tightly. He balanced the budget, kept America peaceful, and initiated a network of multilane interstate highways linking cities. But he tried to give the appearance of being above the political battle. He believed in behind-the-scenes leadership. Eisenhower didn't think the president should be controversial. So he didn't speak out against Joseph McCarthy, even when McCarthy outrageously criticized his friend General Marshall. But he did fly to Korea, as he'd promised when he campaigned for the presidency.

Eisenhower wanted to end the Korean War. Sometimes it takes strength to quit a fight. Eisenhower had that strength. He didn't want any more deaths; he didn't want to risk war with China.

President Eisenhower knew the waste of war. He had seen it with his own eyes. "Every gun that is made, every warship launched," said Eisenhower, "is a theft from those who hunger and are not fed, from those who are cold and are not clothed."

The Korean War came to an end with a truce. Korea was left divided as it had been when the war began. But the United States and the United Nations had proved what they had set out to prove: they would stand up to communist aggression.

▲ Eisenhower conveyed calm and patience as president.

Joseph Stalin died in March 1953, two months after Eisenhower took office as president. Many Russians—who didn't know about all the terrible things Stalin had done and all the innocent people he had killed—wept as though their own father had died.

About 54,000 Americans died in the Korean War. We never officially declared war on Korea and there was no peace treaty.

▲ Nikita Khrushchev threatened the United States, saying, "We will leave you in the dust."

Eisenhower saw a danger ahead for the nation. It was something he was an expert on: military power. In his farewell address he warned of a phenomenon "new in the American experience… an immense military establishment and a large arms industry." He called those two groups (the military and the weapons makers) the "military-industrial complex."

As soon as Eisenhower was out of office, an arms race began in earnest. It was a contest with Russia to see who could build the most weapons. And Republicans and Democrats jumped on the arms wagon. Both our nation and the Soviet Union spent—and went on spending—vast amounts of capital to build guns, bombs, and missiles. It was a theft from those who hungered and were not fed.

Stalin was dead, and no one in the United States knew quite what to make of the new Soviet leaders.

Nikita Khrushchev (KROOSH-chev) had become the first secretary of the Soviet Communist Party in 1953. He once said something like "We will leave you in the dust," but the translator got it wrong, and Khrushchev's words were reported as "We will bury you," which didn't sound friendly. With all the Cold War hysteria, those wrong words got repeated. Fear was in the air; the arms race took off.

Most Americans supported the arms race—which meant more and more weapons, more and more military, for more and more money, which put us further and further in debt. We didn't listen to President Eisenhower. He, a former general, had reduced military spending.

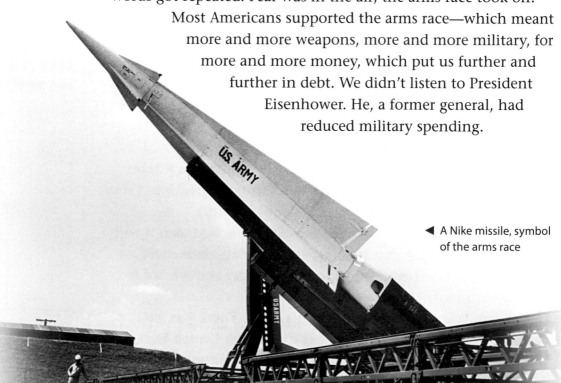

◄ A Nike missile, symbol of the arms race

Good Times?

The Eisenhower years were prosperous. Jobs were plentiful. People had money to spend. During World War II, there had been shortages of consumer goods. Now you could buy bikes, vacuum cleaners, television sets, dishwashers, ballpoint pens, nylon stockings—almost anything you wanted. For three cents you could mail a letter; for five cents you could buy a Coke or a candy bar. There were no big fast-food chains, although they would come soon enough. (Five cents for a Coke wasn't quite as inexpensive as it sounds. Salaries were a whole lot lower then.)

These were good times.

But not for everybody. Some citizens were kept out of the good times. In the South, blacks couldn't eat in the same restaurants as whites, shop in the same stores, use the same bathrooms, drink from the same water fountains, or go to the same schools. It was humiliating—and unfair. But it was the law. It was all because of a Supreme Court decision, back in 1896, called *Plessy v. Ferguson.* That decision said that as long as facilities were equal, they could be separate.

▲ This African American child in a one-room schoolhouse for blacks in Selma, Alabama, knew little of the good times the nation experienced in the 1950s.

It made segregation legal. But the segregated schools, restaurants, and shops weren't equal; anyone could see that. Even if they were, who wants to be separated? Americans were supposed to be free. How can you be free when you can't go where you want to go?

Public facilities like water fountains and restrooms were segregated, and the white-only facilities were always better. ▶

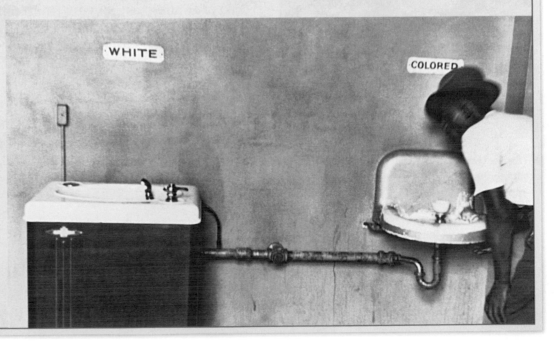

WHITE

COLORED

Houses, Kids, Cars, and Fast Food

Couples had put off having children during the war years—and now they were making up for that. We were having a "baby boom." The war veterans had gone to college under the G.I. Bill of Rights, and the government paid for their tuition. By the '50s, most of those veterans were out of school, married, and having children. Their college degrees helped them find good jobs, usually better jobs than their fathers had ever had (most women—at least middle-class women—didn't work).

Those new families needed places to live, and, in America, every family dreamed of a home of its own. But there was a big housing shortage. What to do? Use some American ingenuity.

William Levitt had it. Before the war, an average builder might build two or three or, at most, five houses a year. Bill Levitt was soon finishing 36 houses a day, which added up to 180 in every five-day week! How did he do it? By analyzing the building process, dividing it into 27 steps, and putting teams of people to work on each step. It was Henry Ford's mass-production idea applied to housing. A team did the same task, over and over, moving from house to house. There

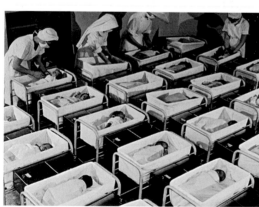

▲ The postwar surge in births during the 1950s and early '60s became known as the "baby boom."

Returning veterans earned college degrees and joined the ranks of middle-class, white-collar workers. ▶

were framers and roofers, tile men and floor men, painters who did all the white painting and others who painted all the green.

Levitt began producing his own nails and making his own cement. He even bought timberland in Oregon and cut his own lumber. By doing all that, he kept his house prices very low.

He had thought all this out while he was in the navy with the Seabees (the navy's builders). Levitt was commissioned to build airfields, practically overnight. Lives depended on his speed. He analyzed, planned, brainstormed with other Seabees, and built the airfields. Later, he said the navy gave him a chance to experiment and learn how to get things done.

Levitt knew that a lot of veterans like himself would be looking for homes after the war. So he bought a huge tract of land on Long Island (near New York City). It was mainly potato fields. Those fields soon became a community called Levittown. Most of Levitt's houses had four and a half rooms and were exactly alike. They were sturdy, available, and a great value—like Ford's Model T. When the first

With its sprawling network of look-alike homes, Levittown, outside New York City, became a model for suburbs all over the country. ▼

▲ As quickly as houses could be built, new homeowners moved in.

Affluent means rich, wealthy.

A 1956 Ford Thunderbird sports tail fins. ▼

advertisement for the first Levittown ran in the *New York Times*, people began lining up. In one day alone, Levitt sold more than 1,400 houses.

Bill Levitt's ideas were soon copied by other builders. The communities they built were part of something that was about to boom: *suburbia*. Suburbs—on the outskirts of the cities—were springing up around the country. Some had low-cost houses, but others were for the affluent. As people moved out of cities, new people—often poor people—moved in. Cities began losing some of their most productive taxpayers just when they needed rebuilding.

In the new suburbs, where there was no mass transportation, something became essential: a car (or two). Well, General Motors and the other auto companies saw to that. Detroit, the home of the auto industry, began building big, fancy cars. They were status symbols with shiny chrome trim, shark-like tail fins. The advertising industry geared up to convince consumers that last year's car, like the hem length on last year's dress, was out of date. Styling changes, not engineering excellence, determined the big sellers.

To most American consumers, bigger seemed better. And bigger and fancier seemed best of all. These young '50s families didn't seem to have a problem paying for the new houses and the big cars. We were becoming an affluent nation. In the old days, most workers had toiled for low wages to enrich factory owners. Now, new union contracts were giving auto workers and others a share of their own productivity. They became some of the best customers for the cars and appliances that were rolling out of the factories. And they set the standards for worker pay in other fields, too.

During this same time, oil was replacing coal as our major source of energy. In 1949, Americans used 5.8 million barrels of oil a day; by 1979 we were using 16.4 million barrels. Oil is much more efficient than coal. Getting it doesn't demand exhausting, killing work. And oil was very cheap. (That changed a few decades later.) Oil began driving the economy. It allowed Americans to get into their big new cars and not worry about how much gas they guzzled.

With a family and a car, chances are you'd want to take a trip. Kemmons Wilson, who was a house builder in Memphis, Tennessee, did just that. It was 1951, and he decided to take his family to Washington, D.C., to see the sights.

You know how kids sometimes behave in the car, don't you? Well, the Wilsons' children were no different from anyone else's. Kemmons and his wife couldn't wait each night to get to a motel and relax. But the motels they found were mostly either disappointing or awful—and they charged extra for each child in the room, even though the Wilsons' kids had brought their own sleeping bags!

Kemmons Wilson decided he would build motels for families. The motels would all be similar, so people would know what they were getting. They would be clean and attractive—and kids could stay free.

Popular singer Bing Crosby had made a movie called *Holiday Inn*. Wilson thought it a great name for a motel. In 1956, when Congress passed a huge $76 billion federal highway program, Wilson's Holiday Inns were ready for all the traffic those new highways brought.

There were suburbs before World War II, but they were mostly pretty communities for the very wealthy. The flow of people from the city to modern suburbia was a mass movement.

As the United States became a car culture, gas stations competed for business with giveaways and excellent service. ▼

Cars, suburbs, and TV watching were changing American habits. But some things hadn't changed much. Most American families never went out to dinner. It was too expensive to eat out with the kids—unless it was a very special occasion. Mothers—especially those suburban moms—were expected to stay home and cook meals.

A lot of working people didn't go out, either. They packed a sandwich in a bag and brought it to work. Two California brothers were going to change that. They were going to build a restaurant that was fast, clean, and very inexpensive—a place where you could feed the whole family without emptying your wallet.

Dick and Mac (Maurice) McDonald had come to California in the Depression '30s. In 1940, they built a drive-in restaurant. People stayed in their cars at the drive-in and waiters, called "carhops," came out and served them. The restaurant appealed to families, especially during the war years, when lots of women went to work and didn't have time to cook.

But the McDonald brothers had a passion for efficiency, and cars were lining up. People were waiting to get service. How could they speed things up?

Well, the carhops would have to go. Then the McDonalds looked at their menu. There was too much choice—that slowed things down. And it took time for the customers to put ketchup and relish on their hamburgers. So the McDonalds decided to put pickles, mustard, ketchup, and onions right on the hamburgers. That really saved time. Instead of regular dishes and silver they changed to

What were people watching on their new television sets in the 1950s? The A. C. Nielsen company, which measures TV watching, says that the number-one show for most of the decade was *I Love Lucy*. Other big shows were *Gunsmoke*, the *Ed Sullivan Show*, *Dragnet*, the *Jackie Gleason Show*, *Wagon Train*, *You Bet Your Life*, and *General Electric Theater*. The host of *GE Theater* was an actor named Ronald Reagan.

▲ Lucille Ball and Desi Arnaz in *I Love Lucy*

paper plates and plastic forks. That was faster. But, most important of all, they organized the kitchen as a production line. It was the Henry Ford idea again, this time applied to hamburgers. Grill men cooked the burgers, milkshake men made shakes, dressers wrapped the burgers, and countermen took orders.

By the middle '50s, people were lined up to eat burgers at the one McDonald's restaurant in San Bernardino, California. The brothers were rich and happy. They didn't need any more money than they had. But some people wanted to open McDonald's restaurants in other places. They wanted to buy *franchises* (that means they were willing to pay for the McDonald's name and expertise). The brothers didn't want the bother.

One day, Ray Kroc came by. He sold milkshake makers, and he wanted to see why the McDonalds were buying so many of them. He was astounded by what he saw: long lines of people waiting to buy hamburgers. The place was spotlessly clean, the hamburgers were good, and they cost 15 cents. Dick and Mac McDonald were looking for someone to handle their franchising. Kroc was eager. Within a few years, he bought the McDonald's name and idea outright.

Ray Kroc began opening McDonald's hamburger stores one after another. Soon they were everywhere. He wanted the hamburgers he sold in Des Plaines, Illinois, to be exactly like the hamburgers he sold in Willmar, Minnesota, or Kalamazoo, Michigan. He wanted every restaurant to be spotless and to maintain high standards. He made rules, lots of rules. McDonald's workers couldn't have beards or mustaches, and they couldn't chew gum. He made sure their fingernails were clean. He didn't like to hire women; he thought they would flirt with the customers. He worked very, very hard. His company grew to be huge, with a McDonald's in almost every town and village, and his worth in the hundreds of millions.

His success was related to the new way of life in America. McDonald's were suburban restaurants, they took advantage of locations on the new highways, and, as more and more women began to get jobs, dinner at McDonald's—or at one of the other fast-food chains that followed—became a regular thing.

▲ Mass production entered the food industry when the first McDonald's restaurant applied the methods to preparing hamburgers.

Ah, Suburbia, Happy Suburbia

Nineteen-fifties suburbia—or its image, anyway—was part Hollywood movie, part TV comedy series, and part slick magazine ad. All these media helped reinforce a sanitized image.

There was Mom (who was pretty), Dad (who was handsome), two kids (who were cute), and Rover (who barked appealingly). A station wagon sat in the driveway. The garage held a lawnmower, bikes, Dad's workbench, roller skates, and the family camping gear and had a basketball hoop above the door.

All the families earned about the same income. If they began earning more, they usually sold the house and moved to a fancier suburb.

Everyone was white. Black people couldn't buy houses in Levittown or most of the other early suburbs. That would change later. Of course separating the races—blacks in the cities, whites in the suburbs—did not lead to harmony between them.

Everyone was young. Grandma and Grandpa were back in their small hometown, which was getting smaller as young couples moved to suburbia. Before, communities had people of all ages to balance each other. In suburbia, children missed having grandparents nearby.

Those picture-pretty suburban families were expected to conform; any who didn't felt out of place. Mothers weren't supposed to work—it spoiled the picture. But some women were bored; there wasn't a whole lot to do in the suburbs—except drive the kids here and there. And Dad got to hate the commuting and the highway traffic. Suburbia wasn't perfect, even though the TV shows and magazine ads made you think it must be.

American magazines and television promoted an idealized picture of the "typical" suburban family. ▼

French Indochina

There was a beautiful country to the south of China. A country that had been ruled by France for about 100 years. The French called the land *Indochina*. The people who lived there called it *Vietnam* and *Laos* and *Cambodia*. Does that sound unusual, for a Western nation to rule an Asian nation? It wasn't unusual at all in the days before World War II. Britain ruled India. The Netherlands ruled Indonesia. The United States ruled the Philippine Islands. That kind of foreign rule is called colonialism, or imperialism.

Most people knew that colonialism wasn't fair. (We had once been an English colony and we hadn't liked it a bit.) Franklin Delano Roosevelt said that nations should determine their own form of government. As soon as World War II ended, we granted independence to the Philippines, but some Asian countries had to fight to become free. India's leaders fought with hunger strikes and nonviolent protests. In Vietnam they fought with weapons.

Vietnam had a leader named Ho Chi Minh. As a young man, he had visited in England, the United States, and France. He knew Western ways. He'd been a poet and a photographer, and he spoke many languages. Back in 1919, he had tried to get President Woodrow Wilson to help the people of Southeast Asia gain their freedom. Wilson didn't respond.

When Ho learned of Philippine independence, he was encouraged. He wrote eight letters to President Truman asking for help in making Vietnam free. Those letters were never answered. Perhaps Truman never saw them. We don't know about that, but we do know that in 1945 Ho Chi Minh founded the Democratic Republic of Vietnam. Some American military men were present at the independence ceremonies. "The Star-Spangled Banner" was played by a Vietnamese band, and Ho Chi Minh spoke words from the Declaration of Independence. When American planes unexpectedly flew overhead, everyone cheered.

> *Imperialism* is the policy of expanding a nation by taking other lands.

Ho Chi Minh studied in Europe, spoke several languages, and knew Western ways. ▼

For much of its early history, Vietnam was ruled by Chinese warlords. When Vietnam rejected Chinese rule, it kept much Chinese culture. Both China and Vietnam were Confucian countries. (See the next page for more about Confucius.) In the 20th century, China turned to communism; so did Vietnam.

But the French didn't want Vietnam to be independent. France had lost the country when Japanese soldiers invaded during World War II. Now that the war was over, the French wanted their old empire back. Ho Chi Minh stood in the way. Ho was a hero to his countrymen. He had fought against the French and then the Japanese; now he wanted to keep France from controlling Vietnam again.

The French asked the United States to help them fight Ho and his forces (called *Vietminh*). They said Ho was a communist, and he was. He had gone to Russia and studied communism there. He believed in freedom for his country (which didn't necessarily mean freedom for the individuals inside the country).

Ho was an independent kind of communist. His goal was to free Vietnam from all outsiders. He needed help. When the Chinese communists began sending supplies to Ho he was happy to have their aid.

Perhaps if Ho Chi Minh had not been a communist we would have stayed out of the affair, but we soon sent military advisers to help the French. Then we gave France $10 million a year to fight Ho and the Vietminh. That was when Harry Truman was president.

Mao Zedong (on left), the leader of communist China, sent supplies to neighboring Vietnam to aid the forces of Ho Chi Minh (on right). ▶

By 1953 (when Eisenhower was president), we were spending $400 million a year to help the French in Vietnam, and before long almost twice that amount. It wasn't enough. The Vietminh kept winning. Vice President Richard Nixon and our top military leaders urged the president to send American bombers to Vietnam. Eisenhower refused.

The French prepared for a major battle. They were confident. They shouldn't have been. Their army was beaten and trapped, and most of the surviving soldiers died in a terrible jungle march. That was more than enough for the French people. They showed in elections that they were ready to get out of Southeast Asia. And, since France is a democracy, the people prevailed. A peace conference was held in Geneva, in Switzerland. Vietnam was divided into two sections: north and south. The division was meant to be temporary (most of the food-growing regions were in the south).

Ho Chi Minh was the leader of North Vietnam. He was now a great popular hero. After all, he had driven the French out of the country. South Vietnam's leaders were chosen by France. According to the Geneva agreement, elections were to be held within two years to reunite the country.

The elections were never held. The South Vietnamese leaders wouldn't allow them. They knew Ho Chi Minh would win. Soon there

▲ Ho Chi Minh became a popular hero in Vietnam. This poster calls for "allegiance to Uncle Ho."

Confucius

Traditionally, the Vietnamese were followers of the ideas of Confucius. It is hard for most Western peoples to understand that Confucianism is not a religion in the same sense as Judaism or Christianity or Islam. Confucius said, "I am simply one who loves the past and is diligent in investigating it." Confucius was a teacher who taught morality, or the way to a good life. That good way is called Tao (DOW). He found its guidelines by studying the wisdom of the past. Americans and other Westerners do much thinking of the future: about invention and progress. Confucians try to perfect systems that have been tried over time. These are very different ways of looking at the world.

Confucius taught the way to a good life. ▶

Ho Chi Minh led Vietnam to independence from French rule and then became president of communist North Vietnam. ▶

was civil war between the communist North and the pro-Western South. (Remember the situation in Korea? Was this the same?)

We were now out of Korea, and many of our nation's anticommunists believed that Vietnam was the place to take another stand against world communism. Those who wanted to send bombers and fighting troops were called "hawks"; those who didn't want to get involved were called "doves."

President Eisenhower said that if we let Vietnam become communist, it would be like watching a row of dominoes fall. The first domino would set off the others. Soon all of Asia would be communist.

Eisenhower's advisers were hawks; they urged him to fight. But none of them really understood Southeast Asia. Hardly anyone in America did. We'd fired our China experts, who might have helped. Eisenhower was wary. "I'm convinced that no military victory is possible [there]," he said. (Remember that statement. You will read more about Vietnam.)

Separate but *Unequal*

Back near the end of the 19th century, Homer Plessy was arrested for sitting in a whites-only railroad car. Was it legal for the railroads to separate the races? What does the Constitution say?

The 14th Amendment says:

No State shall…abridge the privileges…of citizens of the United States…; nor deny to any person within its jurisdiction the equal protection of the laws.

Abridge the privileges—that means take away or limit the rights of citizens. *Equal protection of the laws.* That seems clear. Does keeping people separate on a train abridge privileges? Does it deny anyone equal protection of the laws?

Some Americans weren't sure about that, and they looked to the Supreme Court for guidance. Finally, in 1896, the Supreme Court gave them an answer when it decided Homer Plessy's case.

Bus stations in the South, like this one in Durham, North Carolina, had separate waiting rooms for whites and blacks. ▼

It was an answer that would cause a lot of people a lot of grief. Justice Henry Billings Brown wrote the decision for the majority of the justices. He said that the 14th Amendment called for

> *the absolute equality of the two races before the law, but...it could not have been intended to abolish distinctions based upon color, or to enforce social...equality, or a commingling of the two races.*

Do you understand that? The races were equal before the law, but laws could prevent them from mingling.

Justice John Marshall Harlan disagreed with the majority decision. Supreme Court justices often disagree with each other. The majority rules, but those who don't agree can write their dissenting opinions. In that famous 1896 decision, Justice Harlan wrote:

> *In view of the Constitution, in the eye of the law, there is...no superior, dominant ruling class of citizens.... Our Constitution is color-blind, and neither knows nor tolerates classes among citizens.*

But the majority opinion was the one that counted. The Supreme Court said that if facilities were equal they could be separate. The *Plessy v. Ferguson* decision made segregation legal in schools, restaurants, hotels, and public places in the Southern states. Jim Crow had won the approval of the highest court. Separate but equal was the law.

Charlie Houston and His Students

Charles Hamilton Houston thought the Supreme Court's *Plessy* decision was a mistake. Houston had graduated from Amherst College in 1915, served as an officer in World War I, received his law degree from Harvard, and then earned a Ph.D. Even with all those degrees, Charlie Houston knew he had no chance of getting a job with a big law firm because of the color of his skin.

But Houston had studied law because he wanted to help his people. He wanted to use the power of the courts to end Jim Crow. He became an expert in the law of the Constitution, and then, at Howard University's law school, he trained other black lawyers to be experts, too.

One of Charlie Houston's best students, Thurgood Marshall, said that Houston "made it clear to all of us that when we were done we were expected to go out and do something with our lives." As you'll soon see, Marshall did something with his life—something very important.

Decades after the *Plessy* decision, a number of court cases challenged the idea of separate but equal. Here are the stories behind those cases.

Linda Carol Brown—who was seven years old and lived in Topeka, Kansas—had to walk across railroad tracks and take an old bus to get to school, though there was a better school five blocks from her house. Linda couldn't go to that school because she was black and the schools in Topeka were segregated. Linda's father, the Reverend Oliver Brown, didn't think that was right. He went to court to try to do something about it. Their case became known as *Brown v. Board of Education*.

South Carolina's Clarendon County spent $43 a year on each of its black students. It spent $179 a year on each white student. The white children all had school desks; in two of the black schools there were no desks at all. Harry and Liza Briggs and 20 other black parents sued the Clarendon County school board. They wanted equal funding for the black schools. They sued in the name of 10-year-old Harry Briggs, Jr., and 66 other children. Right away, Liza Briggs was fired from her job. So were most of the other adults who signed the lawsuit that was titled *Briggs v. Clarendon County*.

Barbara Rose Johns, a junior at Moton High School in Farmville, Virginia, was angry about conditions in her school: it had been built for 200 students but held 450. There was no cafeteria and no gym. The highest-paid teachers at Moton received less than the lowest-paid teachers at Farmville's white schools. A committee of black parents had petitioned the county for a new school and been turned down.

Johns decided to act. She had a friend telephone the school principal and tell him he was needed at the bus terminal—at once. Then she called a meeting of all the students. She told the teachers they were planning a surprise event.

▲ Linda Brown, shown sitting at the front of her classroom in the segregated Monroe School in Topeka, Kansas, became the focal point of the landmark Supreme Court decision in *Brown v. Board of Education*. Linda and her younger sister walked along railroad tracks on their way to board a bus to school, although there was a better-funded public school closer to their home.

This painting depicts the Supreme Court justices who presided over the historic case of *Brown v. Board of Education*. ▶

Racism wasn't (and isn't) just a problem of blacks in the South. It is a human problem, and it is found across the land (and across the world, too). Racism is the irrational hatred of those who are different from you. Almost every minority group has, at one time or another, suffered the pain of irrational hatred.

She was right; they were surprised. Barbara Johns talked the students at Moton into going on strike for a better school. They walked out of their classes. A member of the National Association for the Advancement of Colored People (NAACP) came to Farmville. He intended to tell the students that Farmville was not the place to fight segregation. But he was so impressed with their determination that he helped 117 Moton High School students sue the state of Virginia. They demanded that the state abolish segregated schools. Their case was called *Davis v. County School Board of Prince Edward County* because the first of the students listed was 14-year-old Dorothy E. Davis.

Each of those three cases was defeated in court, but that didn't stop the plaintiffs (those who were suing). They appealed the cases.

What does it mean to appeal a law case? Our legal system begins with city and county courts, goes on to state courts and then to federal courts, and, finally, to the Supreme Court. Suppose you go to court and you don't think your trial was fair. You can appeal your case to a higher court. The higher court may reverse the lower court's decision. If it doesn't, you may, in some cases, appeal the case still further, and further, until finally you get to the Supreme Court.

They appealed them all the way to the United States Supreme Court. There they were grouped with two other cases dealing with school segregation: one from Delaware and one from Washington, D.C. Together, the five suits were called by the name of the first of them: *Brown v. Board of Education.*

That case would directly affect all the schools in the 21 states with segregated schools. It would indirectly affect almost every school in the United States. *Brown v. Board of Education* was to become one of the most important cases ever brought before the Supreme Court.

Supreme Court cases are not handled like the cases you see on television. The people involved—the schoolchildren, in this case—don't come before the court. There are no witnesses. Lawyers do all the talking. They often spend months—or years—preparing their cases. Then they present their argument to the nine justices. The Supreme Court justices usually ask questions. Sometimes those questions can be answered at once. Sometimes the lawyers have to come back and re-argue the case.

Anyone can attend a Supreme Court session if he or she is willing to stand in line. The court is in Washington, D.C., right near the U.S. Capitol (which is where Congress meets). On December 9, 1952, all the seats were filled in the Supreme Court chamber and 400 people were turned away. That is unusual, but this was an unusual day. The court was ready to consider *Brown v. Board of Education.*

The NAACP was representing the children. Charlie Houston was dead, but his star pupil, Thurgood Marshall, the great-grandson of a slave, argued their case. Marshall, a hard worker, was a meticulous lawyer with a good sense of humor. He had argued 15 cases before the Supreme Court—and won 13.

The lawyer Marshall faced was John W. Davis. Some people said that Davis was the best lawyer in America. He had argued more cases before the Supreme Court than any living attorney. Davis had run for president against Calvin Coolidge, and everyone seemed to like

"Like an eating cancer," said Thurgood Marshall, "segregation destroys the morale of our citizens and disfigures our country throughout the world." ▼

▲ Chief Justice Earl Warren persuaded his fellow justices to deliver a unanimous decision in the *Brown* ruling.

him (though he lost the election). Even Thurgood Marshall liked Davis; they often ate lunch together.

Supreme Court justices do not decide questions of right and wrong. That can sometimes be a matter of opinion. We live in a society based on law. The Constitution is our highest law. The job of the justices is to decide the meaning of the Constitution. Does the Constitution permit segregation? Or does segregation break the rules laid out in the Constitution? That was the question the justices had to decide.

Marshall and the NAACP lawyers presented two arguments: first they argued that the 14th Amendment—which says *No State shall...abridge the privileges...of citizens of the United States...; nor deny to any person within its jurisdiction the equal protection of the laws*—made the doctrine of "separate but equal" unconstitutional. Then they argued that segregated schools can never be truly equal—separating people, of itself, makes them feel unequal and inferior. The *Plessy* decision was wrong, they said.

John Davis looked at the 14th Amendment and the rest of the Constitution. He said that nothing in it prevented separation, as long as equal facilities were provided. Each state, said Davis, has the right to make its own decisions on social matters such as segregation. He believed the *Plessy* decision was right.

This was a very difficult case. The justices asked questions. They took their time. A year passed. It looked as if the court might be split, with some justices saying segregated schools were unconstitutional and some saying they were not. This issue was dividing the country. If the court were to split, it would make those divisions worse. Then something unexpected happened: the Supreme Court's chief justice died. President Dwight Eisenhower named California's former governor Earl Warren as the new chief justice. Warren was a mild-mannered man who was not expected to be a dynamic chief justice. But a few people who knew him well understood that he had a gift for leadership. They also knew that he had a strong moral sense: he believed in justice and fairness.

Finally, the waiting was over. On May 17, 1954, Earl Warren read the decision in *Brown v. Board of Education*. Here is part of what he read:

It is doubtful that any child may reasonably be expected to succeed in life if he is denied the opportunity of an education. Such an opportunity...is a right which must be available to all on equal terms.... Does segregation of children in public schools solely on the basis of race...deprive children of the minority group of equal educational opportunities? We believe that it does.... We conclude, unanimously, that in the field of public education the doctrine of "separate but equal" has no place. Separate educational facilities are inherently unequal.

UNANIMOUSLY! The new chief justice had convinced all the justices that, because of the importance of this decision, it should be unanimous (which means they should all agree). It was, as the *Washington Post* said the next day in an editorial, "a new birth of freedom." *Plessy v. Ferguson*, a case about a railroad car, had made segregation a fact in almost all phases of daily life in the South.

Brown v. Board of Education, a case about schoolchildren, would provide a way to attack segregation—and not just in the classroom.

◀ Nettie Hunt explains to her daughter Nickie the meaning of the Supreme Court's *Brown* decision. The *New York Times* said of the decision, "The highest court in the land, the guardian of our national conscience, has reaffirmed its faith and the underlying American faith in the equality of all men and all children before the law."

SCHOOL SEGREGATION

INCH BY INCH

But the battle wasn't over. Laws have to be enforced, and some people were determined not to enforce this one. Virginia's Prince Edward County closed all its public schools—for *five years*—rather than integrate the schools. White children were educated in "private" white academies funded with tax money (paid by white and black taxpayers). Black children were denied any schooling at all. Prince Edward County wasn't alone in its mean-spiritedness. Most Southern communities refused to integrate schools. In Norfolk, Virginia, all public schools were closed for a year. Most children—black and white—didn't have any schools to go to.

◄ A political cartoon titled "Inch by Inch" depicts the difficulty of enforcing the Supreme Court's ruling on integration in public schools. Most Southern school districts refused to integrate.

Emmett Till

Emmett Louis Till was 14 when he was found, brutally beaten, shot in the head, wired to a heavy weight, and dumped into Mississippi's Tallahatchie River.

Why? Because he had allegedly dared to say a flirtatious word to a white woman.

It was 1955, and many differences existed between ways in Chicago and the ways of the white-dominated South. His mother had warned the young man from Chicago when she put him on a train heading for Mississippi and his Southern cousins. "If you have to get down on your knees and bow when a white person goes past, do it," said Mrs. Till.

One day, Emmett went into a store, bought some candy, and then allegedly turned to the wife of the owner (who wasn't there), and said, "Bye, baby." The store owner's wife would also say that Emmett also touched her.

Very soon after, two white men—the store owner and his brother-in-law—beat and murdered

Fourteen-year-old Emmett Till from Chicago was murdered in Mississippi. The nation was shocked when his murderers were found not guilty. ►

Emmett Till. Why? Because, one of them later said, "He thought he was as good as any white man."

The two white men were found not guilty by an all-white jury. Across the nation, all people of decency were outraged.

Myrlie Evers, widow of civil rights leader Medgar Evers (another murder victim), said that the Emmett Till killing showed that "even a child was not safe from racism and bigotry and death."

Decades later, the wife of the store owner admitted that she lied about part of her story in court. In 2018, the U.S. Department of Justice reopened its investigation of Emmett Till's killing.

◄ Ruby Bridges was one of the first African American children to attend an all-white elementary school in the South. This painting by Norman Rockwell, titled *The Problem We All Live With,* depicts Ruby Bridges as she walks to school, guarded by marshals.

It was a difficult time for moderate Southern whites. They had always lived with segregation. Strong voices were shouting that the Southern world they knew and loved would end if they agreed to integrate their schools. (It was the same message that had been used to defend slavery 100 years earlier.) Those who spoke out against segregation often lost their jobs and friends. Some white people were scared.

Where were the voices of reason? The moderate Southern leaders seemed to have gone into hiding. But, remember, these were conforming times. All over the nation, people were keeping silent while others were abused.

In a few areas—especially in the states bordering the North—integration proceeded, usually without incident. White children had no trouble going to school with black children. It was the adults who were creating problems. They were dragging out all the old, tired arguments.

In some places, when black children marched into integrated schools, grownups insulted them or threw rocks. Because of that new medium—television—everyone, all over the world, could see the rocks and the taunting faces. Decent folks hid their heads in shame. *Brown v. Board of Education* may have been a new birth of freedom, but the baby was having a hard time breathing on its own.

MLKs, Senior and Junior

Mike King was a Georgia sharecropper's son who was teased when he went to school because he smelled of the barnyard. Muscular, energetic, and ambitious, he headed off to the big city, Atlanta, where he worked on the railroad. In Atlanta, he discovered that what he really wanted to do was preach. So he did, on Sundays, in small Baptist country churches. Then he learned of a girl, Alberta Williams, a student at Spelman College, a talented organist, and the daughter of the Reverend A. D. Williams, the leading black preacher in Atlanta. Before they even met, he decided he would marry her.

In the segregated South, the church was the center of the black world. It was the place where you took your troubles and your heart and found friends and support in an often unkind world. The minister was apt to be the most respected and best-educated man in the black community.

There was no way a rough country boy could marry the daughter of the Reverend Williams. Mike King decided he would get an education. So, at age 20, he went to a public school and sat at a big desk in a fifth grade classroom. A few years later he was finished with high school, but that wasn't enough. To be accepted in the Williams family he needed a college degree. So he went to Morehouse College—where the Reverend Williams had studied—took the entrance tests, failed them, and was turned away. But there was no stopping Michael Luther King. He worked hard and got a college degree; he got the girl he wanted; and, eventually, he got his father-in-law's church.

He and Alberta, who was church organist, took their three children everywhere and beamed with pride at their accomplishments. His older son, named for him and called M.L., was a small, wiry, athletic kid who loved to play ball and had lots of friends. When M.L. was five, his father changed their names. Each became Martin Luther King, after the German priest, Martin Luther, who had founded Protestantism.

Martin Sr. and Alberta made sure their son had a good education. At age 15, he entered Morehouse College. Martin intended to be a doctor, but he changed his mind: he would become a minister.

▲ Martin Luther King, Jr., appears (front row, right) in an early photo with his family.

What's in a Name?

In the United States, *negro, black, colored, Afro-American,* and *African American* are all words used to describe those who are descended, in whole or in part, from people of African origin. Words, like other things, have fashions. Negro was the preferred term for many generations. Today, African American—or black—is most people's choice.

◄ Indian nationalist and spiritual leader Mohandas Gandhi (center front, beneath the crossed poles) leads villagers and workers on a march.

Martin Luther King, Jr., chose Crozer Seminary, in Pennsylvania, to study theology—about religion. That school had an astounding mix of students—white and black, from North and South, some Asian Americans, several American Indians, and some from other lands. For a privileged boy from a protective family, living with all those people was an education in itself.

Martin Luther King, Jr., became the valedictorian—the top student—in his class at Crozer. There he discovered that he had a passion for words and ideas and a talent for public speaking. At Morehouse, King had read Henry David Thoreau's essay, "Civil Disobedience." Thoreau believed in the power of nonviolence. He believed in the power of even "one honest man" to create great change in the world.

At Crozer, King learned about India's great leader Mohandas (Mahatma) Gandhi, and that Gandhi had been inspired by Thoreau. Gandhi was a shining example of the honest man Thoreau had believed in. Gandhi led millions of people in nonviolent boycotts and marches to protest British rule in India. When British soldiers taunted and beat and jailed Gandhi and his followers, they didn't fight back with fists or guns; they just kept peacefully marching and protesting. Gandhi's reasoned courage and calm dignity turned away the guns and cannons of a mighty empire. Gandhi showed the world the power of goodness and right action. India became free. Martin Luther King was fascinated to discover that Gandhi had been full of rage when he was young and had learned to control his anger. King was often angry. Could he teach himself self-control? Could he teach others?

To *boycott* something is to refuse to use it or have anything to do with it.

To *taunt* is to jeer, tease, and goad with words.

▲ Behind Martin Luther King, Jr., is a portrait of Gandhi, who, King said, taught him that "there is more power in socially organized masses on the march than there is in guns in the hands of a few desperate men."

Martin Luther King, Jr.'s new learning seemed to expand his ideas on Christianity and Christian love. In his father's world, Christianity was simple and sure; at Crozer, King found a Christianity that was questioning.

He still wasn't finished with school. After Crozer he went to Boston University for more study and reading and for a Ph.D. (that made him the Reverend *Dr.* Martin Luther King, Jr.). His professors wanted him to become one of them: a teacher and a scholar. But Martin wanted to be a preacher. He had an idea that a minister could do things to make the world better. He wanted to fight injustice. He wanted to lead his people—the black people—because he thought they had a message for all people. Segregation and racial hatred were wrong. Injustice and unfairness were wrong. Social cruelties and meanness hurt everyone.

The more Martin Luther King, Jr., thought about Thoreau, and Gandhi, and about Christian ideas on loving your enemies, the more he began to believe in the power of peaceful protest. When he thought about America's founding idea, that "all men are created equal," he wondered if nonviolent action could be used to bring that equality to all people. Could nonviolence overcome the evil of segregation? He knew it wouldn't be easy.

How *do* you face evil?

You can turn away from it, which is the easiest thing to do.

You can fight it with weapons or fists—which is harder, and may hurt or kill people.

The hardest way of all is nonviolence. It means standing up to evil without weapons. It means taking punches and not returning them. Now that takes courage.

Martin wasn't sure how he would lead his people—he just knew that was what he wanted to do. In the meantime, his father wanted his son as assistant pastor at his fine big church in Atlanta, Georgia. But Martin Jr. decided he would start his career at a small church in a quiet city. He had no idea that an explosion—the civil rights movement—was about to begin in that quiet city.

It was Montgomery, Alabama, and soon everyone in America would know about it.

Rosa Parks Was Tired

Rosa Parks, who worked as a tailor's assistant in a department store in Montgomery, Alabama, was a small, soft-voiced, 43-year-old woman who wore rimless glasses and pulled her brown hair back in a bun. Parks had been secretary of the Montgomery chapter of the NAACP, so she was well known to Montgomery's black leaders. She was also well respected. Rosa Parks was refined and reliable.

But on the evening of the first day of December in 1955, Mrs. Parks was mostly just plain tired. She had put in a full day at her job. She didn't feel well, and her neck and back hurt. She got on a bus and headed home.

Rosa Parks ▼

In 1955, buses in all the Southern states were segregated. Laws said that the seats in the front were for whites, those in the back for blacks. Parks sat down in the section for blacks. Then, when all the seats filled up, the driver asked Parks to stand and give her seat to a white man (that was customary in Jim Crow Alabama). Rosa Parks wouldn't budge. She knew she might get in trouble, she might even go to jail, but suddenly she found herself filled with determination. She stayed in her seat.

◀ In the segregated South, blacks had to sit in the back of the bus.

▲ Rosa Parks is fingerprinted after her arrest. Four days later, she was convicted of violating Montgomery's segregation laws and fined $14. On the same day, the bus boycott began and all over town black citizens organized carpools to get to work.

The bus driver was filled with rage. He called the police. Rosa Parks was soon arrested and on her way to jail. She knew that blacks were beaten and abused in Montgomery's jail. It didn't seem to matter to her. She was tired of riding on segregated buses. She was tired of being pushed around. She was even ready to go to jail.

When the ministers and black citizens of Montgomery heard of her arrest, they were stunned. Of all people—mild-mannered, dignified Mrs. Parks in jail? E. D. Nixon, who had been president of the local NAACP chapter, raised bond money to get her out of jail. But she would have to go on trial for breaking the law—the segregation law.

Rosa Parks knew that some of Montgomery's black leaders (members of the NAACP and a group of professional women) were trying to find a way to do something about segregation on the city's buses. E. D. Nixon asked her if the NAACP could use her case to fight segregation. They both knew that might put her life in danger. Blacks who stood up for their rights were sometimes lynched. Parks talked to her husband and her mother. Then she thought a while and said quietly, "I'll go along with you, Mr. Nixon."

As soon as Jo Ann Robinson heard that Rosa Parks had been arrested, she began organizing a boycott of the buses. Robinson felt humiliated and angry each time she had to sit in the back of a bus. She had longed to do something about Jim Crow buses. Now she was ready to act. She decided to ask all Montgomery's blacks to stay off the buses for one whole day as a protest. Robinson and some friends stayed up most of the night (it was a Thursday). They printed

The Civil War was fought over an idea. It was property rights against human rights. Human rights won. But it was only a partial victory. This was another battle in the same war for human rights.

In America, people accused of a crime do not have to stay in jail before their trial because, according to our laws, people are considered innocent until proved guilty. A judge sets an amount of money, called "bail," that an accused person must pay to get out of jail. Bail is a way of guaranteeing that they will appear in court. The amount of the bail usually varies with the severity of the crime, and whether the accused seems likely to run away. Bail, also called "bond money," is returned at the time of the trial.

leaflets—35,000 of them—telling the black community to keep off the buses the next Monday, the day of Rosa Parks's trial.

Montgomery's leading negro ministers agreed to support the one-day boycott. In their sermons on Sunday they urged everyone to stay off the buses on Monday. They knew that wouldn't be easy. Those who rode the buses were mostly the poorer citizens. They were people who needed to get to work. Some were elderly. It was December and cold. Some could find rides, but many would have to walk miles. And they all feared white violence. It was customary to intimidate blacks who tried to stand up for their rights. It was fear that made segregation work.

But something unexpected happened in Montgomery. Like Rosa Parks, most black people no longer seemed afraid. They had had enough. They stayed off the buses on Monday. And also on Tuesday. And then all week. And all month. And on and on, in rain and cold and sleet and through the heat of summer. They stayed off the buses. They shared rides; they worked out elaborate carpools; they walked. Houses were burned, churches were bombed, and shots were fired, but Montgomery's black people stayed off the buses. The jails filled with people whose only crime was riding in a carpool; still the boycott continued.

When E. D. Nixon went to get Rosa Parks out of jail, two white friends went with him. They were Virginia and Clifford Durr. Durr, a lawyer, helped the boycott movement and, because of that, lost many white clients. The Durrs were not the only whites who sided with the marchers. White minister Robert Graetz's house was bombed. Others lost their businesses or had to put up with insults and threats.

◀ African Americans in Montgomery boycotted the bus company for 381 days.

Montgomery's black citizens had always thought of themselves as ordinary folk, but they were proof that ordinary people can do extraordinary things. They were lucky: what they were doing was important, and they knew it. They were doubly lucky: they had remarkable leadership. The community had several strong leaders, but one was outstanding.

That leader was a 26-year-old minister, newly arrived in Montgomery, with a pretty, musically gifted wife named Coretta and a two-week-old daughter. He was Martin Luther King, Jr.

When King was asked to lead the boycott, he accepted. He was a beginner—as a minister and a leader—and he didn't know what he would have to do. But he and others found out that when it came to strength and vision and courage, Martin Luther King, Jr., had what was needed.

And so a great leader, a just cause, and an inspiring idea came together at the same time and made history.

The cause began with Rosa Parks. It was the cause of fairness. Segregation is unfair. Segregation is humiliating. Segregation is wrong.

The idea was nonviolence. King had been considering that idea, and he wasn't the only one. A number of others—black and white—believed Gandhi's methods would work in America. It was King who took the idea, spoke it in powerful words, and inspired others to act on it.

"We are not here advocating violence," he said in Montgomery. "The only weapon that we have...is the weapon of protest...[and] the great glory of American democracy is the right to protest for right." And so, while the segregationists screamed bad words and kicked cars and set off bombs, Montgomery's black community protested with calm, unflinching courage. They didn't scream back. They maintained their dignity.

Newspaper reporters began to come to Montgomery to see what was happening. Television crews came, too. Soon people around the nation, and in other nations as well, were watching the people of Montgomery marching. They marched to

"Where segregation exists," said Martin Luther King, Jr., "we must be willing to rise up en masse and protest courageously against it." He added, "I realize that this type of courage means suffering and sacrifice. It might mean going to jail. If such is the case, we must honorably fill up the jails of the South." ▼

work; they marched to well-organized carpool centers. When they were arrested, they marched to jail. TV watchers also saw and heard the screamers and rock throwers. And they listened to Martin Luther King, Jr.'s eloquent words:

> *There are those who would try to make of this a hate campaign. This is not a war between the white and the Negro but a conflict between justice and injustice. If we are arrested every day, if we are exploited every day, if we are trampled over every day, don't ever let anyone pull you so low as to hate them. We must use the weapon of love.*

The weapon of love won the battle. Thirteen months after Rosa Parks's arrest, the Supreme Court ruled that segregation on Alabama buses was unconstitutional. The boycott was ended! Martin Luther King, Jr., E. D. Nixon, Ralph Abernathy (a black minister and boycott leader), and George Smiley (a Texas-born white minister) rode the first integrated bus—and they all sat up front together.

The people of Montgomery not only changed their world, they changed their times.

The boycott over, Rosa Parks rides the bus again—this time, in the front. ▼

Three Boys and Six Girls

The fight to see that all Americans—black, white, Hispanic, Asian, female—would be treated fairly was called the "civil rights movement." Some of its most important battles were fought by school students.

After the Supreme Court announced its decision in *Brown v. Board of Education* in 1954, the court said integration should take place with "all deliberate speed." What does that mean? The Southern states decided that it meant with the speed of a snail. So, in the Deep South in 1957, there were still no classrooms where black boys and girls and white boys and girls sat together. Then a federal judge ordered schools in Little Rock, Arkansas, integrated.

Little Rock's Central High School was built in 1928. Some people, then, called it the finest public high school in the nation. Twenty-nine years later, it was still a good school. It had generous playing fields, modern facilities, and more than 2,000 students. But not one black child had ever gone to Central High. In Arkansas, as in all the Southern states, laws said that blacks could not go to public schools with whites.

Melba Pattillo wanted to go to Central High. She wanted the best education she could get in her community. She was not, as she recalled later, seeking to "change history."

But 15-year-old Melba would change history. She was one of nine black children to integrate Central High. At first, she didn't expect problems. Neither did most other people. Little Rock's citizens thought their city had good race relations. But some people in Little Rock decided to fight integration. They used threats, rocks, and nasty words.

Others, who might have shown some courage, kept quiet. Arkansas's governor, Orval Faubus, announced that he would call in the National Guard. Most people thought the guardsmen would protect the black students, but Faubus meant to use them to keep the nine out of Central High. He knew that aiding integration would make him lose white votes. (And blacks weren't able to vote, so they didn't matter to him.)

On the first day that the nine black students entered Central High, a mob was waiting, yelling angry threats. To avoid the mob, most of the black students entered through a side door. But slim, shy Elizabeth Eckford faced the mob alone. Elizabeth was wearing

▲ Many Southern school districts ignored the Supreme Court's 1954 *Brown* ruling that outlawed segregated schools. Here, African Americans picket along a sidewalk outside a segregated school.

In 1957, Dr. Seuss published *The Cat in the Hat*, Althea Gibson became the first black athlete to win a tennis championship at Wimbledon, Smith Corona introduced a portable electric typewriter, teenage girls were wearing poodle skirts and teased hair, Dick Clark helped make rock 'n' roll respectable on TV, and nine black students integrated Little Rock High School.

a starched new black-and-white cotton dress for her first day at school. She had not gotten the message that the black students were to enter school together. So she was by herself, at the opposite end of the building from the others.

Elizabeth must have been scared, but she held her head high and tried to walk up to the school door. The guardsmen stared at her. Adults screamed awful words. A woman spat. Some boys threatened to lynch her. Elizabeth ran back to the curb, and a *New York Times* reporter put his arm around her. "Don't let them see you cry," he whispered. A white woman (who was on her side) took Elizabeth home.

▲ Elizabeth Eckford, one of the Little Rock Nine, arrives at Central High School amid hostile shouts and armed guards.

Three black reporters weren't as lucky. They were beaten by enraged whites. One of them, Alex Wilson, was a former marine and more than six feet tall. He was hit with a brick and "went down like a tree."

In the nation's capital, President Eisenhower said he didn't want to take sides. He believed in persuasion. But there was no persuading the lawbreakers who stood outside Central High that day and the next.

Most of the students known as the Little Rock Nine: from left, Carlotta Walls, Gloria Ray, Ernest Green, Jefferson Thomas, Thelma Mothershed, Terrance Roberts, and Minnijean Brown. (At right is Jane Hill, who decided to attend a different high school. Not pictured here are Melba Pattillo and Elizabeth Eckford.) ▼

Nine Brave Kids

In 1987, 30 years after they entered Central High, the Little Rock Nine came together for a reunion. Elizabeth Eckford, now a social worker, was the only one who had stayed in Little Rock. Thelma Mothershed was a teacher in Illinois, Terry Roberts a professor at UCLA, Minnijean Brown a writer and mother of six, Jeff Thomas a Defense Department accountant in California, Ernie Green a vice president of a New York investment firm, Carlotta Walls a Denver realtor, Gloria Ray a magazine publisher living in the Netherlands, and Melba Pattillo a communications consultant and author living in San Francisco. Do you think they might have been strengthened by their struggle? The *Chicago Defender* said: "The Supreme Court ruling would have been meaningless had these Negro boys and girls failed to follow the course mapped out for them by the law.... They should be applauded by all of us."

▲ National Guard troops maintain order outside Central High School.

▲ Ernest Green, one of the Little Rock Nine, adjusts his cap on graduation day in 1958. Green was the first black graduate of Central High School.

Finally, the president acted. "Mob rule cannot be allowed to override the decisions of our courts," he said. Reluctantly, he ordered federal troops sent to Little Rock. Then Melba Pattillo, Elizabeth Eckford, and the other black students entered through the front door.

Ernest Green remembered the convoy that took him to school. There was a jeep in front and a jeep behind.

> *They both had machine gun mounts…. The whole school was ringed with paratroopers and helicopters hovering around. We marched up the steps…with this circle of soldiers with bayonets drawn…. Walking up the steps that day was probably one of the biggest feelings I've ever had.*

At the end of that year, Ernest became the first black person to graduate from Central High. "I figured I was making a statement and helping black people's existence in Little Rock," he said. "I kept telling myself, I just can't trip with all those cameras watching me. But I knew that once I got as far as that principal and received that diploma, I had cracked the wall." He was right.

PART 3

CONFLICT AT HOME AND ABROAD

Passing the Torch

It had been cold all week in Washington, D.C., and Thursday night—January 19, 1961—snow fell thick and heavy. Washington, southern in its graciousness and geography, handles snow poorly. Everywhere cars stalled and people shivered.

That evening the army and navy were called. Three thousand servicemen, using 700 snowplows and trucks, worked through the night. The next day the wind was mean and the temperature stayed below freezing, but the streets were clear. Wooden bleachers were set up outdoors in front of the Capitol. At noon, when some 20,000 invited guests filled those bleachers, the winter sun reflecting off the banks of new snow seemed unusually bright. It was Inauguration Day.

The new president delivers his inaugural speech, hatless and coatless. ▼

Most of the presidential party wore scarves and mittens with their top hats and formal clothes. But the president-elect seemed to generate his own warmth—a quality he had in abundance. He took off his overcoat before he spoke. Then John Fitzgerald Kennedy put his hand on his grandfather's Bible and swore to uphold his mighty responsibilities. At 43, he was the youngest president since Theodore Roosevelt and the youngest man ever elected president. Next to him stood 70-year-old Dwight D. Eisenhower, at the time the oldest man ever to be president.

The contrast between the two was as strong as the winter sun. Genial, likable Ike was the son of a poor Midwestern creamery worker. But his easy manner was an outside face; inside was a core of steel. Eisenhower had worked his way through an army career to the nation's top job.

Harvard-educated JFK, the patrician son of a wealthy businessman, had been given every advantage our society has to give. But the silver spoons that fed him had not made him lazy. Quite the opposite. He, and the other members of the large Kennedy family, were trained to serve their country, to achieve, and to do their best.

The wind blew as Robert Frost, America's favorite poet, read part of a poem he had written for this occasion. He spoke of "a Golden Age of poetry and power, of which this noonday's the beginning hour."

A "Golden Age of poetry and power." Would this handsome young president bring it about? There were many who believed he could. Not since the first days of Franklin Roosevelt's New Deal had so many eager people clamored to join the political process. The new cabinet (the president's top advisers) was going to be bipartisan. That meant it would include people from both political parties. Some of Kennedy's college professors were leaving their classrooms to become government officials.

> To *clamor* means to agitate noisily for something.

Thousands of Americans wanted to be part of the excitement that seemed to be building. It was amazing, the number of people who hoped to work to help their nation. John Kennedy had already suggested a "peace corps," a volunteer agency that would let Americans unselfishly share their experience and knowledge with less fortunate nations.

The young president, with his intense blue eyes, his thick head of hair, and his engaging smile, stepped up to the lectern and began

◀ President Kennedy urged the creation of the Peace Corps. This Peace Corps volunteer in a poor district of Ankara, Turkey, helped residents form a library, nursery school, community center, and clinic. By 1963, about 5,000 volunteers were serving two-year stints in more than 40 developing countries.

▲ President Kennedy's charm, youthful appearance, and quick wit appealed to many people.

to speak. "We observe today not a victory of party but a celebration of freedom," he said in strong, self-confident New England tones.

Let the word go forth from this time and place, to friend and foe alike, that the torch has been passed to a new generation of Americans, born in this century, tempered by war, disciplined by a hard and bitter peace, proud of our ancient heritage, and unwilling to witness or permit the slow undoing of those human rights to which this nation has always been committed.... Let every nation know, whether it wishes us well or ill, that we shall pay any price, bear any burden, meet any hardship, support any friend, oppose any foe to assure the survival and the success of liberty.... Let us begin anew... remembering on both sides that civility is not a sign of weakness.

Then he challenged his listeners:

If a free society cannot help the many who are poor, it cannot save the few who are rich.... And so, my fellow Americans, ask not what your country can do for you, ask what you can do for your country.

On that bright January afternoon, hope vibrated in the air. Our new president had big dreams that everyone could share. He intended that the nation reach for greatness within itself. He was surrounding himself with men and women who would be called "the best and the brightest." He expected to get things done. Everyone talked of his charisma (kuh-RIZ-muh).

Charisma is an exceptional ability for leadership and for securing the devotion of large numbers of people.

And so, when he noticed in the inaugural parade that there were no black cadets among the Coast Guard marchers, his first act as president was to call an aide and ask him to do something about that. The next September there was a black professor and several black cadets at the Coast Guard Academy.

This man, John F. Kennedy, was determined to be an active president, a good president, a president who would inspire the nation.

Rachel Carson, Ecologist

Rachel Carson wrote of science and the natural world, and she did it so well that all who read her books gained a new awareness of their environment. Although, at first, no one paid much attention to what she wrote.

In July 1951, she published *The Sea Around Us*, a book about reefs and islands and sea creatures and coral and sea plants. To her surprise, the book became a huge best-seller.

▲ By the end of the '60s, at least five state legislatures, alarmed by Rachel Carson's warnings about a poisoned world, had banned or limited the use of the pesticide called DDT.

Eventually it was translated into 32 languages. The book was enormously influential. It introduced the ideas of ecology and conservation to large numbers of people. (Ecology—which comes from the Greek word meaning habitation—is the scientific study of the interactions between living things and their environment.)

The Sea Around Us made Rachel Carson famous; the last book she wrote, *Silent Spring*, brought her enemies. It took courage to write that book. It was a look at a grim subject—pesticides—and how they were poisoning the earth and its inhabitants. In *Silent Spring*, Carson attacked the chemical and food-processing industries, and the Department of Agriculture.

Those powerful interest groups lost no time in fighting back. Rachel Carson was mocked and ridiculed. But the fury and fervor of the attacks only brought her more readers. President Kennedy asked for a special report on pesticides from his Science Advisory Committee. The report confirmed what Carson had written, and it made important recommendations for curtailing and controlling the use of pesticides.

The public, which had been generally unaware of the danger of the poisons sprayed on plants, was now aware. Modestly, Rachel Carson said that one book couldn't change things, but on that she may have been wrong.

Being President Isn't Easy

The small island of Cuba, near Florida, had terrible problems. Its government was corrupt, criminals were making fortunes on the island, and most Cubans were very poor. So when Fidel Castro came along and took charge, in 1959, many Cubans and Americans were hopeful. But when they learned that Castro was a communist—a Marxist-Leninist-Soviet communist—most stopped cheering. Castro did clean up much of the corruption in Cuba. He also improved the schools and race relations. But he was a dictator. The Cuban people were not free to oppose him or his ideas.

Many Cubans fled Cuba for the United States. They didn't intend to stay here. They wanted to go back to their own country and overthrow Castro. Most Americans would have liked that. The idea of a communist nation with ties to Russia sitting 90 miles off the coast of the United States made people in this country very nervous.

As soon as John F. Kennedy became president, he learned that the CIA—the Central Intelligence Agency—had been secretly training Cuban refugees as warriors

▲ A portrait of Karl Marx looms behind Fidel Castro. Many Americans hoped Castro would bring democracy to Cuba, but he embraced communism instead.

Castro cheers with other rebels in 1957. In 1959, the rebels overthrew the corrupt Cuban government. ▶

◀ A U.S. U-2 spy plane took aerial photographs of a nuclear missile site built by the Soviets in Cuba.

Labels on image: LAUNCH POSITION, MISSILE-READY TENTS, MISSILE ERECTORS

and planning to land them on the island. The CIA experts said that the Cuban people would then rise up, join the invaders, and throw out dictator Castro. President Kennedy didn't want to seem soft on communism. After Joseph McCarthy, no one did. He told the CIA to go ahead.

The invasion, at a place called the Bay of Pigs, was a fiasco (fee-ASS-ko), which means it was a flop, fizzle, bomb, washout, dud, botch, bungle, failure. Nothing worked right. The invaders were captured; the Cuban people didn't rise up; America—and Kennedy—looked foolish. The young president took all the blame himself.

Around the world people wondered, "Is he strong enough to be president?" Russia's leader, Nikita Khrushchev, was sure he wasn't. It seemed a good time to bully the United States. Premier Khrushchev decided to do something bold. He decided to put nuclear missiles in Cuba. They would be aimed right at America's most important cities and military targets. Some missiles were already in place when spy planes flying over Cuba brought news that missile sites were being prepared. Then Russian ships were sighted carrying more missiles.

What should the president do? The wrong move could start World War III. Both Russia and the United States had weapons that could destroy the world as we know it.

What would you do? The joint chiefs of staff (our top military leaders) wanted to bomb Cuba. Kennedy said no to his

The CIA (Central Intelligence Agency) was established by Congress in 1947 and is America's foreign sleuthing operation. CIA agents are apt to be spies, or foreign-intelligence gatherers. During the Cold War, the CIA became very influential, employing thousands of agents overseas and many others at its headquarters in Langley, Virginia (near Washington, D.C.). It spent its large budget without congressional scrutiny. (See what you can find out about what the CIA does today. Do you think we still need a spying organization?)

▲ President Kennedy faced the real possibility of nuclear war with the Soviet Union.

The U.S. Navy was charged with maintaining a blockade around Cuba to keep Soviet ships from delivering their cargoes. ▼

experts. He would not drop the first bomb, but he did announce that American troops were ready to invade the island if the missiles were not removed.

Khrushchev was in a tough spot, too. Castro wanted the Russians to launch a missile at the United States. Khrushchev said no to that. But he did tell the Russian military experts in Cuba that they could use nuclear weapons if there was an invasion.

Kennedy was firm. He said the missiles had to be removed. He gave Khrushchev time to make a decision. Secretly, Kennedy agreed to remove U.S. missiles from Turkey. (Missiles there were a threat to Russia.) For 13 days the world held its breath, wondering if there would be a nuclear war. Then the missile-carrying Russian ships turned around and sailed home. The Cuban missiles were removed. The crisis was over.

Everyone knew that no one could win a nuclear war. Kennedy wanted both Russia and the United States to sign a treaty to stop testing nuclear bombs. We began talking with Russia about disarmament (reducing or doing away with weapons).

Then, suddenly, Russia announced that bomb tests would begin again. Those tests put radioactive particles into the atmosphere—and that poisoned the air. Kennedy appealed to the United Nations. But Russia's tests continued. Finally, Kennedy said that the United States would have to begin testing again. Then he made a great speech at American University in Washington. The president said that we needed to change our thinking about the Soviet Union. He said we needed to work together, not continue as enemies. Some Americans couldn't imagine getting along with Russia. Kennedy spoke to them:

> *Some say it is useless to speak of world peace. I realize that the pursuit of peace is not as dramatic as pursuit of war...but we have no more urgent task.... We all inhabit this small planet. We all breathe the same air. We all cherish our children's future. And we all are mortal.*

A few weeks later, Khrushchev accepted the U.S. proposal for a test-ban treaty. "This treaty...is particularly for our children and grandchildren," said Kennedy, "and they have no lobby in Washington."

A *lobby* is a group that tries to persuade politicians to do what it wants. Some people think lobbies are a danger (most give congressmen money for campaign expenses). Others say that lobbying for your own interests is what democracy is all about.

Meanwhile, things were still a mess in Vietnam. Remember, governments in the North and South were fighting for power. North Vietnam was backed by communist China and communist Russia; we were sending aid to South Vietnam. The North seemed to be winning.

President Kennedy sent his vice president, Lyndon Johnson, on a fact-finding trip. When Johnson returned, he said the same thing that almost all our military and State Department experts were saying: if we wanted to see the communists defeated we would have to send more money and more supplies and more experts to train the South Vietnamese. So JFK sent the first American troops (called "advisers") to Vietnam. Except for a few lonely dissenters, no one asked if it was right to fight communists in Vietnam. Just about everyone in the early 1960s seemed to think we had to. By 1963 we had 11,000 military advisers in Vietnam; we were spending a million and a half dollars a day supporting that war.

Meanwhile, the struggle for civil rights continued in the American South.

An American military adviser instructs South Vietnamese villagers in the use of rifles in 1962. At the time, few Americans knew where Vietnam was. ▼

Some Brave Children Meet a Roaring Bull

It was hot, very hot, in the summer of 1962 in Birmingham, Alabama. But that didn't seem to make any difference to the city's white leaders. They closed all the city's public recreational facilities because they didn't want to see them integrated. That meant 68 parks, 38 playgrounds, 6 swimming pools, and 4 golf courses were locked up, and no one in Birmingham—kindhearted or mean-spirited, young or old—could enter the parks or swim in the city pools. For the wealthy, there were private pools and clubs, but for most people, there was no escaping the heat.

Birmingham, Alabama's largest city, had plenty of moderate, clear-headed citizens, but the South's moderates were used to keeping quiet. Perhaps they feared mob action, or the disapproval of some of their friends, or the violence of the Ku Klux Klan. The Klan had helped elect Eugene "Bull" Connor as Birmingham's commissioner of public safety (police chief). Connor was about as big a bully as the South has ever produced. Besides that, he wasn't very smart. Bull Connor helped the civil rights movement a whole lot, although that wasn't what he intended to do.

Civil rights protesters march in downtown Birmingham, Alabama, in 1963. ▼

This is what happened: Birmingham's black citizens were marching, protesting, and demonstrating. They wanted the same rights as everyone else. They wanted to be able to eat in any restaurant. They wanted an end to segregation. They wanted to vote. Those were all their civil rights. They were demonstrating peacefully and nonviolently, but Bull Connor threw them in jail.

Martin Luther King, Jr., came to Birmingham, joined the marchers, and he was thrown in jail. Around the nation, people began to be concerned. A Southern jail was a dangerous place for a black civil rights leader. King decided to write a letter from Birmingham jail and explain the reasons behind the civil rights movement.

The Highest Respect for Law

Martin Luther King, Jr., wrote a letter from the Birmingham jail. He addressed it to eight clergymen—Christian ministers and a Jewish rabbi—who had criticized the civil rights demonstrations and wondered why Dr. King had come to Birmingham. Here is part of what King said.

> *I am in Birmingham because injustice is here.... I cannot sit idly by in Atlanta and not be concerned about what happens in Birmingham. Injustice anywhere is a threat to justice everywhere.... What affects one directly affects all indirectly. There are two types of laws: just and unjust. I would be the first to advocate obeying just laws.... One who breaks an unjust law must do so openly, lovingly, and with a willingness to accept the penalty. I submit that an individual who breaks a law that conscience tells him is unjust, and who willingly accepts the penalty of imprisonment in order to arouse the conscience of the community over its injustice, is in reality expressing the highest respect for law.*

▲ Dr. Martin Luther King, Jr., sits behind bars in the Birmingham jail.

He didn't have any writing paper so he wrote on the margins of a newspaper and on toilet paper. He chose his words carefully. His powerful and persuasive letter explained what the marches were all about. He said it was unjust laws.

But Dr. King and the other leaders knew something dramatic was needed to capture the nation's attention. Demonstrators were being sent to jail every day, yet no one was doing anything about it. Thousands of demonstrators were needed. Most blacks knew they would lose their jobs if they marched. Where could they find thousands of people who would march and not worry about losing their jobs?

In the schools.

"We started organizing the prom queens of the high schools, the basketball stars, the football stars," said Reverend James Bevel. Those student leaders got others interested.

Bevel had already helped organize a demonstration in Nashville, Tennessee. College students there sat down at lunch counters and politely asked for items on the menu. When they weren't served, because of the color of their skin, they stayed in their seats—until the police took them off to jail. Across the South, black and white students took part in *sit-ins* at lunch counters. Some people poured ketchup on the students' heads; others hit and kicked them. President Kennedy said, "The new way for Americans to stand up for their rights is to sit down." (But privately, JFK was urging Dr. King to ease up on the confrontations. He didn't want trouble.)

In Birmingham, boys and girls from the high schools, junior highs, and elementary schools wanted to march. "We held workshops to help them overcome the crippling fear of dogs and jails, and to help them start thinking on their feet," said Bevel, who taught the children the ways of nonviolence.

In Montgomery, when a woman was asked why she got involved in the bus boycott, she had said, "I'm doing it for my children and grandchildren." In Birmingham, Martin Luther King, Jr., said, "The children and grandchildren are doing it for themselves."

Some 600 children there marched out of church singing, and Bull Connor arrested them all. The next day another 1,000 children began a peaceful march. Connor called out his police dogs. Firemen turned on high-pressure hoses.

▲ Black and white students and a professor stage a sit-in at a segregated Woolworth's lunch counter in Mississippi's state capital, Jackson, in 1963. The whites behind them drenched them with soda, ketchup, and mustard.

"All you gotta do is tell them you're going to bring the dogs," Birmingham police chief Bull Connor told the press. "I want to see the dogs work." ▶

The fire hoses were so strong they ripped bark off trees. When the water hit the children they were thrown on the ground and rolled screaming down the street. Television cameras hummed and people, worldwide, saw what was happening to Birmingham's children. Police dogs bit three teenagers so badly they had to be taken to the hospital. A small girl and her mother who knelt to pray on the steps of City Hall were arrested and taken to jail. Seventy-five children were squeezed into a cell built for eight prisoners. They sang freedom songs.

Can you see why Connor helped the civil rights movement? Decent people were outraged. Most hadn't realized how bad things were for blacks in the segregated South. Now they could see for themselves on TV. In Washington, President Kennedy remembered stories his grandfather had told him about anti-Catholic mobs who burned Catholic houses in 19th-century Boston. Kennedy knew that racial and religious hatred had no place in America. He asked his brother, Attorney General Robert "Bobby" Kennedy, to work to bring justice to all Americans. Bobby Kennedy would devote much of his energy to that cause.

▲ Firemen turn high-pressure hoses on Birmingham civil rights demonstrators. "Every channel of communication," said a reporter, "has been fragmented by the emotional dynamite of racism, reinforced by the whip, the razor, the gun, the bomb, the torch, the club, the knife, the mob, the police."

On Sunday, September 15, 1963, a bomb exploded with the force of 12 sticks of dynamite during Sunday school at Birmingham's 16th Street Baptist Church. On May 22, 2002, a jury found 71-year-old Bobby Frank Cherry—a former Ku Klux Klansman and the last living defendant—guilty of that horrible crime.

Relatives mourn one of the four young girls killed in the bombing of the 16th Street Baptist Church in Birmingham, Alabama. ▶

Standing with Lincoln

The civil rights leaders were human, and so there were rivalries and jealousies. They disagreed among themselves. Those from older organizations, like the NAACP (National Association for the Advancement of Colored People), were at their best working through the courts and trying to change the laws. That was a slow process; it took skilled leadership. The lawyer Thurgood Marshall and the labor chief A. Philip Randolph were that kind of leader.

Martin Luther King, Jr., had helped organize the SCLC (the Southern Christian Leadership Conference). Its appeal was to the mass of moderate churchgoing blacks; most of its leaders were ministers. But many young people were impatient with both of these approaches, which seemed too slow-moving. They formed the Student Nonviolent Coordinating Committee—the SNCC, which people pronounced as "snick." SNCC and the Congress for Racial Equality (CORE) organized many of the sit-ins in college communities.

Some black groups wanted to fight with fists, weapons, and anger. Everyone knew that if they got their way, much of the high purpose of the civil rights movement would be lost. Leaders like Martin Luther King, Jr., had made civil rights a cause for all Americans. It was

A protester practicing passive resistance is carried away by police during a CORE demonstration. ▶

▲ President Kennedy stands on a platform to survey the Berlin Wall.

about equality. It was about justice and freedom for all. It wasn't just for blacks—although most of the leadership was black.

For years, A. Philip Randolph had talked of a freedom rally in the nation's capital. Perhaps it would bring the diverse black leaders together. Perhaps it would bring black and white people together. Perhaps it would influence Congress.

President Kennedy had sent a civil rights bill to Congress. Would it be passed? No one was sure. A march would show Congress and the president the importance of the civil rights movement. Many thought that Kennedy was paying more attention to affairs in Cuba and Vietnam than to the problem of unfairness at home. When President Kennedy gave a speech in West Berlin, Germany, about political freedom, it inspired cheers from people around the world.

▲ More than 250,000 people, including 60,000 whites, gathered in Washington, D.C., to demand an end to racial inequality in America.

▲ Marchers held hands and sang "We Shall Overcome."

"We Shall Overcome" became the anthem of the civil rights movement. The song is said to have originated in the 1940s at Tennessee's Highlander Folk School, where black textile workers gathered together.

We shall overcome,
We shall overcome,
We shall overcome someday.
Oh, deep in my heart,
I do believe.
We shall overcome someday.

But some Americans weren't enthusiastic. They knew there was a kind of freedom that was missing right here in America.

Exactly 100 years had passed since Abraham Lincoln signed the Emancipation Proclamation. Some white people were still telling black people to be patient. Martin Luther King, Jr., said, "We can't wait any longer. Now is the time."

A. Philip Randolph was 74. If ever he was to have his march, it had to be soon. And so it was decided: on August 28, 1963, there would be a march for freedom in Washington, D.C. Black leaders hoped that 100,000 people would participate. The marchers were going to demand four things: passage of the civil rights bill; integration of schools by year's end; an end to job discrimination; and a program of job training. Bayard Rustin, who was a whiz at organizing, was in charge.

Rustin got to work. He had 21 drinking fountains, 24 first-aid stations, and lots of portable toilets set up on Washington's grassy Mall. Workers made 80,000 cheese sandwiches. Movie stars, singers, high-school bands, preachers, and politicians practiced speeches and songs. The speakers and entertainers were to stand on the steps of the Lincoln

Memorial and look toward the tall, slender Washington Monument and, beyond that, to the nation's Capitol.

Two thousand buses headed for Washington, and 21 chartered trains. Sixty thousand whites came. Television crews, high in the Washington Monument, guessed that there were 250,000 people altogether.

It was a day filled with song, and hope, and good will. Finally, in the late afternoon, the last of the speakers stood on the steps of the Lincoln Memorial. It was Martin Luther King, Jr. He began with a prepared speech, which was formal and dignified, as was his nature. Then something happened inside him. Perhaps he responded to the crowd. Perhaps his training as a preacher took over. Whatever it was, he left his written speech and began talking from his heart. *"I have a dream,"* he said.

> *I have a dream that one day down in Alabama…little black boys and black girls will be able to join hands with little white boys and white girls as sisters and brothers. I have a dream today!*

See page 331 for the complete text of Martin Luther King, Jr.'s "I Have a Dream" speech.

Dr. King's powerful words were heard across the country. ▼

The President in Dallas

President Kennedy had to deal with a Congress controlled by an alliance of northern Republicans and southern Democrats. They voted as a bloc—against change. Kennedy, a liberal Democrat, wanted to take the country in new directions. The conservative Congress stood in his way.

The president spoke to the American people of a "New Frontier" that would go beyond FDR's New Deal. Kennedy had legislation that he wanted passed: civil rights bills, tax-cut bills, and health-care bills. There were also bills on equal pay for women, aid to the cities, aid to poor rural areas, manpower training, and a minimum wage. At first, the president was frustrated. Some people called his ideas "socialist." Fear of change, especially in the field of civil rights, caused his popularity to drop.

But by 1963, the president saw signs that his ideas were being heard. John F. Kennedy seemed to know how to inspire people. Remember that charisma? It was working.

The president believed he could get enough votes in Congress to pass his bills. And Kennedy believed that the next election might bring him a Congress with even bigger favorable numbers. He expected to win a second term in the presidential elections in 1964.

President John F. Kennedy spoke of a "New Frontier" for America. ▼

He hoped Congress would support his New Frontier. Except for that situation in Vietnam, things were looking good.

But there was trouble in Texas—political trouble—and Texas's votes would be important in the coming election. The Texas Democratic leaders couldn't seem to get along with each other. So when Vice President Lyndon B. Johnson, a Texan, asked Kennedy to go on a peacemaking mission, the president felt it his job to go.

Kennedy's press secretary got a letter. DON'T LET THE PRESIDENT COME TO DALLAS, it said. TEXAS IS TOO DANGEROUS, the letter writer added. The secretary put the letter aside. Everyone knew there was a group of noisy hatemongers in Dallas, but this president didn't seem to worry. And so, on a day filled with sunshine, he and Jackie waved goodbye to their two children and flew off to the Lone Star State.

▲ "Dallas is a very dangerous place," Arkansas senator J. William Fulbright told Kennedy before the president left on his Texas trip. "I wouldn't go there." But the crowds greeting the president in Fort Worth were enthusiastic.

▲ First Lady Jacqueline Kennedy holds the bouquet of roses she received shortly after she and the president arrived at the Dallas airport.

Things started wonderfully well. The crowds in San Antonio and Houston and Fort Worth were unusually warm and encouraging. At Fort Worth, unexpectedly, Kennedy went out into a parking lot and shook as many hands as he could. It bothered the Secret Service men, who were there to protect him, but the president liked contact with people.

Later in the day, when Air Force One, the presidential plane, touched down at Love Field in Dallas, thousands of people were waiting to cheer the president and First Lady. Jacqueline Kennedy was handed a big bouquet of roses and asters. The weather was so fine and the crowds so enthusiastic that the plastic bubble top was taken off the presidential limousine. The bulletproof side windows were rolled down. Texas's governor, John Connally, and his wife sat in the front seat of the big car; the Kennedys sat behind. They were on their way to a luncheon, and they took the busiest route through the city, so they could see the most people. Crowds lined the streets: a few among them were protesting, but most were cheering. When the car passed an old, seven-story schoolbook warehouse, Mrs. Connally turned around and said to the president, "You can't say that Dallas isn't friendly to you today!"

▲ Lyndon Johnson is sworn in as 36th president of the United States. "He did everything he could to be magnanimous, to be kind," said Jackie Kennedy.

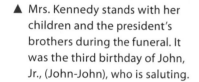

▲ Mrs. Kennedy stands with her children and the president's brothers during the funeral. It was the third birthday of John, Jr., (John-John), who is saluting.

But President Kennedy never answered. Two bullets had pierced his head.

For the rest of their lives, most Americans would remember exactly where they were on November 22, 1963, when they heard the news. Again and again, they would stare at their TV screens and see the motorcade, the president falling into his wife's lap, the press at Parkland Hospital, and Jacqueline in her blood-stained suit.

At 1 p.m., John F. Kennedy was pronounced dead. At 2:30 p.m., Lyndon B. Johnson was sworn in as chief executive on Air Force One. That plane carried him, and the martyred president, back to the nation's capital. And the world wept.

Ruby's Revenge

Dallas police captured Lee Harvey Oswald in a movie theater after he shot a policeman who noticed his suspicious behavior. Oswald, who had lived in Russia and Cuba, was charged with the shooting of President Kennedy and Governor Connally (who was wounded). Two days later, going through a jail passageway, Oswald was shot and killed by Jack Ruby, a Dallas nightclub owner. The debate about whether others were involved in JFK's assassination continues to this day.

Millions were watching on TV as Jack Ruby (right) shot Lee Harvey Oswald (center) on his way to the county jail. ▶

LBJ

The new president was big. Taller than six feet three inches, he had big bones, big ears, a big nose, big hands, and big feet. His voice was big, his ego was big, and when it came to his ambition—it was bigger than big. His ambition was colossal.

Ego (EE-go) is a person's sense of self.

He wanted to be a great president, right up there with Washington and Lincoln. No, he wanted more than that. He said he wanted to be "the greatest of them all, the whole bunch of them."

Johnson's dream was to wipe out poverty in America. He wanted to see blacks, whites, Hispanics—all people—treated as equal citizens. He wanted old people to be cared for. He wanted no barriers to hinder the handicapped. He wanted every child in the country to get a good education. He wanted to see an America where *all men [and women] are created equal.* And he worked for those goals with more energy and political savvy than any president before or since. He understood, as few have, that helping the poor and the disadvantaged would enrich the whole nation.

Lyndon Baines Johnson came from Texas, from the scruffy Hill Country near Austin, a region so isolated when he was a boy that no one had electricity at home, and almost no one had running water indoors or an indoor toilet. If you wanted to take a bath, or do the dishes, or wash clothes, you had to pump water from a well in the yard, carry it inside the house, and heat it over a fire. At the first school Lyndon went to, all the grades were in one room, with just one teacher. Most of the children didn't wear shoes. But the Hill Country people didn't think of themselves as poor. They had food to eat and roofs over their heads—and they knew and cared about each other.

Lyndon B. Johnson was a president with huge ambitions. ▼

Lyndon Johnson—five years old in this photo—grew up in a scruffy, isolated part of Texas. ▶

▲ Johnson, on the right, was a member of the debate team at Southwest Texas State Teachers College.

▲ President Johnson poses in front of Junction Elementary, the one-room school he attended in Johnson City, Texas. The town was named for his ancestors.

From the time he was a little boy it was politics that fascinated him. That wasn't surprising. His mother was the daughter of a Texas secretary of state. His father, Sam Ealy Johnson, served in the Texas legislature.

By the time Lyndon was six he was attending political rallies and handing out pamphlets. When he was 10 he would go with his father to the legislature and "sit in the gallery for hours watching all the activity on the floor."

But when he was ready to go to college, his father was in debt. The family farm had failed. Lyndon borrowed $75 to help pay his expenses. After a year he had to drop out and teach in order to earn money to finish. He taught Mexican American children that year and saw real poverty—worse than anything he knew. He never forgot those children.

Back at college, he got a job carrying trash and sweeping floors. He ended up working as an assistant to the college president, who later laughed and told him, "You hadn't been in my office a month before I could hardly tell who was president of the school—you or me."

When Lyndon Johnson graduated, the college president said, "I predict for him great things in the years ahead." But he had no idea he was talking to a future president of the United States.

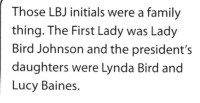

Those LBJ initials were a family thing. The First Lady was Lady Bird Johnson and the president's daughters were Lynda Bird and Lucy Baines.

The Biggest Vote in History

Some people are born to be preachers and some to be teachers and some to be ballplayers. Lyndon Johnson was born to be a politician. He was 29 when he was first elected to Congress, and he set out like a sprinter in a running race. Right away, he arranged to meet President Franklin Roosevelt. Afterward, FDR called an assistant and said, "I've just met a most remarkable young man...this boy could well be the first southern president [in a century]."

As a congressman, Johnson worked 16-hour days and sometimes longer; he expected his aides to work right along with him. That was nothing new for him, but one of his assistants had a nervous breakdown. Naturally, Johnson got a lot done and impressed some Washington old-timers.

All that energy meant benefits for his district. He got the government to help finance slum-clearance projects and low-cost housing in Austin, the state capital. And he insisted that Mexican Americans and blacks have a fair share of the new houses. Money he got for the region helped farmers go from backbreaking horse-and-plow farming to 20th-century farm machinery. He brought electricity to the Texas Hill Country.

Farming wives soon had washing machines. Farming families could turn on the lights. "Of all the things I have ever done," said Johnson 20 years later, "nothing has ever given me as much satisfaction as bringing power to the Hill Country of Texas."

A congressman represents one district in a state. Some states have many congressmen; the number depends on the state's population. But each state has only two senators; each senator represents the whole state. Twelve years after entering Congress, Lyndon Johnson was elected to the Senate. Four years after that, he was elected leader of the Democratic Party in the Senate.

Andrew Johnson, who was president right after the Civil War, and who also succeeded a martyred leader, was the last Southern president until Lyndon Johnson.

When Johnson ran for Congress, his campaign's slogan was "He Gets Things Done." ▼

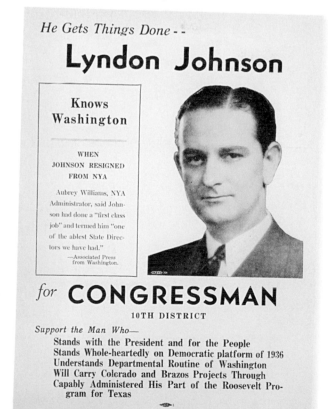

He Gets Things Done --

Lyndon Johnson

Knows Washington

WHEN JOHNSON RESIGNED FROM NYA

Aubrey Williams, NYA Administrator, said Johnson had done a "first class job" and termed him "one of the ablest State Directors we have had."
—Associated Press from Washington.

for **CONGRESSMAN**

10TH DISTRICT

Support the Man Who—
Stands with the President and for the People
Stands Whole-heartedly on Democratic platform of 1936
Understands Departmental Routine of Washington
Will Carry Colorado and Brazos Projects Through
Capably Administered His Part of the Roosevelt Program for Texas

▲ A 1964 cartoon pokes fun at Johnson's Southern roots.

A cyclone in the Senate chamber might have been less noticed. When Lyndon Johnson let loose with his never-stop Texas energy, he usually got whatever it was he wanted. But he wasn't all bluster. He knew how to compromise. During the Eisenhower presidency he worked closely with the Republicans. He helped them get bills passed; they helped him get favors for Texas.

President Kennedy's programs had been stalled in the Republican Congress. President Johnson knew how to trade and maneuver and twist arms. He soon began to get Kennedy's programs passed, and then he added his own vision—it extended the New Frontier and the New Deal. He called it the "Great Society." It was a vision of a place where there was no poverty; where all children were well schooled; where health care was a birthright; where jobs and job training were attainable by all. If he could make all that happen—well, he would be the greatest president.

The American people didn't know quite what to make of Lyndon Johnson. Sometimes he just seemed like a big, crude country boy who had stumbled into the presidency. Some people made fun of him. Johnson was hurt. He wanted everyone to admire and love him.

Near Johnson City, Texas, LBJ rides a horse at his ranch, which became known as the "Western White House." ▶

A campaign poster reflects the president's desire to have the support of the entire country. ▼

▲ When he was inaugurated in 1965, Johnson had big ideas for the nation.

He didn't want to be an accidental president. He wanted to be elected president himself. He soon had that chance. In 1964 he took his ideas to the American people. He ran for the presidency on his own. He didn't just want to be elected; he wanted the biggest popular vote in the history of the country.

Well, he got what he wanted: the biggest popular vote ever! And he also got a Congress that was Democratic; it would support his programs. Now he had an opportunity few presidents have had. He had that grand vision of a Great Society. He had support from the people to get things done. And he had the ability and energy to make it happen.

The president was triumphant. But he had already done something that would tear down much of what he had carefully constructed. He had told the American people and Congress that the North Vietnamese had attacked an innocent American ship in the Gulf of Tonkin. That wasn't quite true, and he knew it. (Keep reading and you'll hear more about the Gulf of Tonkin—and that untruth.)

January 8, 1964. President Johnson tells Congress that he is declaring a "war on poverty." He outlines a plan that includes aid to Appalachia, youth employment programs, improved unemployment insurance, a domestic peace corps, and expansion of the area redevelopment program. Later, his budget puts the cost of the war on poverty at $1 billion. Actual expenditures in fiscal 1964–1965 are slightly more than $600 million. The deficit for that year is the lowest in five years. (A government has a *deficit* when it spends more money than it brings in—from taxes, import duties, etc. What is a fiscal year?)

Johnson's Great Society

In the mid-20th-century, the United States was thriving. We were called an "affluent society." That means we were rich. Many Americans had cars, bikes, television sets, hi-fi sets, and nice houses. But some people were left out. Some people went hungry. They didn't get a fair chance to go to a good school or to get a good job. Were they to blame for that?

What should be done about poverty? That problem was as old as society and not easy to solve.

Lyndon Johnson thought something could be done about poverty, and he meant to do it. He intended to build his Great Society. It would take money, the talent to get bills passed in Congress, and the leadership to make Americans understand that ending poverty would make everyone richer.

Johnson revved up his jet-engine personality and blasted away.

The Civil Rights Act of 1964 was passed—it outlawed most discrimination, helping women as well as minorities. Head Start helped little children prepare for kindergarten. The Job Corps found work for school dropouts. Upward Bound helped needy children go to

Hi-fi is short for high fidelity—meaning true sound reproduction. It was what everybody called stereo systems when they first became popular in the late '50s and early '60s.

According to the Census Bureau, between 1960 and 1990, poverty was reduced by 39 percent—from 22.2 percent of the nation's population to 13.5 percent. That was still too many poor people, but many fewer than there would have been without antipoverty programs.

Johnson was determined to establish programs to eliminate the kind of poverty seen here in Alabama in 1965. ▶

college. The Neighborhood Youth Corps trained unemployed teenagers. The Teacher Corps trained schoolteachers. Medicare helped old people pay their hospital bills. Medicaid helped those without much money afford a doctor.

Johnson went to the Statue of Liberty to sign a bill that ended narrow, racist immigration quotas. Because of an immigration bill passed early in the century, only people from some privileged regions, like Western Europe, were able to come to the United States in large numbers. Just a few from other regions—Asia, for instance—were allowed to enter and become citizens. Johnson's new law let new groups of immigrants (especially Asians and Latinos) broaden the American family.

The president began beautification programs and environmental protection programs. Congress and the president worked together. FDR had accomplished a lot during his first 100 days in the presidency; Johnson got even more laws passed.

▲ The Head Start program was designed to help needy families get children ready for kindergarten.

Major Great Society Programs			
Civil Rights	Civil Rights Act	1964	Outlawed discrimination in public facilities and employment
	Voting Rights Act	1965	Guaranteed voting rights for blacks
War on Poverty	Volunteers in Service to America (VISTA)	1964	Sent volunteers into communities throughout the country to combat poverty through education and job training
	Food Stamp Program	1964	Provides aid to low-income families to buy groceries
	Project Head Start	1965	Provides education, nutrition, and health services to children from low-income families
Health	Social Security Act of 1965 (Medicare)	1965	Provides federal funds to cover many medical costs faced by senior citizens regardless of income level
	Medicaid	1966	Provides federal funds to cover many medical costs for people who receive welfare
Education	Elementary and Secondary Education Act	1965	Helped schools with a large population of poor children buy supplies and establish special programs
Environment	Clean Air Act	1963	Provided federal funds to conduct research and create programs to control air pollution
	Wilderness Preservation Act	1964	Protects national forest wilderness areas

A wounded U.S. Marine gunnery sergeant, Jeremiah Purdie, is led past a stricken comrade after a fierce firefight during the Vietnam War. ▶

By 1967, the Vietnam War was costing the country $70 million a day.

All the new programs cost money. But we had the money. We were a rich nation. Johnson knew that. We could afford the Great Society. We could afford the war on poverty—until something else began taking most of our money. That was the war in Southeast Asia.

American soldiers were now fighting in Vietnam. But things weren't going the way we hoped they would go. North Vietnam was fighting back. That little nation didn't seem to be frightened by America's power.

Being president had turned out to be harder than Lyndon Johnson expected it to be. His military and political advisers kept telling him to send more men and more weapons to Vietnam. But some of America's citizens were saying that the war was a mistake. They thought we needed to quit the war. Johnson didn't like that advice at all; he didn't want to be a quitter.

And then there was the black community. President Johnson thought that African American people, and other minorities, would be thrilled with the Great Society programs. They were pleased. But they weren't satisfied; they wanted more. They wanted what everyone else had. They wanted to be equal partners in America. Why, they even wanted to vote!

When it came to voting, Lyndon Johnson asked the black leaders to be patient. He explained that it wouldn't be easy to get a voting act through Congress. Change would have to come one step at a time, he said. But some people were fed up with being patient.

A King Gets a Prize and Goes to Jail

Martin Luther King, Jr., was in the hospital. He wasn't seriously ill; it was a case of exhaustion. It was Tuesday, and he'd given three speeches on Sunday and two on Monday, and then there were all those trips to jail, and the marches, and the pressures. But when the phone rang he felt a whole lot better. Matter of fact, he felt great.

His wife, Coretta, had big news: Martin had been awarded the Nobel Peace Prize. That prize is given each year to the person, from anywhere in the world, who has contributed most to peace. Along with the great honor, there is a sizable cash award. Theodore Roosevelt had won the Nobel Peace Prize and so had Woodrow Wilson and Jane Addams. Martin Luther King, Jr., at 35, was the youngest person ever to receive it. (King gave his Nobel Prize money to the civil rights movement.)

Some Americans were furious, and they wrote to the Nobel committee in Sweden and told them so. But most Americans were proud. Newspaper columnist Ralph McGill, writing in the *Atlanta Constitution*, said Europeans understood King better than most Americans; they saw in him "the American promise," with its message for the whole world. When King flew to Europe to receive the Peace Prize, Norwegian students sang, "We Shall Overcome." King realized that his message had become part of a universal language of freedom.

King was soon back in the United States— and in jail again. He was in Selma, Alabama, trying to help black citizens vote.

President Johnson's Civil Rights Act didn't solve the voting problem. It did allow black people to check into any hotel they desired,

"Nonviolence is the answer to the crucial political and moral questions of our time," said Martin Luther King, Jr., in his Nobel acceptance speech. ▼

sit on buses wherever they wished, and eat in any restaurant. But in much of the rural South, blacks still couldn't vote. In 1964, when blacks tried to register to vote in Alabama or Mississippi or some other Southern states, they were likely to be beaten or to lose their jobs—even though the 15th Amendment to the Constitution says that every citizen has the right to vote. Those who kept trying to register were given impossible questions to answer or asked to pay a poll tax they couldn't afford.

Selma was an Old South cotton town on the banks of the Alabama River. More than half of its 30,000 people were black.

In the 1960s, the streets in the black section of town were made of red dirt; those in the white section were paved.

The leaders of Selma's black community asked Dr. King (and his organization, the SCLC) to come to town. In 1965, when King and the SCLC arrived, SNCC workers had already been in Selma for more than a year. They had worked hard to try to get blacks signed on the voting rolls. SNCC had doubled the number of registered black voters to 333 (out of 15,000 of voting age).

A few SNCC members weren't happy that King was asked to come to Selma. They wanted to stay in charge. But John Lewis, SNCC chairman, was not one of them. He was thrilled that Dr. Martin Luther King, Jr., was coming to town. So were the majority of Selma's citizens.

Nobel Prizes

The 19th-century Swedish chemist Alfred Nobel invented dynamite, which he thought was so dangerous it would end all wars. It didn't, but it did earn a lot of money for Nobel. A year before he died, he shocked his relatives, who hoped to inherit his wealth, when he changed his will, leaving his fortune to establish prizes

▲ The Nobel medal features a likeness of Alfred Nobel.

in physics, chemistry, medicine, literature, and peace. The Peace Prize was to go to "those who, during the preceding year, shall have conferred the greatest benefit on mankind."

Today, Nobel Prizes are awarded each year in Sweden for outstanding achievement in physics, chemistry, physiology, medicine, economics, and literature, as well as peace. Many consider the Nobels the most prestigious prizes that there are. They include a gold medal and a substantial sum of money as well as great acclaim.

Martin Luther King, Jr., spoke out at Brown's Chapel. "Give us the ballot," he cried. A group of Selma's black citizens marched to the courthouse to try to register. They weren't allowed inside. When SNCC workers tried to bring them sandwiches and water, the workers were hit with billy clubs. That just made Selma's black citizens more determined.

More than 100 black teachers marched. Martin Luther King, Jr., marched with 250 citizens who wanted to register to vote. They were all thrown in jail. King, too. When they heard of Dr. King's arrest, 500 schoolchildren marched to the courthouse. They were arrested. Two days later 300 more schoolchildren were arrested.

The evening television news covered it all. King wrote a letter from jail. He said, "This is Selma, Alabama. There are more Negroes in jail with me than there are on the voting rolls." Fifteen congressmen came to Selma. They announced that "new legislation is going to be necessary." President Johnson held a press conference and said, "All Americans should be indignant when one American is denied the right to vote."

Coretta Scott King went to the jail to visit her husband. She brought a message from Malcolm X, who was in Selma. Malcolm, a black leader who was electrifying urban audiences with hard facts and a spirit of militancy, had been invited to Selma by SNCC's leaders. His ideas were different from King's. Malcolm had never recognized the power and force of nonviolent action. But Malcolm seemed to be heading in a new direction. He told Coretta, "I want Dr. King to know that I didn't come to Selma to make his job difficult." Then he added, "If the white people realize what the alternative is, perhaps they will be more willing to hear Dr. King."

The alternative was violence. Speaking to a big crowd in Brown's Chapel, Malcolm said, "White people should thank Dr. King for holding people in check, for there are others who do not believe in these [nonviolent] measures."

Malcolm had broken with the Black Muslims, who believed in the separation of blacks and whites. He'd gone to Mecca in Saudi Arabia—the center of the Muslim world—where he converted to orthodox Islam. That experience moved him deeply.

▲ Malcolm X urged black people to be proud of their blackness and their African roots. He had been a leader of the Nation of Islam, or Black Muslims, but left the organization over the advocacy of violence by some members.

Muslims are followers of Islam and its prophet, Mohammed. Islam, like Judaism and Christianity, is based on belief in one God. Mecca, in Saudi Arabia, is Mohammed's birthplace. It is considered Islam's holiest city and its religious center.

It caused him to change some of his ideas—especially ideas that called for hate and violence. He told a journalist about that change in himself.

> *The sickness and madness of those [early] days. I'm glad to be free of them. It is a time for martyrs now. And if I'm to be one, it will be in the cause of brotherhood. That's the only thing that can save this country. I've learned it the hard way—but I've learned it.*

Two and a half weeks after his trip to Selma, Malcolm X was martyred—killed by members of the radical political group, the Black Muslims—a victim of the violence that he had once tolerated. Malcolm's new belief in brotherhood made the loss of this brilliant Muslim especially tragic.

A *martyr* is someone sacrificed to a cause.

Malcolm X drew large audiences, particularly among young blacks in urban areas. Here, a crowd gathers at a rally in New York's Harlem neighborhood. ▼

From Selma to Montgomery

The tension in Selma was awful. Marchers, and even reporters covering the marches, were being roughed up and beaten. Where could they go for protection? Not to the police. The police and state troopers were doing most of the beating. When 82-year-old Cager Lee marched, a state trooper went for him and whipped him until he was bloody. Jimmy Lee Jackson, Cager's grandson, carried his grandfather into a café. But the troopers weren't finished; they stormed right into the café. One trooper hit Jimmy's mother, and another shot Jimmy Lee Jackson in the stomach. He died seven days later.

That murder was too much for the civil rights workers to bear. They felt responsible. There was no stopping them now. The murder was also too much for some of Selma's white citizens. Seventy of them marched in sympathy to the courthouse.

Six hundred people—men, women, and children, most black, some white—gathered at Brown's Chapel. They were prepared to march the 58 miles from Selma to Alabama's capital, Montgomery. They intended to face Governor George Wallace and demand that all of Alabama's citizens be protected in their right to vote.

Hosea Williams, a young firebrand, was in charge. (Martin Luther King, Jr., was in Washington consulting with the president.) First they prayed, and then they began their march, singing as they went. They marched six blocks from Brown's Chapel to the Edmund Pettus Bridge. No one stopped them; all was quiet except for their voices. They knew that once they crossed the bridge they would be on the road to Montgomery.

When they mounted the sloping crest of the bridge they were stunned by what they saw: Alabama state troopers were lined up, gas masks in place, bullwhips and billy clubs raised. The troopers didn't give anyone time to decide what to do. They moved forward; some were on horseback, some on foot.

A long line of African American marchers walks by a sign welcoming visitors to Selma, Alabama. The demonstrators were soon confronted by state troopers, who used clubs and tear gas to break up their march to Montgomery. ▼

209

SNCC leader John Lewis (center) tries to ward off a blow from a state trooper during the attempted march from Selma to Montgomery on March 7, 1965. He and 16 others were hospitalized. ▶

Then they released tear-gas bombs. Eight-year-old Sheyann Webb said:

> I saw people being beaten and I tried to run home as fast as I could…. I saw horses behind me…. Hosea Williams picked me up and I told him to put me down, he wasn't running fast enough.

But something new had come to this out-of-the-way Southern town. That something was television coverage. Camera crews were filming the action. Television stations across the nation interrupted their regular programs to show scenes of policemen on horseback clubbing peaceful marchers.

How would you feel if you watched all that on television? Most good people were sickened. So, when Martin Luther King, Jr., sent telegrams to prominent clergymen saying "Join me for a ministers' march to Montgomery," ministers came from many places and many faiths. White-bearded Rabbi Abraham Heschel came from the Jewish Theological Seminary. From the United Nations came world leader Ralph Bunche (he, too, had won a Nobel Peace Prize). And Unitarian minister James Reeb came from Boston.

Reeb did not go back to Boston. The nightmare of brutality wasn't quite finished in Selma. Reeb and some other white ministers made the mistake of eating in a black café. For Reeb it was a fatal mistake. He was clubbed to death when he came out of the restaurant.

President Johnson was shocked and said:

What happened in Selma was an American tragedy. At times, history and fate meet in a single place to shape a turning point in man's unending search for freedom. So it was at Lexington and Concord. So it was a century ago at Appomattox. So it was last week in Selma, Alabama.

The president announced that he was sending a voting rights bill to Congress. Then he spoke to the 70 million people who listened on television. "It's not just Negroes," he said. "It's really all of us who must overcome the crippling legacy of bigotry and injustice. And," he finished with these words from the civil rights theme song, "*WE SHALL OVERCOME.*"

"We were all sitting together," said a black leader who heard the president speak. "And Martin was very quietly sitting in the chair, and a tear ran down his cheek. It was a victory like none other."

Six days later, 4,000 people—black and white—marched from the Pettus Bridge in Selma to Montgomery, camping out at night and singing songs of freedom. This time National Guardsmen protected them. By the time they reached the capital, 25,000 people had joined the march.

Rosa Parks was there, and so were many of those who, 10 years earlier, had walked through winter's bluster and summer's heat rather than ride Montgomery's segregated buses. Martin Luther King, Jr., had been an unknown preacher then. Now he was world famous.

Where are Lexington and Concord? Why are they famous? What about Appomattox?

By the time marchers reached Montgomery, 25,000 people, black and white, had joined the march. ▼

War in Southeast Asia

The war in Vietnam was costing billions of dollars a year. Someone said we had to make a choice between *guns* and *butter*. (Guns symbolized war and butter stood for goods and helping programs.) At first, President Johnson thought we could have both. But the guns got more and more expensive. Soon we were spending more in Vietnam than on all the welfare programs combined. Funds for the Great Society had to be cut. Many of its programs were eliminated.

The Vietnam War was a civil war but we made it our war. It became a battle between the most powerful nation in the world and a small country of farmers. It was bombers, helicopters, and rockets in a nation with water buffalo and barefoot runners. What were we fighting for? It was supposed to be for freedom and democracy. But since we didn't know much about the country we were fighting in, we backed corrupt leaders in South Vietnam who robbed the treasury and bossed everyone around.

Helicopters played a key role in the American combat strategy in Vietnam. They could move troops quickly to and from the fighting. But many helicopters were lost due to enemy fire or mechanical failure. ▶

▲ U.S. troops in Vietnam faced difficult conditions and a determined enemy.

▲ An American soldier crawls through the mud of a rice paddy to avoid heavy Viet Cong fire.

It is easy to see mistakes after you've made them; that is called "hindsight." No nation wants to make mistakes. We didn't enter the Vietnam War in order to do wrong. It was that issue of communism that caught us. The North Vietnamese were getting money and supplies from communist China and from the Soviets, too. Many Americans feared that the Chinese communists would control a united Vietnam. Because we hadn't studied much Vietnamese history, we didn't know that the Chinese and the Vietnamese didn't get along very well.

Most of the advisers to presidents Eisenhower, Kennedy, and Johnson believed we should fight in Vietnam. They believed it was America's role to stand up to any communist nation, anywhere. They believed that all communist nations were part of a large conspiracy. If Vietnam was allowed to become communist, everyone seemed sure that all of Southeast Asia would soon follow.

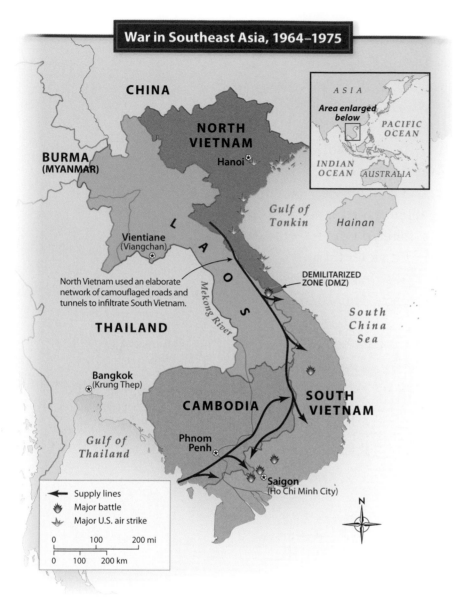

War in Southeast Asia, 1964–1975

CHINA

NORTH VIETNAM

BURMA (MYANMAR)

Hanoi

ASIA

Area enlarged below

PACIFIC OCEAN

INDIAN OCEAN   AUSTRALIA

Gulf of Tonkin

Hainan

L A O S

Vientiane (Viangchan)

North Vietnam used an elaborate network of camouflaged roads and tunnels to infiltrate South Vietnam.

DEMILITARIZED ZONE (DMZ)

Mekong River

THAILAND

South China Sea

Bangkok (Krung Thep)

CAMBODIA

SOUTH VIETNAM

Gulf of Thailand

Phnom Penh

Saigon (Ho Chi Minh City)

Supply lines
Major battle
Major U.S. air strike

0   100   200 mi
0   100   200 km

N

▲ Communist North Vietnamese forces received supplies, weapons, and ammunition through a series of hidden trails and tunnels in neighboring Laos and Cambodia.

We got into the war in Vietnam one step at a time. It wasn't the fault of the Republicans or the Democrats—it was bipartisan. In the early 1960s, war hawks in both parties were screaming that we needed to fight. Our presidents didn't want to be called soft on communism. Besides, they remembered Hitler, the terrible tyrant who started World War II. If Hitler had been stopped early, that war might not have happened. But the leader of North Vietnam, Ho Chi Minh, was no Hitler (though he wasn't a democratic leader, either).

We sent more than half a million Americans to do battle in a faraway land. We got deeper and deeper into the Vietnamese jungle—and then we didn't seem to know how to get out. First there was that little step of Truman's. Then Eisenhower invested more money and sent more advisers. And Kennedy sent much more money and lots of advisers.

President Johnson didn't know what to do. His advisers were pushing him to enter the war in a big way. Barry Goldwater, who was the Republican candidate for president in 1964, ran a get-into-the-war campaign and even talked about using nuclear weapons. Johnson ran as the peace candidate. But Johnson didn't want to look like a coward. Something happened soon after he was elected that gave him an excuse to become a warrior.

An American ship was on a secret mission in the Gulf of Tonkin. It wasn't supposed to be there. A torpedo was fired at the ship. Two days later there was a second report of torpedoes. It turned out to be untrue. Maybe a sailor saw a flying fish. President Johnson said an American ship had been attacked. He got Congress to pass a resolution that let him go to war. It was called the Gulf of Tonkin Resolution. The Vietnam War went into high gear.

We began bombing North Vietnam. Before we finished we dropped more bombs on that small country than we had on both Germany and Japan during all of World War II.

We sent soldiers. Lots of them. Most of our soldiers were decent and many were heroic. Many helped the people of Vietnam. But imagine trying to fight in a hot jungle where you can't even see the enemy. Some soldiers became angry and violent. Many were introduced to drugs in Vietnam. Some used their weapons on innocent villagers as well as on enemy soldiers. The war became a national nightmare.

The Pentagon (which is the name for our military control center) just couldn't understand how guerrilla fighters who had their ammunition carried over jungle trails on the backs of old men and women could beat a modern army supplied by helicopters. The military chiefs kept telling the president that if we just sent a few thousand more soldiers and dropped a few more bombs it would all

Guerrilla (say it like "gorilla") fighters usually strike in small groups, often in surprise raids. They often fight for a political cause against a larger regular army.

A Farming Village in Vietnam

Early on the morning of March 16, 1968, the men of Charlie Company entered the farming village of My Lai (me-LY), on the northeast coast of South Vietnam. The American soldiers shot everyone they could find: old men, pregnant women, children, babies—504 civilians in all.

Then the soldiers shot all the domestic animals—water buffaloes, pigs, chickens—and burned the place down. Their officers didn't seem to think they had done anything wrong. But a few of the soldiers had refused to participate.

Later, officers and men lied about what they had done. Only after a newspaper reporter (Seymour Hersh) wrote the truth did Americans at home understand what their soldiers had done.

Lieutenant William Calley, Jr., who had directed much of the massacre (and who personally killed 109 Vietnamese, including babies), was the only soldier convicted of a crime. He was court-martialed and sentenced to life in prison at hard labor. But President Nixon intervened and Calley was released after three years of house arrest.

If Americans had any illusions about the war, My Lai shattered them and left a lasting legacy of shame.

be over. But the old men and women and the guerrilla fighters, who seemed to know how to vanish into the jungle, finally made the great and mighty United States give up and go home.

We thought we were doing the right thing when we began. But we didn't understand what the war was all about.

It was about freedom. The Vietnamese wanted to be free of foreign rule. They wanted to choose their own leaders. They wanted freedom even to make the wrong decisions. This was a nasty civil war. We soon made it much worse. We made it a high-tech war. We brought in grenades, rocket launchers, jellied-gasoline explosives (called "napalm"), and chemicals (called "defoliants") that took all the leaves off the jungle trees—and we still couldn't beat the Vietnamese.

We should have known that could happen. After all, we ourselves started out as a little pipsqueak nation that defeated the great and mighty British empire. Didn't we remember that people fighting for their own freedom are apt to be unbeatable? What had happened to us?

Children from Trang Ban, South Vietnam, flee after their school was burned with napalm during an American raid. ▼

An Unwilling Guest at the Hanoi Hilton

It was July 18, 1965, and U.S. Navy Commander Jeremiah A. Denton, Jr., was flying a bombing mission over North Vietnam. As he dropped his bombs over the target, near Hanoi, he felt a jolt. His plane had been hit. The controls were dead. Denton descended into the Ma River, was picked up by Vietnamese soldiers, and became a POW: a prisoner of war.

At home in Virginia, Denton's wife, Jane, and his seven children learned that he had been captured (other pilots had seen him eject from the plane). They didn't know that he was put in solitary confinement—which means he was all alone in a tiny cell with only a concrete bed, wooden stocks that held his legs, and a bucket for a toilet. They didn't know that he was physically tortured, mentally tortured, starved, and taken on a march through Hanoi where people hit him and spat on him. Or that he sometimes lost all sense of who he was.

He was one of the first POWs. Eventually some 700 Americans were captured and held in several prisons near Hanoi. They gave the prisons names like the Hanoi Hilton, Dogpatch, Heartbreak, Alcatraz, and Briarpath. The prisoners kept their sanity and their pride in themselves and their country by defying their captors. They maintained military discipline.

The American people disagreed about the war—its purpose and necessity—but everyone was in agreement when it came to the POWs. We wanted them home. The Vietnamese soon realized that they had important hostages. They filmed some of the POWs, intending to show that they were being well treated. Commander Denton kept blinking his eyes. Most people thought it was the bright camera lights, but Denton was blinking the word *torture* in Morse code.

▲ Though hampered by chains, an American airman helps his fellow prisoner as they are marched through the streets of Hanoi, North Vietnam's capital.

International law sets standards for the treatment of prisoners. Torture is forbidden. Four people who saw the film recognized the code and called government officials.

The North Vietnamese were not the only ones who tortured prisoners. The South Vietnamese army also committed terrible atrocities.

Jeremiah Denton's plane had been shot down in 1965. Seven years later, he and other POWs finally left the Hanoi Hilton, Heartbreak, and Alcatraz. They were going home. These men had endured great hardship and had survived. (One of them, John McCain, would become Arizona's senator and a spokesman for political change.) They flew to Clark Field in the Philippines. On the first plane to land, Jeremiah Denton—now Captain Denton—was asked to speak. He stood straight and spoke clearly: "We are honored to have had the opportunity to serve our country under difficult circumstances. We are profoundly grateful to our commander in chief and to our nation for this day. God bless America!"

LBJ in Trouble

Lyndon Johnson was losing his dream of a Great Society, but he didn't know how to stop the war in Vietnam. He didn't seem able to admit that he had made a mistake. He had started with that fib about an attack in the Gulf of Tonkin. But one lie usually leads to another.

During a battle in Vietnam, a wounded medic treats a fellow American soldier. ▼

President Johnson had said, "We are not going to send American boys nine or ten thousand miles away from home to do what Asian boys ought to be doing for themselves." But he was already planning to do just that. He said all the bombing was "aimed at military targets." But newspaper reporters told of houses, schools, and stores flattened by bombs. President Johnson kept saying that we were winning the war and it would soon be over. TV made people realize he wasn't telling the truth. For the first time in history, ordinary people could see exactly what war was like. The TV screen showed dead American soldiers and dead Vietnamese.

At first, it was mostly students on college campuses who began demonstrating against the war. Then more and more American people began to join them. Martin Luther King, Jr., was now leading antiwar protests as well as civil rights marches. Ministers of many faiths were doing the same thing. The college protests began to get ugly and violent. Another big social change was happening in America, but most Americans seemed unaware. It was a long and massive migration of African Americans from South to North, from rural to urban. Farm mechanization,

◄ As time went on, Vietnam took its toll on the president. "I feel like a hitchhiker caught in a hailstorm on a Texas highway," said LBJ. "I can't run. I can't hide. And I can't make it stop."

On May 4, 1970, some 600 students at Ohio's Kent State University protested against the U.S. invasion of Cambodia. The National Guard was called in, and the nervous guards opened fire. When it was over, four students were dead and 10 hurt. This photograph captures the anguish of a student as she kneels over the body of a slain fellow student.

especially the invention of the mechanical cotton-picker, forced many Southern blacks to seek work elsewhere. Between 1910 and 1970, 6.5 million blacks moved from the South to the North. Of that number, 5 million moved after 1940. They moved to Chicago, New York, Detroit, and Los Angeles. Others, who didn't go north, moved to the South's urban centers: Atlanta, Norfolk, Little Rock, Memphis, and Houston. A people with a tradition and culture based on farming became city folk. By 1970, more than three-fourths of black Americans lived in cities.

All those people were moving into cities that were already crowded. They were being squeezed into places that weren't prepared. They needed good schools, they needed opportunity, they needed all the things America does so well—and it wasn't happening.

Black people themselves didn't quite understand what was going on. Most Americans thought segregation was a Southern problem. Its historical roots were Southern. It was the legacy of slavery. The civil rights movement was something happening in the South, wasn't it? Why should anyone worry about racial problems in the North? They didn't exist, did they? Segregation in the North? Urban ghettoes? Poor schools? Poor jobs? The problems of the big cities? What problems?

Going to Jail to Fight War
Dorothy Day was the founder of the *Catholic Worker*, a newspaper devoted to educating the public about the plight of the poor and uneducated. The *Catholic Worker* sponsored soup kitchens and hospitality houses for the poor. When she was in her sixties, Day stood outside a missile base and tried to block its entrance to protest against an industry that built weapons of destruction. At the same time, she urged Americans not to pay their income taxes, because tax money supported the war in Vietnam. (Henry David Thoreau had done the same thing at the time of the Mexican War.) Day was willing to go to jail for her beliefs—and she did.

▲ Northern cities like New York, Detroit, and Chicago, and other cities like Los Angeles, weren't prepared for the huge influx of people. Many inner cities became poverty-stricken, crime-ridden slums.

All those people packed into cities were like powder in a firecracker. And then the cities, especially those in the North, started exploding. America's cities had been neglected. In many, schools were terrible, transportation was terrible, crime made life frightening, and there weren't enough jobs for those who wanted to work. City people were fed up.

President Johnson was trying to improve the cities but not everyone was willing to wait for his programs to work. Things had been too bad for too long. In 1965, riots in the Watts section of Los Angeles lasted six days and left 34 dead. Newark, Chicago, Cleveland, and other cities erupted with riots of their own. America's cities were like volcanoes filled with frustration and pain. The riots may have eased the frustration; they didn't do much to help the pain.

A government-appointed commission warned, "Our nation is moving toward two societies, one black, one white—separate and unequal." Black protests began changing direction. New leaders

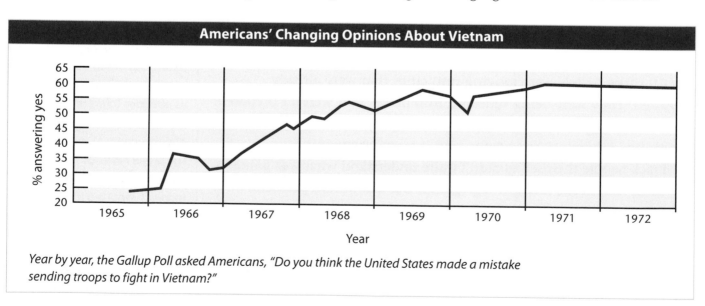

Americans' Changing Opinions About Vietnam

Year by year, the Gallup Poll asked Americans, "Do you think the United States made a mistake sending troops to fight in Vietnam?"

A National Guardsman stands at the ready at a Detroit intersection during the summer riots of 1967. A terrible new slogan replaced the South's "We shall overcome." It was "Burn, baby, burn" as frustration and despair erupted from the sidewalks of the Northern cities.

▲ Mexican Americans and other Latino groups became vocal in demanding their civil rights. Here, two members of the activist group called the Brown Berets stand in uniform.

appeared; many were angry young people. They had no patience with nonviolence. The new leaders didn't talk about brotherhood and love; they talked of power, separation, and sometimes hate.

Black Power voices were followed by Brown Power, or Mexican American, voices. These were people who wanted their full rights as citizens. So did the female half of the population. Women had been demanding equal pay for equal work and not getting it. Women's rights leaders joined the protest fray. Some were just angry; others had clear ideas and programs.

By 1968, the country seemed to be coming apart.

Conscience of the Court

Thurgood Marshall was a lawyer who argued that segregation was wrong in *Brown v. Board of Education* and won that Supreme Court case. Lyndon Johnson liked and respected him. They both were filled with energy, good humor, and a desire to make their world better. But when the president invited Marshall to the Oval Office in 1967, Marshall didn't have any idea why he'd been summoned. They chatted a bit and then the president said, "You know something, Thurgood?"

"No sir," said Marshall. "What's that?"

"I'm going to put you on the Supreme Court."

Thurgood Marshall was to be the first black justice ever appointed to the highest court. He would be an independent-minded justice, a great justice, a justice one lawyer described as the "conscience of the court."

▲ Justice Thurgood Marshall was the first African American appointed to the Supreme Court.

Friedan, Schlafly, and Friends

Television programs (and newspaper and magazine articles) can tell you a lot about a time—or at least the way people of that time saw themselves. And in the '50s, the number-one TV program was *I Love Lucy.* Lucy was a dippy dame—a white, middle-class wife and mother—who didn't work, was kind of bored, and was always getting into mischief with her neighbor, Ethel. One day, Lucy and Ethel decided to get jobs on the production line at a candy factory. As the chocolates passed by—zip-zip fast—Lucy and Ethel got farther and farther behind. So they began stuffing chocolates in their mouths and then in their dresses—and it was all a big laugh.

There were mixed messages in that *Lucy* show. Did women belong in the candy factory or at home? Lucy and Ethel always seemed to be trying to break away from the household routine. But they usually goofed up. And behind the show was the real Lucille Ball, who was not only one of the most gifted comedians this country has produced but a powerful businesswoman as well.

In January 1953, more people saw *I Love Lucy* on Monday nights than watched President Eisenhower's inauguration in the same month. ▶

"The suburban housewife," wrote Betty Friedan, "was the dream image of young American women and the envy, it was said, of women all over the world."

▲ Betty Friedan wrote of an "identity crisis" among American women.

The reality of the '50s was that most middle-class white women—like it or not—did stay home. A lot of them lived in the new suburbs, in new houses, with new washing machines. Most TV programs told you that as long as Mom didn't venture out into the big world, her life was close to perfect. The shows were all full of happy suburban couples and cute kids: *Ozzie and Harriet, Leave It to Beaver,* and *Father Knows Best* (note that title) were three very popular shows that portrayed terrific, happy households.

Yet when Betty Friedan decided to write an article about suburban women, she found that many of them were not happy—and they didn't know why. She called it the "problem that has no name." Then she investigated and said that women weren't being given a chance to develop their talents. They were taught to "keep their place." If a woman had the potential to be a brain surgeon, if she wanted to be a veterinarian, if she thought being an architect would fill her life with pleasure—well, too bad. Those, and most professions, were for males only. Women had a separate—and unequal—role in society.

Betty Friedan couldn't get that article on discontented women published, so she decided to turn her research into a book. She called it *The Feminine Mystique.*

That book, published in 1963, put in words what a lot of women had been thinking. More than a million copies were sold. It made people think—some men as well as women. It carried an idea—that all people, including women, have the natural right to develop their potential. It told how the media (advertising, TV, radio, newspapers, and magazines) were manipulating women in order to keep them at home where they could be sold vacuum cleaners and dishwashers. Friedan's book came along at the same time that other things were happening to make women reconsider their role in society.

Suburban women may not have been working, but many other women were at work. It had begun during World War II (from 1941 to 1945), when about 6.5 million women who had not worked before got jobs. It was patriotic. Men were fighting; women were needed on production lines. Many women found they liked working. Some had no choice: they had to work.

After the war, many of those women kept working. Others began to work, too. But attitudes didn't change. Working women were paid less than men. And they hardly ever got the best jobs. Many were teachers, but women were not superintendents of schools. Many were nurses, but very few were doctors. And those who worked had to put up with prejudice against working women.

When the civil rights movement erupted in the '60s, women became some of its hardest workers. And they often found that the men in the movement expected them to make coffee, do the cleaning up, and not make major decisions. That was infuriating. Women knew that they had minds and talents equal to men's. The civil rights movement was all about equal rights. So some women took the activism they learned as civil rights workers and brought it to the women's liberation movement.

Some women thought Betty Friedan didn't go far enough. Friedan wanted women to be equal partners in American society. But the radical feminists, as they were called, saw male-dominated institutions as hopeless. The radical feminists developed feminist publishing houses, health organizations, child-care centers, food

Beginning in the 1960s, the women's movement changed American society. ▼

▲ New York congresswoman Bella Abzug (wearing her trademark hat) and Betty Friedan (in a red coat) lead the last lap of a 2,610-mile marathon to support an equal rights amendment to the Constitution.

cooperatives, and other women-run institutions. Some said they hated all men. Although they were few in number, their extreme ideas got a lot of publicity.

By 1970, seven years after the publication of *The Feminine Mystique*, women activists were demonstrating for equal job opportunities and equal access to all-male clubs, restaurants, and schools. Feminists were making daily headlines in the newspaper—competing with the civil rights movement and the war in Vietnam.

The demonstrations reflected a whole new attitude on the part of women.

Some women began to get good jobs in banking, law, engineering, and other previously male-only fields. Women were now newspaper editors and TV anchors. But that news was only part of the picture. Things did not go well for all women—especially poor, black, or Hispanic women.

▲ Phyllis Schlafly, national leader of the Stop the Equal Rights Amendment movement, addresses a rally.

It was the women who were educated and talented who were going places. If you were poor, it was difficult to get a really good education. Women without training or skills—who made up a majority—were usually stuck in dead-end, low-paying jobs and still suffering from sex discrimination. (Actually, the same thing was happening to men. Education was becoming more and more important for all as the 21st century approached.)

Some women didn't agree with the feminists. Many women were *traditionalists*: they thought that a woman's primary role *was* as a wife and mother and that a career took away from that role. The traditionalists emphasized the differences between men and women. Phyllis Schlafly (SHLAFF-lee), a spokeswoman for the traditionalists, attacked the women's liberation movement.

Schlafly was part of a powerful political force, the conservative "New Right," which developed in response to the turmoil of the times (the Vietnam War; growing rates of drug use, crime, and divorce; and new sexual ideas). The ideas of the New Right reached many Americans through something new: television church programs. TV preachers like Jerry Falwell, Pat Robertson, and Tammy and Jim Bakker were speaking to millions of Americans.

It was a Supreme Court decision that gave the New Right a focus. In 1973, in the case of *Roe v. Wade*, the Supreme Court said that a woman, in consultation with her doctor, could decide to end her pregnancy. That means she could choose to have an abortion. That decision gratified some Americans and outraged others.

Feminists said that women were finally in control of their own bodies. Antifeminists said that abortion was murder and at odds with traditional religious values.

Does all this sound confusing? Well, change is rarely orderly. Women were sorting out new ideas. Men were, too. Fathers were enjoying their children and participating in home activities in ways that other generations had not done. And some of the statistics carried good news for women.

In the '50s and '60s, women had made up between 5 and 8 percent of the students in medical, law, and business schools. By the mid-'80s, they were at 40 percent and heading upward. Educated women could now make choices. They could work as veterinarians or as housewives. They could be Supreme Court justices, brain surgeons, or, like that pioneer Lucille Ball, television producers. For women— of all races and backgrounds—there was now a hard question to consider: just how do you manage a job, marriage, children, a home, friends, and community involvement?

A Great Professional

In the 1950s, tennis was a country-club game. Mostly, it was a sport for the wealthy. Billie Jean Moffitt (who became Billie Jean King when she married) didn't belong to a country club. She learned to play tennis on public courts in California. King was a fighter. She fought her way to the top of the tennis world, she fought against elitism in tennis, she fought for equality for women in sports, and she fought for professionalism in tennis.

In 1968, the prizes for the winners of men's tennis tournaments were as much as 12 times higher than the women's. The U.S. Lawn Tennis Association and most male tennis players said that women's tennis wasn't as good as men's tennis. They said that spectators weren't interested in watching women.

Billie Jean King said they were wrong. She and eight other top women players quit the tournaments sponsored by the USLTA. They formed their own tour. They took a chance.

▲ Tennis great Billie Jean King returns a volley.

They proved that women's tennis could attract a following. Crowds cheered the women on. Finally, the USLTA began to change its sexist practices.

When Billie Jean King retired in 1984, she had won nine U.S. championships and a shelf full of other trophies. She'd helped bring respect and professionalism to women's athletics.

Picking and Picketing

Lucía and María Mendoza, 18 and 17, stumbled out of bed at 2 a.m., dressed in the dark, went into the kitchen of their adobe house, made a lunch of tacos and soda pop, and filled a thermos with hot soup. Then they woke their dad and their younger brother. Soon the four of them were heading north, toward the border between Mexico and the United States. They were on their way to pick lettuce in California. Each of them expected to make $16 that Tuesday. It wasn't much, but it was more than they could earn at home. They would use short-handled hoes that kept them bent over all day. It was hot, dusty, backbreaking work. The Mendozas were soon part of a line of cars making for the picking fields.

These Mexican farmworkers were entering the United States legally. They were wanted to help harvest crops to feed people across the nation. But some of them would stay in the United States illegally. Hundreds of thousands of them had already done it. Most of those

These migrant workers are picking grapes in California. One farmer said, "We need Mexicans for their labor, for the same reason you need a mule." ▼

illegal immigrants had little schooling and few marketable skills. They were crowded in cities in poor districts (*barrios*). Their children needed to go to school. They needed job training and help. All that cost taxpayer money. Some Americans resented them.

Many said the Mexicans took jobs from American citizens, especially from Mexican Americans. It wasn't their fault that they took those jobs. The growers wanted them instead of Americans because they would work for less money. They could live on less. Life in Mexico was cheaper than life in the United States.

Once they were across the border, the Mendozas parked their car and walked to a place where workers were hired for agricultural jobs. By 3:30 a.m. they were settled just behind the driver in an old, rattletrap bus heading north toward lettuce fields. Most of the 46 passengers tried to sleep. They knew they had a long ride ahead of them, and it was still dark. Later, one passenger would remember that they had been going very fast when the driver missed a curve and the bus became airborne—crashing into the bank of a canal, bouncing off that bank to the other bank, and settling in a shallow waterway. All the seats in the old bus flew out of their sockets in a mess of arms, legs, twisted metal, and broken glass. Nineteen passengers were trapped in the bottom of the bus; they drowned in two and a half feet of water. The four Mendozas were among them.

César Chávez wept for Lucía and María and the others who lay in silent caskets. Chávez was an American of Mexican heritage. Like most of the 2,000 mourners at a special funeral mass for the victims, he was a devout Roman Catholic. Everyone knew Chávez. He was the leader of the Farm Workers Association and famous. They knew he cared about people, especially farmworkers. They wanted to hear what he had to say. Speaking in Spanish, Chávez told them:

> *This tragedy happened because of the greed of the big growers who do not care about the safety of the workers and who expose them to grave dangers when they transport them in wheeled coffins to the field.*
>
> *The workers learned long ago that growers and labor contractors have too little regard for the value of any individual worker's life. The trucks and buses are old and unsafe. The fields are sprayed with poisons. The laws that do exist are not enforced. How long will it be before we take seriously the importance of the workers who harvest the food we eat?*

▲ César Chávez devoted his life to helping migrant farmworkers.

▲ Huddled in a miserable shack in California, this migrant woman and child likely moved to an equally awful hovel on another farm within weeks.

Chávez knew all about harvesting food. He had been a migrant worker himself, traveling from bean fields to walnut groves to grape arbors, following the harvest of the seasons. That meant living in a tent or whatever room could be found. When he was a boy, it meant changing schools as often as he changed picking fields. It meant sometimes not having shoes or a bathroom to use. By the time César graduated from eighth grade he had attended 38 different schools.

There was something special about Chávez, although it was hard to decide quite what it was. He had a pleasant, round face with brown skin and dark straight hair—there was nothing out of the ordinary about that. He was a gentle man, and he didn't boast or call attention to himself. But when he had a job to do he did it carefully and well. He could be trusted; he was honest, thoroughly honest. So when people needed help, they often turned to him.

Fred Ross, an organizer who came to California to try to help the farmworkers, heard about César Chávez and gave him a job with the Community Service Organization, which helped poor people deal with many kinds of problems.

Chávez was soon helping those people find housing, medical care, food, and, if they needed legal aid, a lawyer. He got them to register to vote, and he made them realize the power of the vote. Then he began to think about starting a labor union for farmworkers. A labor union is an organization of people, usually all doing the same kind of work, who get together to try to make life better for themselves. Factory unions are easy to organize—most of the workers are together in one place—but getting agricultural workers organized isn't easy at all.

In California, farmworkers labored on thousands of farms that stretched the length of the state. Chávez knew that many growers took advantage of workers. They paid them little, they ignored unsafe conditions, they got their children to work even though that was against the law, and sometimes they cheated them on their pay. By themselves the workers had no power, but if Chávez could organize them into a union, they could demand fair wages and safe conditions.

César Chávez had a wife, eight children, and that steady job with the CSO. When he told his wife he wanted to quit his job to try to start a union, what do you think she said? She knew the family might go hungry if he had no regular work. What would you say? Helen Chávez said okay. She understood that if *La Causa*—the cause—were successful, it would help millions of people. And, knowing César, Helen Chávez thought there was a good chance it would be successful.

It was 1962, and César Chávez started going from farm to farm, talking to workers. Three years later, his Farm Workers Association voted to join Filipino farm workers in a strike against the grape growers. The workers refused to pick grapes until they got better pay and better working conditions. Then the growers hired other pickers. Union members marched near the grape fields with signs that said *Huelga!*, which means *strike* in Spanish. Chávez convinced some of the new pickers to stop work and strike with them.

California's biggest industry is agriculture, and grapes are the biggest money crop. Before *La Causa*, those who picked the crops got little benefit from the riches they helped create.

César Chávez marches with migrant workers. They trusted him because he was one of them; he had lived their life and understood its hardships. ▼

▲ César Chávez insisted that the farmworkers movement use the nonviolent tactics of Gandhi and Martin Luther King, Jr. When Chávez broke his 1968 fast, presidential primary candidate Robert Kennedy visited him to show support for the cause.

AFL-CIO is the abbreviation for the American Federation of Labor and Congress of Industrial Organizations.

Grapes began rotting because no one was picking them. The growers were furious; union members were attacked and beaten. The police helped the growers.

César Chávez had been inspired by Gandhi, Martin Luther King, Jr., and his own religious beliefs. He insisted that the farmworkers fight with peaceful marches and prayers. Nonviolence, he told them, took more courage than violence. He also believed that it achieved more. It appealed to the conscience of good people everywhere.

Chávez needed to draw attention to La Causa. He decided that a 300-mile march across much of California might just do it. He got university students and religious leaders to agree to march with the farmworkers. Look at a map and find someplace that is 300 miles from your home. Now imagine walking that far. Chávez's feet became blistered and his legs swollen. He could hardly walk—but he kept going. Television cameras whirred. Suddenly everyone knew about La Causa.

Some farm owners called César Chávez a communist (he wasn't), but most people believed he was on the side of justice and fairness. Finally, a few growers signed contracts with the union—but most still would not. (About this time, the Farm Workers Association was renamed the United Farm Workers; it became part of a national union—the AFL-CIO.)

Chávez announced a boycott. He was going to ask people across the United States not to buy grapes grown in California. But boycotts work slowly, and some of his union members were impatient. They wanted to use violent methods.

Chávez had to do something to control them and to make the growers pay fair wages. He did what Gandhi did. He went on a fast. For 25 days he ate no food. Finally, 26 growers signed contracts with the union.

César Chávez started eating again.

Troubled Cities

There had been enormous changes in the two decades since the end of World War II. Martin Luther King, Jr., could look at the South with some satisfaction. Where segregation had once flourished, blacks and whites now worked together, voted together, went to school together, ate in restaurants together, and rode on buses together. The changes were amazing to those who knew the Old South. The new racial harmony had helped bring industry and a progressive spirit to the South. The region was thriving.

Flourish means grow and thrive.

But when King decided to take his movement north—into big-city ghettoes—he discovered problems that were tougher than any he had faced before. He had believed that the methods that worked in the South would work in other regions, too. But the situation was different in America's Northern cities.

In the South, the problem had been Jim Crow laws and police-enforced segregation. The solution was to get the laws changed and to get the police to enforce those laws. The job wasn't finished, but the laws were in place and the direction was clear.

A *ghetto* is a city neighborhood where poor people live crowded together, usually in bad conditions. It comes from an Italian word used to describe a walled section of a city where Jews were required to live apart from the rest of the townspeople.

There were no Jim Crow laws in the North or West. The urban nightmare had nothing to do with laws. The problem there was economic.

The cities were filled with poor people— black, white, brown—who weren't being given a chance to rise out of poverty. Usually they went to schools that were tattered and poor, where they didn't get good training for the new kinds of jobs that technology was bringing. But there were hardly any jobs in the inner cities, anyway. Many city people were almost without hope. Young blacks in cities were full of frustration and rage.

Children play in the dirt and debris of a crowded slum on New York City's Lower East Side. ▶

▲ As President Johnson sent more young Americans to Vietnam, more and more people turned against the war, while the war's ever-increasing cost made it hard to pay for Johnson's domestic reforms.

And urban whites? When King marched in the Chicago area he was met with white hatred more vicious than anything he had encountered in Mississippi or Alabama. Many of the city's whites were poor, too. They were competing with blacks for jobs—and there weren't enough jobs to go around. Instead of coming together, black people and white people seemed to be growing further and further apart. Some leaders, on both sides, were encouraging hatred.

President Johnson still hadn't found a way to get out of Vietnam. He was putting pressure on those, like Martin Luther King, Jr., who protested against the war.

It was a tough time for King. John Kennedy's brother, Robert (Bobby) Kennedy, was telling him he needed to bring his battle for justice north. Kennedy said the same thing to the ministers and the others who had gone south.

Martin Luther King, Jr., decided to begin a new campaign. It would be a campaign against poverty. King's program was aimed at "all the poor, including the two-thirds of them who are white." Poverty was not just a black problem or just a white problem—it was a national disgrace. King planned to bring poor people to Washington. This would not be a one-day march. They would stay; they would camp in the city; the government leaders would have to pay attention.

King believed that eliminating poverty made economic sense and was the right thing to do. If you turn the poor into purchasers, King said, they will solve many of their own problems. The vast amounts of money that the nation spent on military goods could be used to make life better for all people. "Poverty has no justification in our age," he said. "War is obsolete." He believed that nonviolence was the way nations must learn to solve their differences. But time was running out for King and his nonviolent ideas.

King talked over his problems with Bobby Kennedy. So did César Chávez. Kennedy really seemed to care about poor people. Few other politicians did. The senator was now on the campaign trail, attempting to win the Democratic nomination for president. It looked as if he might do it.

◀ Bobby Kennedy campaigns for the Senate in Philadelphia. He said, "All of us…have a great lesson to learn—the importance of getting a dialogue going between people in the North and South."

Civil Rights for Native Americans

The civil rights movement inspired Indian leaders. They, too, had faced discrimination and persecution. They knew that many who were Indian pretended to be otherwise because they were ashamed of their heritage. But that was changing.

In the state of Washington, tribes held "fish-ins" to protest restrictions on their treaty-given right to harvest salmon. In Minneapolis, urban Indians created AIM (the American Indian Movement) and shouted of Red Power. In San Francisco, like-minded Indians formed Indians of All Tribes, and when the Bureau of Indian Affairs refused to listen to their grievances, they seized an abandoned federal prison on Alcatraz Island in San Francisco Bay and held it for a year and a half.

Traditionally, Indians had focused on their tribal identity. Alcatraz was a *pan-Indian* action. That means that Indians from tribes that had sometimes been one another's enemy were now banding together—although it didn't happen easily. Many tribes, especially those on reservations, were still determined to go their own way.

The militant activists went from Alcatraz to the Bureau of Indian Affairs in Washington, where they staged a protest occupation in 1972. Next they took over a trading post at Wounded Knee, South Dakota, where there had been a terrible massacre of Indians in 1890.

Those very dramatic takeovers accomplished what was intended. They made non-Indians aware of Indian grievances. And they made some Indians rediscover and take new pride in their heritage.

Native Americans also achieved success in the courts. Again and again the courts decided in their favor in disputes over rights granted in treaties (many signed 100 or more years earlier).

In 1971, Aleuts, Eskimos, and other native Alaskans won 40 million acres of land and nearly $1 billion in settlements of long-standing claims. In Maine, Penobscots received $81 million for claims based on a law passed in 1790. Several other tribes received similar awards.

Part of the former federal prison on Alcatraz Island in San Francisco Bay burns in the last days of Indian occupation of the island in 1971. (The Indians who occupied Alcatraz offered to pay $24 in beads and cloth for it, the price paid for Manhattan 300 years earlier.) ▶

Overall, however, things were still not good for many Native Americans. Alcoholism devastated whole peoples. Unemployment was high on reservations and among urban Indians.

But some Indian entrepreneurs were taking a new look at Indian reservations, which were nations within a nation and thus not subject to most state requirements. Indian business people realized that the status of reservations allowed for activities that were often illegal outside, like gambling. In the 1980s and '90s, casinos began to bring enormous wealth—which meant jobs, good schools, and nice homes (along with controversy and power)—to some Indian reservations.

Other things were happening: in Washington, D.C., the Smithsonian Institution returned Indian skeletal remains and funeral objects to their rightful owners. In Colorado, voters elected an American Indian, Ben Nighthorse Campbell, as a representative to the U.S. Congress

Wilma Mankiller served as the first female chief of the Cherokee Nation. ▶

(and as a senator in 1992). And in Oklahoma, Wilma Mankiller, the first female chief of the Cherokee Nation, spoke of her "firm belief that 500 years from now there will be strong tribal communities of native people in the Americas where ancient languages, ceremonies, and songs will be heard." If so, all the peoples of the land will be richer for it.

◀ An AIM activist stands at Wounded Knee on the Pine Ridge Reservation in South Dakota.

Up to the Mountain

Martin Luther King, Jr., was preparing for the Poor People's Campaign in Washington when the garbage workers in Memphis, Tennessee, went on strike. They needed help, and King agreed to lead a march on their behalf. That march had hardly begun—King was in the front row—when teenagers at the back of the line began smashing windows and looting stores.

King was furious. "I will never lead a violent march," he said. "Call it off." A staff member urged the marchers to turn around and return to the church where they had begun. Dr. King left. But the police and the rock-throwing youths weren't finished. By the time they were, 155 stores were damaged, 60 people were hurt, and a 16-year-old boy had been

Memphis's black garbage workers formed a union and went on strike. They struck because some black workers—but no white workers— had been sent home one day when it rained. When the rain stopped, the whites went back to work and were paid a full day's wages; because they had been sent home, the blacks were paid for only a few hours. ▼

◄ A police officer uses his nightstick on a youth reportedly involved in the looting that followed the breakup of a march led by Dr. Martin Luther King, Jr., in Memphis, Tennessee. Black leaders accused the police of brutality while police officers said they did what was necessary to restore order.

killed by police gunfire. It was the first time that anyone had been killed in a march led by Martin Luther King, Jr. He felt sick that a boy had died. He was horrified by the violence. But he couldn't step aside.

King decided that he had to lead a peaceful march in Memphis. Some of Dr. King's aides thought Memphis was too dangerous. J. Edgar Hoover, the head of the FBI (the country's federal law-enforcement agency), hated Dr. King. He was using illegal methods to tap King's phone, and he was starting rumors and planting false articles in newspapers. Later, the truth came out about Hoover, but right now Dr. King was receiving death threats in the mail. That didn't stop him. He was going to go back to Memphis.

The night before his trip, King turned on the television. President Johnson was making an announcement. First Johnson said that he was cutting back on the bombing of North Vietnam and would try to get a settlement of the war. That was a surprise—and a relief. Then Lyndon Johnson stunned the nation. "I shall not seek and I will not accept the nomination of my party for a second term as your president," he said. The big man who wanted to be the greatest of all presidents, who wanted to end poverty, who wanted to do his best for America, had failed.

A few days later, in Memphis, Dr. King spoke before a huge crowd at a church rally. He didn't have a written speech; he just spoke from his heart. King said, "Only when it is dark enough can you see the stars."

Those who heard him that day would always remember his next words:

I would like to live a long life. But I'm not concerned about that now. I just want to do God's will. And He's allowed me to go up to the mountain. And I've looked over. And I've seen the Promised Land. And I may not get there with you. But I want you to know tonight that we as a people will get to the Promised Land....
I have a dream this afternoon that the brotherhood of man will become a reality.

The next evening, after making plans for the Memphis march, Martin Luther King, Jr., went out onto the balcony off his room at the Lorraine Motel to breathe some fresh air before dinner. His friend Ralph Abernathy heard something that sounded like a firecracker. But it was no firecracker. Martin Luther King, Jr., had been shot dead.

Robert Kennedy heard the news in Indianapolis just before he was to speak to a black crowd in a troubled section of the city. The people on the street had not heard the awful news. "Cancel the talk," the mayor of Indianapolis urged. The police refused to protect the senator. But Kennedy would not leave. He climbed onto the flat back of a truck under some oak trees and told the crowd of the tragedy in Memphis. Then he said:

Martin Luther King dedicated his life to love and to justice for his fellow human beings, and he died because of that effort. In this difficult day, in this difficult time for the United States, it is perhaps well to ask what kind of a nation we are and what direction we want to move in. For those of you who are black—considering the evidence there evidently is that there were white people who were responsible—you can be filled with bitterness, with hatred, and a desire for revenge. We can move in that direction as a country... black people amongst black, white people amongst white, filled with hatred toward one another.

Throughout all of history, violence has marred human life. No one is really free in a violent society. Martin Luther King, Jr., dedicated his life to a protest against violence and hatred and unfairness. He understood that freedom brings responsibility. That understanding helped enlarge the quest for life, liberty, and the pursuit of happiness in his time.

▲ Dr. King stands with other civil rights leaders on a motel balcony in Memphis, Tennessee, on April 3, 1968. The next day, he was assassinated just a few feet away. (From left are Hosea Williams, Jesse Jackson, King, and Ralph Abernathy.)

Or we can make an effort, as Martin Luther King did, to understand and to comprehend, and to replace that violence, that stain of bloodshed that has spread across our land, with an effort to understand with compassion and love.

He told his listeners that he understood their anguish because he had lost a brother to an assassin's bullet.

What we need in the United States is not division; what we need in the United States is not hatred; what we need in the United States is not violence or lawlessness, but love and wisdom, and compassion toward one another, and a feeling of justice towards those who still suffer within our country, whether they be white or they be black.... The vast majority of white people and the vast majority of black people in this country want to live together, want to improve the quality of our life, and want justice for all human beings who abide in our land.

A New Kind of Power

Martin Luther King, Jr., was carried to his grave in a casket of polished African mahogany on a plain farm cart pulled by two mules. The cart and the mules reminded people that King's ancestors had farmed America's land with courage and dignity. The mahogany symbolized his African heritage. Weeping at the graveside were leaders from around the world, who had come to pay tribute to the man who had earned a Nobel Peace Prize with his message of love and brotherhood and peace.

Martin Luther King, Jr.'s final journey to Atlanta, in a mule-drawn farm cart, was broadcast by satellite to millions all over the world. ▼

▲ In the days following Dr. King's assassination, cities across the country erupted in riots. Decades later, black neighborhoods in many cities had still not recovered economically.

But, at the very time King was being lowered into the ground, 130 cities around the nation were burning. Rioters—looting and shooting—were killing people and destroying homes and businesses; 65,000 troops had to be called in to put down the riots. Almost all the victims were black.

When the fires cooled, 39 people were dead. The rioters said they were responding to the murder of Martin Luther King, Jr. But was that the right thing to do in memory of a man who had dedicated his life to nonviolence? Hadn't they heard his message?

Most black people had. Every poll showed that the majority of African Americans approved of the ideas of Martin Luther King, Jr., and disapproved of violence. But a black minority—a strong, active minority—was listening to other voices. Mostly those voices were young, male, urban, and angry. They were Black Power leaders; they wanted to change their world, and it certainly needed changing.

Some of them seemed to want power so they could get even for the terrible oppression of slavery and segregation. Some, disgusted by all oppression, wanted to separate themselves from whites. But some others wanted to bring respect and power to a black community that could then act on equal terms with whites.

A Year of Headlines, 1968

Jan — **January 31** North Vietnam launches the Tet Offensive.

Feb

Mar — **March 31** President Lyndon Johnson announces that he will not seek reelection.

Apr — **April 4** Martin Luther King, Jr., is assassinated in Memphis, Tennessee; riots erupt in cities across the country.

May

Jun — **June 4 and 5** Robert Kennedy wins the California Democratic presidential primary and addresses supporters in Los Angeles; minutes later he is shot and dies the next day.

Jul

Aug — **September** Members of NOW and other women's rights groups protest the Miss America Pageant in Atlantic City, New Jersey.

Sep — **October 18** U.S. athletes and medalists at the Olympic Games in Mexico City raise their fists in a black-power salute during the playing of "The Star-Spangled Banner"

Oct

Nov — **November 5** Richard Nixon wins the presidency; college campuses nationwide observe Turn in Your Draft Card Day.

Dec — **December 21** Apollo 8 begins the first U.S. mission to orbit the moon.

That first idea didn't go far. Most black people had no intention of being oppressors. A few did want to separate themselves from the rest of America's citizens, which, after the sacrifices of the civil rights time, was difficult for many to understand. But that idea of power through respect—now that was appealing. Soon blacks—and whites, too—were studying African American history. They were also learning about Africa and its history. They were wearing African-inspired clothes. They were telling stories of slavery from the slaves' point of view. They were taking pride in an inheritance full of stories of achievement. They were voting and electing blacks as sheriffs and mayors and congresspeople.

Black writers were bringing new sensitivities to readers. They were not just writing for African Americans; they were writing for all people. In 1940, Richard Wright published *Native Son*; five years later, his *Black Boy* was a main selection of the Book-of-the-Month Club. Ralph Ellison—whose ancestry was black, white, and Native American—wrote *Invisible Man* (1952), a novel about the ways in which society can ignore the ordinary person and make him feel invisible and powerless. In a stunning first novel titled *Go Tell It on the Mountain* (1953), James Baldwin wrote about the religious awakening of a boy living in Harlem.

Richard Wright, author of *Native Son* and *Black Boy* ▶

Black women were among the best writers of the time. Zora Neale Hurston (who was part of the pre-World War II artistic movement known as the Harlem Renaissance) was rediscovered and celebrated. Hurston's great novel *Their Eyes Were Watching God*—which is both funny and profound—inspired many other writers. Toni Morrison was one of them. She won the Nobel Prize for Literature—there is no higher honor. Alice Walker, Maya Angelou, and Paule Marshall, too, found power in words and ideas.

Before he was killed, Malcolm X found power as a speechmaker. Malcolm had quit school, become a thief and a drug peddler, and landed in jail. He was frustrated; he wanted to turn his life around. But he couldn't express himself because he didn't have control of the English language. He decided to do something about that. He got a dictionary from the prison school and carefully copied every word onto a tablet. "With every succeeding page," he recalled, "I also learned of people and places and events from history." As his vocabulary grew, so did his sense of power and confidence.

In 1960, blacks had very little political power. In that year there were only a few more than 100 black elected officials in the whole United States; by 1993 there were more than 8,000, including 40 members of Congress. Thurgood Marshall and Clarence Thomas had been appointed justices to the Supreme Court.

Between 1950 and 1990, the number of African Americans in white-collar jobs—which means those who work in offices—leapt from 10 percent to 40 percent of all black workers. Black men and women were engineers, doctors, lawyers, politicians, ballplayers, government workers, and artists. Many lived in beautiful houses and belonged to fancy clubs. As to entertainment and sports, Bill Cosby and Earvin "Magic" Johnson were hard to top (until Oprah Winfrey, Michael Jordan, and Tiger Woods came along).

▲ Maya Angelou, poet and author of *I Know Why the Caged Bird Sings*

Michael Jordan became a popular superstar as he brought unprecedented attention to the game of basketball. ▶

▲ Thousands of people lined the railroad tracks as a train carried the slain Robert F. Kennedy from his funeral in New York to his burial at Arlington National Cemetery near Washington, D.C.

Although most people still seemed to think in racial terms, that concern was hiding the real problem—poverty in this prosperous land. Martin Luther King, Jr., had seen that. Bobby Kennedy understood that America would never truly be a land of the free if some people were trapped in poverty and inequality. "Today, in America," he said, "we are two worlds." They were the worlds of rich and poor. He said he hoped to build a bridge between those worlds.

Kennedy decided he would run for president; there were many who believed he would win. And so he set out, giving speeches across the country. Young people flocked to his side. Wherever he went, however, along with the cheers there were also hate pamphlets.

In California, two months after Dr. King's funeral, Kennedy won the Democratic primaries in California and South Dakota. On June 5, 1968, in front of a cheering crowd, he thanked some of those who had helped him: his staff, his friends, his wife, and César Chávez. Then Robert Kennedy, heading for a press conference, took a shortcut through the hotel kitchen. A shot rang out—and the man who might have been president was no more. It was the end of an era.

> *Each time a man stands up for an ideal, or acts to improve the lot of others, or strikes out against injustice, he sends a tiny ripple of hope, and crossing each other from a million different centers of energy and daring, these ripples will build a current which can sweep down the mightiest walls of oppression and resistance.*
>
> —Robert Kennedy, speaking in South Africa

PART 4

NEW CHALLENGES, NEW DIRECTIONS

The Counterculture Rocks

In the '60s, a group of young people—mostly college age and middle class—started living differently from most Americans. They wore different clothes; they marched; they demanded power in their schools and colleges; sometimes they went off to live in their own little communities, called "communes"; and some refused to serve in the army because they didn't believe in fighting.

They were part of something that was called the "counterculture." It had nothing to do with counters, and a few people (who felt threatened by those who weren't in the mainstream) said it had nothing to do with culture, either. But according to the dictionary, *culture* is "behavior patterns, arts, beliefs, institutions, and all other products of human work and thought characteristic of a population." And that was what the counterculture was all about: behavior patterns. People in the counterculture just didn't behave as most other people did in the 1960s.

One meaning of the word *counter* is "against," and those in the counterculture stood against many of the ideas that guided the Vietnam era. Some people called them "hippies"; some people called them strange.

◀ In a used school bus or Volkswagen van, often painted in wild patterns, some hippies traveled from one counterculture event to the next.

▲ In August 1969, a music festival near Woodstock, New York, was expected to attract 50,000 people. Ten times that number came to the three-day event that featured over 30 popular rock bands. Despite rain, lack of sanitation, and inadequate food and water, the young people at Woodstock stayed committed to the event's theme— "Three Days of Peace and Music."

Mostly, they were energetic and idealistic. They were Jewish and Catholic and Protestant and Muslim and Buddhist. They had skin tones that were chocolate and honey and peach and mustard. They were male and female. None of that seemed to matter. What did matter was music and protest and ideas.

They thought the Vietnam War was wrong and immoral.

They were civil rights marchers and they helped register new voters. Many wore their hair long and their clothes loose and colorful. Many lived in California, and they made other Americans realize that much of the nation's population had shifted west—and that maybe its ideas had shifted, too. They had big dreams: they wanted to make America live up to its ideals, and they might have achieved more if it hadn't been for some of their experiments, like drugs, which turned to disaster.

Someone who won't serve with the military because of deep religious convictions (whose conscience tells him or her that it is wrong to fight) is called a "conscientious objector."

The drug culture was one part of the counterculture, and it did untold harm to many— those who experimented with drugs at the time, and thousands who came after them. The '60s produced the first generation in America to make taking drugs fashionable among a large group in society. But drugs take a terrible toll. Drugs led to the early deaths of many musicians and entertainers.

▲ Bob Dylan wrote songs that became anthems for the counterculture.

But people in the counterculture did change things. They questioned everything, refused to conform, and made their favorite music—rock music—a national passion. Rock was a throbbing, pulsing, new kind of sound that took advantage of the electronic wizardry that was just being developed. It was urban music. It merged sounds from the music of blacks and whites. It was speeded up, and loud, and had a beat that was repeated and repeated so you couldn't get it out of your head. Some of it was political music. Some of it was disturbing music.

The most influential musician of the Vietnam era was a young songwriter and performer who called himself Bob Dylan (although his real name was Robert Allen Zimmerman). Dylan was a poet who played a guitar and a harmonica and wrote music and lyrics

Rock wouldn't have happened, at least not quite the way it did, if it hadn't been for an unusual man—a very rich white man—who had so much money that he could do whatever he wanted. And what he wanted was to listen to black music (especially jazz), and learn about black culture, and make recordings of the music that was now becoming his, too. John Henry Hammond, Sr., was born in 1910 but he might have been a child of the '60s, he was so far ahead of his times. He dropped out of Yale College and drove around the country in a convertible in search of black musical talent, and he put that talent on record. Because of John Hammond, a whole young generation could turn on the radio and hear music that had African ancestry.

▲ Jazz great Billie Holiday

One of Hammond's first great discoveries was an amazing black jazz singer named Billie Holiday.

But Hammond understood that talent has no color. He signed recording contracts with some terrific white musicians, too, including Pete Seeger, Bob Dylan, and Bruce Springsteen.

▲ When the Beatles sang, millions of teenage girls screamed, wept, and fainted. The Beatles became the most influential musicians of their time.

about the worries of the times. He was against the war and for civil rights, and his songs "Blowin' in the Wind" and "The Times They Are A-Changin'" became theme songs for the counterculture.

Four English musicians—charming and inventive and electric—became the most important popular musicians of their time (maybe of all time). They were called the Beatles, and they were full of energy and terrific tunes. The Beatles had listened to a lot of black music on the radio in Liverpool, England, the big industrial port city where they grew up. They loved its drumbeat, its rhythm, and its energy and emotion. "It was the black music we dug," said Beatle John Lennon. They took that music and turned it into something that was all their own.

It was hard for anyone to ignore the Beatles. But there were many other good musicians, too. Aretha Franklin, the daughter of a Detroit Baptist minister, was one of the

Aretha Franklin began singing as a child in her father's church. ▼

superstars. She managed to take gospel and blues and merge them together into something that was sad and raw and cool all at the same time—it was called "soul." Franklin, like most of the rock stars, came from an ordinary background. It was her talent that was extraordinary.

Not everyone liked rock—in fact, some people hated it. The lyrics were often about sex or drugs, and the volume of the instruments—which were usually electrically amplified—could be earsplitting. But a lot of people, especially young people, kept their amplifiers turned way up.

The Motown Sound

▲ The Supremes and other Motown groups enjoyed a long string of radio hits.

Berry Gordy was a hardworking guy who drove performers mercilessly, but he had a great ear and he produced a fountain of black music that white listeners (and lots of others) ran to record stores to buy. Gordy was from Detroit, which was then the auto capital of the world, known as Motown to many. So when it came to naming his record company—why, Motown it was.

Gordy found talent in inner-city Detroit and turned it into gold. His discoveries included Martha and the Vandellas, Smoky Robinson and the Miracles, the Temptations, the Supremes, the Jackson 5 (including Michael Jackson), Stevie Wonder, and Marvin Gaye. The Motown sound, with its pounding beat, dominated the radio waves. By 1977, Gordy's company, Tamla-Motown, was the largest black-owned conglomerate (collection of smaller companies) in the United States.

Nixon: Vietnam, China, and Watergate

In the second half of the 20th century, 1968 stands out as a pivotal year. Things changed dramatically in 1968.

It was the year of those two awful assassinations. It was the year of the Tet Offensive in Vietnam. *Tet* is the Vietnamese New Year, a very big holiday. The North Vietnamese launched an attack during Tet; a lot of American soldiers were killed, and we realized we weren't winning that war (although our leaders had been telling us that we were).

The year 1968 was one of urban riots and protests on college campuses. It was the year a computer named Hal starred in a movie and people gasped when they considered where technology might lead. It was an election year, and the end of a liberal era and the beginning of more conservative times. It was the year Richard Milhous Nixon was elected president.

Nixon's ancestors were Quakers. Richard, a quiet, dark-eyed, serious boy, got good grades in school; in high school he learned to

> It was after Tet that American public opinion changed. After Tet, most Americans no longer supported the war.

> In 1971, the 26th Amendment to the Constitution was ratified. It said that 18-year-olds could vote. Are you getting ready?

◀ In 1962, after he lost the race for governor of California, Richard Nixon told reporters, "You won't have Nixon to kick around anymore, gentlemen, because this is my last press conference." Six years later he ran for the presidency and won easily.

President Nixon inspects a military unit during his groundbreaking trip to China. Nixon was the first U.S. president to visit the communist country. ▶

debate and to act. Then he went to Whittier College in California, was president of the student council, and got a scholarship to Duke University Law School (across the country in North Carolina). He served in the U.S. Navy during World War II.

It was politics that always seemed to interest him. So, as a young lawyer, when he got chances to run for Congress and then for the Senate, he grabbed them. But he used mudslinging and dirty tricks in his campaigns. For example, he accused some of his opponents of being communists, when he knew they weren't.

In Congress, Nixon became known as a tough anticommunist. He impressed people: he was smart, industrious, serious, and ambitious. Dwight D. Eisenhower asked him to be his vice president, and he did a good job in that office. People began talking about the two Nixons. One was very capable. The other Nixon didn't seem to care about truth and honor.

When he became president, he brought those two personalities with him. Richard Nixon the statesman talked of "law and order," and, after months of riots in our cities, that was just what most Americans wanted to hear. But the other Richard Nixon had no respect for the law when it affected him.

He claimed he had a plan to end the war, but he never said what that plan was. Then he kept us fighting in Vietnam for almost five more years (he was reelected in 1972). He took the war into

United States Involvement in Vietnam, 1945–1975

1945 Ho Chi Minh declares Vietnam an independent nation; Allied powers divide the nation into North Vietnam and South Vietnam; France fights to regain colonial control of Vietnam.

1950 President Truman authorizes funds for military equipment and advisers to aid the French.

1954 President Eisenhower cites the "domino theory" to justify increased support for noncommunists in South Vietnam; France withdraws from Southeast Asia after defeat at Dien Bien Phu.

1961 President Kennedy sends Special Forces units and military advisers to aid the South Vietnamese against the Viet Cong.

1963 Buddhist monks protest corruption in and oppression by the South Vietnamese government of Diem; Diem is assassinated in a military coup.

1964 President Johnson authorizes secret bombing raids on the Ho Chi Minh Trail in Laos; 85 percent of Americans support U.S. military action in Vietnam; Congress passes the Gulf of Tonkin Resolution.

1965 The war escalates as U.S. combat troops arrive in Vietnam and bombing raids increase; antiwar protests begin in the United States.

▲ Helicopters helped evacuate South Vietnamese from Saigon when the city fell to the communists in April 1975. The fall of South Vietnam's capital marked the end of the war for the United States.

1968 More than 460,000 American troops are serving in Vietnam; the Viet Cong launch the Tet Offensive; public support for the war declines.

1969 President Nixon initiates peace talks in Paris; U.S. troop strength peaks at more than 540,000 before withdrawals begin.

1970 Four student protesters at Kent State University in Ohio are killed by National Guard troops; President Nixon reduces troop strength but extends bombing into Cambodia.

1972 The last American combat troops withdraw from Vietnam.

1975 Chaos erupts in Saigon as North Vietnamese troops enter the city; the last Americans are evacuated; Vietnam is united as a communist country.

neighboring Cambodia and Laos without telling Congress that he planned to do it. He dropped more bombs than any president in our history, although he said he wanted to be a peacemaker. The antiwar demonstrations had been bad when Lyndon Johnson was president; they were worse for President Nixon.

Nixon's intelligent, reasonable side helped him lead the nation in a new foreign-policy direction. Nixon was a pragmatist, which means a "practical thinker," and he understood that the world was changing and

A political cartoon accuses Nixon of lying by depicting the president as Pinocchio.

that it was time to try to work with the communist nations. So he went to China and improved relations with that enormous nation. Then he went to Moscow (Russia's capital), the first American president to do so, and once again showed concern for world harmony.

We got out of Vietnam much as we had gotten in—one step at a time. It was called "phased withdrawal." But, after Saigon, the capital of South Vietnam, fell to northern forces, we finally withdrew completely. We had lost a war—although we didn't quite admit it. We were confused and humbled and weary. We needed to feel good about ourselves again, but something was going on at home that left us even more upset and dismayed. The problem, again, was one of leadership.

Something happened to Richard Nixon that is important for you to understand. It happened because of that distrustful side of his nature. He imagined enemies.

He seemed to think that because he was president, he was above the law. But he was missing the whole point of American democracy. No one is above the law—not even the president.

Richard Nixon forgot that the president is a servant of the people. He allowed his staff to play dirty, illegal tricks on his opponents. Burglars broke into Democratic Party headquarters and stole documents. Burglars broke into a psychiatrist's office and stole the confidential records of someone Nixon disliked. People tapped telephone lines and listened to private conversations. Money was gathered and used in illegal ways. Lies were told about people Nixon disliked. The government's tax office was used against his enemies. All of those things were against the law.

Washington Post reporters Bob Woodward (left) and Carl Bernstein investigated and reported on the Watergate scandal for more than two years. ▼

When some of that wrongdoing became known, people in the Nixon White House did something even worse. They paid hush money to keep some people quiet and to have others lie in sworn testimony to judges and juries. It was the bottom moment in the history of the presidency. It was called "Watergate" because the Democratic Party headquarters were in Washington's fancy Watergate apartments. Nixon's dirty-tricks workers burglarized those Watergate headquarters. They rented a room in a nearby hotel so they could spy on the Watergate.

▲ Former White House counsel John Dean testifies before Congress.

▲ By October 1973, Nixon's approval rating had hit a low of 17 percent. Ten months later, facing impeachment and informed that he had lost almost all support in the Senate, Nixon resigned.

Shameful as it was, there was something positive about Watergate: our democratic system worked. When two *Washington Post* reporters (Bob Woodward and Carl Bernstein) found out about the burglaries and the dirty tricks, they told of them. It took great courage to accuse a president and his aides.

Richard Nixon almost got away with criminal acts—but he didn't. The president was not above the law. Nor were other people in his administration. Vice President Spiro Agnew admitted to filing a "false and fraudulent" tax return. Agnew left office, was fined $10,000, and was sentenced to three years' probation. Fifty-six men in the Nixon administration were convicted of Watergate-related crimes. Some went to jail. The Constitution writers had prepared for this kind of emergency by giving Congress the power to impeach and try a president.

In the House of Representatives, articles of impeachment were prepared. President Nixon was charged with lying, obstructing justice, and using the Internal Revenue Service (the tax office) and other government agencies illegally. Nixon was going to be impeached. After that, he would face a trial in the Senate for "high crimes and misdemeanors." He chose to leave the presidency instead. He resigned as president of the United States—the only man ever to do so.

Mercury, Gemini, and Apollo

In 1957 the Russians sent a satellite called Sputnik into space. Sputnik was a shock. It made us feel that we were falling behind Russia when it came to technology and science.

Russia's Sputnik got us energized. We didn't want our communist foes to take over space.

In April 1961, the Russians sent a cosmonaut, Yuri Gagarin (guh-GAR-in), rocketing into space. The United States had a space agency, NASA (the National Aeronautics and Space Administration), and a space program—but we were behind the Russians, and we couldn't stand that idea.

President John F. Kennedy made a speech announcing our intention to put a man on the moon "before the decade is out." We were off on a space race.

This moon trip became the will of a nation. It took the talent of thousands of brains, it took the lives of some astronauts (who were killed in explosive misfires), and it cost $25.5 billion, which came from the earnings of America's citizens.

The first step toward the moon was the Mercury project, named for the swift messenger of the ancient Roman gods. Alan B. Shepard was squeezed into a spacesuit in a space capsule called Freedom 7, just big enough to hold him.

Shepard blasted into space with a great roar and arched back to his home on Earth with a mighty splash into the ocean. The flight of Freedom 7 lasted 15 minutes.

After the six Mercury missions came Gemini, named for twin stars. They were two-man flights intended to test rendezvous (meeting) and docking techniques. The Gemini spacecraft was a big improvement over Mercury. It was bigger and could be steered by the astronauts. The Gemini astronauts walked outside the capsule—into outer space—with a cord that firmly tied them to their vehicle.

Earthrise over the surface of the moon, seen from the orbiting Apollo 11 spacecraft ▼

▲ Astronaut Buzz Aldrin poses on the surface of the moon.

▲ American heroes (left to right) Neil Armstrong, Michael Collins, and Buzz Aldrin return from the moon.

▲ Apollo 11 mission commander Neil Armstrong (photographed by Buzz Aldrin, lunar module pilot) stands by an American flag placed on the moon in July 1969.

On the morning of July 16, 1969, five months before President Kennedy's deadline of the end of the decade (Richard Nixon was now president), the sun was bright and the skies were clear at Cape Canaveral on Florida's east coast.

Three men sat strapped inside a narrow capsule on top of a rocket that stood as tall as a 30-story building. Neil Armstrong, a civilian pilot, was in the left seat. Edwin E. Aldrin, known as Buzz, sat in the middle. Michael Collins, another air force officer and test pilot, was to pilot the command ship, which would orbit the moon while the other two men descended to the lunar surface in the landing vehicle.

The rocket—named Saturn—belched fire and lifted off. After two and a half minutes Saturn was 41 miles above Earth, traveling at 5,400 mph (miles per hour) when its first stage fell away.

After circling the globe twice, the astronauts were cruising toward the moon. It would take three days to get there. (Three days was the time it took Thomas Jefferson to make the 90-mile trip, in a horse-drawn carriage, from his plantation at Monticello to his plantation at Poplar Forest.)

When two men stepped out of the landing vehicle onto the moon's surface, because of television, we were there—all the peoples of the earth. It was an American spaceship, but it was a world event.

Neil Armstrong stepped onto the moon's crunchy soil and said, "One small step for man, one giant leap for mankind." It was an understatement. The man in the moon was now real, and we were standing with him.

A Congressman and a Peanut Farmer

▲ "To me," said Gerald Ford, "the presidency and the vice presidency were not prizes to be won but a duty to be done."

Gerald Ford was never elected president or vice president, and yet he became president of the United States. How did that happen?

This was the way: President Nixon chose him to replace Spiro Agnew when Agnew resigned as vice president. Then, when Nixon resigned, Ford became president.

Ford, a popular, pleasant man, was a congressman from Michigan and House minority leader. That means he was the Republican leader in the House of Representatives (where there was a Democratic majority). When he became president, he put his feet into two hornet's nests: the messes that were left from Watergate and Vietnam.

He said he would heal the "long national nightmare," and he was talking about the scandal of Watergate. He promptly granted Nixon an unconditional pardon for any wrongdoings against the United States. Some people howled in protest—they thought Nixon should be put on trial—but others believed the country was better off spared that agony; they were glad to forget the national nightmare. Then Ford pardoned draft protesters who had refused to fight in Vietnam, although there were some conditions attached to their pardons.

During Gerald Ford's presidency the last U.S. troops and support workers were evacuated from Vietnam. Vietnam would take its place in history as America's worst foreign-policy defeat.

As president, Gerald Ford didn't break new ground or excite the imagination of most Americans. His wife, Betty Ford, did. She spoke out openly on controversial subjects, especially the rights of women. She talked of her own problems with cancer and alcoholism and discussed the pressures on young people to use drugs. But that wasn't enough to get her husband elected. In 1976, when Ford tried to win an election for president, he lost.

◀ First Lady Betty Ford was known for speaking out on controversial issues.

James Earl "Jimmy" Carter became the 39th president. A peanut farmer, Carter had graduated from the U.S. Naval Academy at Annapolis and become governor of Georgia. When he decided to run for president he was hardly known outside his state. But Jimmy Carter was determined. Soft-spoken and deeply religious, Carter told the American people, "I will not lie to you." And, as far as we know, he never did.

Carter was a Southern Democrat with progressive views on civil rights and moderate ideas on economics. But he was an outsider when it came to dealing with the government in Washington. He brought his friends from Georgia with him to the capital. They had some good ideas, and President Carter thought Congress would go along with those ideas. But Jimmy Carter hadn't learned the ways of Congress. He couldn't get things done. It was frustrating for him and for the country.

Besides, he was unlucky. While he was president, a worldwide energy crisis made prices—especially the price of oil and gas—in the United States zoom way up. (It was an inflationary time.) Then the ruler of Iran, the shah, was overthrown and replaced by a fundamentalist Muslim religious leader, the Ayatollah Khomeini, who preached hatred of the United States. The Iranians captured some Americans and held them as hostages for 444 days. President Carter ordered a daring rescue mission, but it fizzled into an embarrassing mess of poor planning and failed equipment. As if that weren't bad enough, the Soviet Union invaded Afghanistan, another Muslim country in Central Asia, and, when we protested, relations with Soviet Russia became icy.

▲ President James Earl "Jimmy" Carter

◀ In Iran's capital city, Tehran, militants stormed the U.S. embassy and took 52 hostages. For the next 15 months, they often humiliated the hostages by parading them, bound and blindfolded, in front of Iranian photographers and TV cameras.

▲ Carter invited Egypt's president, Anwar Sadat (left), and Israel's prime minister, Menachem Begin (right), to a summit meeting. The treaty they agreed to was a big breakthrough for these angry neighbors.

President Carter did serve as a peacemaker between Egypt and Israel. And he did get Congress to agree to turn the Panama Canal over to Panama at the end of the century (which was a new Good Neighbor policy). And he did support measures to help protect our natural environment.

Jimmy Carter tried to solve problems of national debt and energy conservation by asking people to make sacrifices. Maybe he didn't know how to ask—or maybe Americans weren't ready to make sacrifices. When Carter ran for reelection, he was defeated.

A Tangled Tale

Why did Iran's Ayatollah Khomeini preach hatred of America? It's a complicated story, but here's a bit of it. When Eisenhower was president, Iran had a democratically elected ruler, Mohammed Mossadegh, who was trying to exist outside the influence of Western powers. But Britain and the U.S. wanted influence. Iran is oil-rich. So we helped overthrow Mossadegh and return the shah of Iran to power through secret—and illegal—activities of our CIA (Central Intelligence Agency). The CIA helped train and support the shah's secret police, who tortured and murdered political opponents.

Then the shah was overthrown, to be replaced by the anti-American and repressive government of the Ayatollah Khomeini. Khomeini took American citizens as hostages, defying the Carter administration. Later, the Reagan administration sold arms to Iran in the hope of getting other hostages released in Lebanon. This is a tangled tale.

▲ Iran's Ayatollah Khomeini

Taking a Leading Role

The next president was a great communicator—in fact, that was what people started calling him. His name was Ronald Reagan, and he was in his 70s during most of his presidential years.

Although he was old enough to be a grandfather, few people thought of Ronald Reagan as an old man. He was boyish, easygoing, likable, and friendly. He had a great sense of humor. And he knew how to use television as no president had before him.

After the turmoil of the '60s and '70s and the unsettled presidencies of Ford and Carter, many Americans thought Ronald Reagan just right for the times. He called himself "Mr. Normal," and he didn't seem to take himself too seriously. As for ready wit, hardly anyone could touch him. But he didn't joke when it came to ideas. He knew exactly what he believed, and he explained those beliefs clearly and simply. In a complex world that was harder and harder to understand, he seemed reassuring and honest and old-fashioned.

It was 1981, and Reagan was about to bring about a radical change of direction in American politics—and be very popular doing it. Few presidents have been as effective.

In the "Reagan revolution," as it has become known, many of the ideas begun 50 years earlier with the New Deal were overturned. By Reagan's time, many welfare programs designed to help the poor and needy had become bureaucratic dead ends. Reagan opposed

▲ President Ronald Reagan, known as the "great communicator," waves as he boards the helicopter known as Marine One.

During the Depression, when hardly anyone could find a job, the young Ronald Reagan got a job as a radio sportscaster. After that he went to Hollywood and became a movie actor, appearing in family films about cowboys, football, and wartime heroics. But politics fascinated him, so he began with the politics of moviemaking and became a labor leader in the filmmaking community, and, eventually, governor of California.

Before he became president, Ronald Reagan was an actor, which helped make him a brilliant and persuasive speaker. ▶

the antipoverty programs of the New Deal and the Great Society, which he referred to as the "welfare state." He rejected the liberal philosophy that government should take an active role to solve social problems. Instead, he firmly held to the conservative belief that unrestricted capitalism can lead to opportunity and prosperity that helps everyone.

One of Ronald Reagan's conservative heroes was Calvin Coolidge. Coolidge's economic policy had been called "trickle-down" economics by its critics. It was based on the idea that economic freedom helps create wealth that then trickles down to all levels of society. Reagan's economics had a similar goal. It was called "supply-side" economics.

Reagan was antitax, antiunion, and fiercely anticommunist. He wanted to reduce the size of the government. He wanted to cut spending on welfare programs, eliminate most government regulations on business, take the national government out of the field of education, and balance the budget. He also wanted to build up the armed forces and increase military spending.

How did things turn out? By the end of the '80s, the United States was the world's greatest superpower, and very wealthy. But many inner-city schools, bridges, roads, and buildings were falling apart,

Assassination Attempt

March 30, 1981—shots were fired, and a Secret Service man pushed President Reagan to the floor of the limousine. "Jerry, get off me. You're hurting my ribs," he said. But a bullet had gone through his lung and was three inches from his heart. That was why his ribs hurt. When he coughed, blood came up, and the limousine sped for the hospital. As the president was being wheeled to an operating room, he saw his wife, Nancy. "Honey, I forgot to duck," he said. When he saw the doctors who were removing the bullet he said, "I hope you fellas are Republicans." Ronald Reagan had spunk (and a sense of humor).

A series of photographs shows the sequence of events as shots were fired. ▶

much of our population was poorly educated, and access to good health care was not equal to that in many developed nations.

Balancing the budget was one of his key goals. A *balanced budget* means that your annual spending equals your annual revenues (taxes provide revenues for the government). If you spend more than you earn, you have a *deficit* (DEF-uh-sit); if you spend less, you have a surplus. A deficit means you have to borrow to pay the bills. That puts you in *debt*.

The national debt in 1979 (under Carter) was very high. Reagan believed that if his administration cut taxes and public welfare programs and eliminated as much government regulation of business as possible, it would stimulate the economy and tax revenues would increase. He thought that would pay for the huge increase in military spending that he believed necessary.

Congress enacted the largest single tax cut in our history. Programs directed at the poor and the middle class were reduced. At the same time, Congress embarked on a $1.6 trillion military expansion. What happened to the national debt? It went from $383 billion in 1980 to $2.3 *trillion* in 1988. Reagan's deficits totaled more than the deficits of all the presidents before him combined. That wasn't his intention.

"Government is not the solution to our problem," Reagan said. "Government is the problem." Many agreed. Too often, Americans dealing with their government faced a frustrating, often arrogant, unresponsive bureaucracy. Bureaucracies—in big business, big schools, and big government—seemed to define the 20th century. What could be done about it? Was there a creative answer? How do you conduct public business wisely without oppressive regulations?

The Republican administration decided to cut or cut back the watchdog agencies that oversee business; it weakened already weak union power; where it could, it turned public lands and agencies over to private interests; it lifted restrictions on TV and the public airwaves. The intent was to actively encourage private interests. The theory was that if private interests and competition benefited they would pass some of those benefits on to the public.

But some companies were unprepared for the responsibilities that went with new freedom. For example, savings-and-loan associations, which were created to lend money to ordinary people to buy homes, began making speculative investments. When the value of their investments went down, many of the savings and loans became insolvent (which means they went bankrupt and were unable to pay their debts). That cost taxpayers an estimated $481 billion. At the Department of Housing and Urban Affairs, scandals cost the taxpayers further billions of dollars.

While military spending went up, libraries, public radio and television, museums, national parks, and other public institutions found themselves with less government aid. Spending on education also dropped.

None of this seemed to affect Reagan's popularity. After Vietnam and some flawed presidencies, his optimism and vitality restored many citizens' confidence in themselves and in their country. Whatever the problems, he believed this nation would solve them.

"If men were angels, no government would be necessary," said James Madison. He explained: "In framing a government...the great difficulty is this: you must first enable the government to control the governed, and in the next place oblige it to control itself."

What is the difference between a billion and a trillion? Try this to get a picture in your mind. Go to a blackboard (or imagine one). Write zero on one side, one trillion on the other, and put a line between. Now you have a number line that stretches from zero to a trillion. Where do you think the one billion mark will fall on that number line? Pick a spot.

Did you put it right near the zero? One billion is just one-thousandth of a trillion. If you make one thousand marks on the board, the first of them will represent one billion. All the rest of the number line is the difference between one billion and one trillion. So when our national debt went from billions to the trillions, it was a big hike.

◀ President Reagan and General Secretary Gorbachev sign an arms control treaty at the White House in 1987.

Again and again, Reagan spoke out on the dangers of Russian communism. He called the Soviet Union an "evil empire." At the same time, he preached the virtues of democracy. Speaking in England to both houses of Parliament, he said:

> *Let us be shy no longer. Let us go to our strength. Let us offer hope. Let us tell the world that a new age is not only possible but probable.... For the sake of peace and justice, let us move toward a world in which all people are at last free to determine their own destiny.*

And then something astonishing happened. President Ronald Reagan and Russian premier Mikhail Gorbachev (gor-buh-CHOFF) began talking to each other. They met at Geneva, Switzerland, in 1985, and in Reykjavik, Iceland, in 1986. Their talks led to historic arms control agreements.

Two Very Different Decades

The 1960s had been a decade of high drama, with marches in the streets and sit-ins at lunch counters. The '80s were different. This time the drama was so quiet that sometimes hardly anyone noticed. Mostly the revolution took place in corporate headquarters, on Wall Street's money exchanges, in people's minds, and in Congress—but it was effective. Some called it a conservative reaction to the excesses of the liberal decades that preceded it. Goals changed. Business was the focus of the '80s. Most voters no longer thought government should be used to solve social problems. Labor unions lost power.

In West Berlin, President Reagan gave a speech in front of the Berlin Wall. He concluded, "Mr. Gorbachev, tear down this wall!" ▶

During the Cold War, the Soviet Union and its allies were referred to as the Eastern Bloc. Many Eastern Bloc governments were communist regimes, manipulated or controlled by the U.S.S.R. The United States and its allies were sometimes referred to as the Western Bloc but more often as "Western nations" or simply "the West." The Western nations—such as Great Britain and France—were anticommunist.

The following year, the president went to Berlin, Germany. That city was divided into two parts. In West Berlin, people were free to come and go and practice democracy. In East Berlin, a communist government had walled in its own people. There, a strong, well-guarded wall kept East Germans from visiting friends and neighbors in the West. The Berlin Wall was a bald example of communist repression. It imprisoned a whole people. President Reagan stood before the wall and said, "Mr. Gorbachev, tear down this wall!"

Although few people in the West realized it, forces were at work in the Eastern Bloc nations that would cause that wall to tumble. Mikhail Gorbachev, who was a communist but also a pragmatic leader, was aware that Russia needed to change. Ronald Reagan, the Cold Warrior, was now anxious to become a peacemaker.

In 1988, Reagan went to Moscow, this time as a friend of the Russian premier. A beaming Gorbachev took his guest around Red Square, pointing out the sights. Smiles and handshakes replaced the Cold War chill. These two leaders surprised everyone when they realized they had a chance to change history. They could end the insane arms race that had been so costly for both nations and had affected the whole world. They found ways to do it. And, as you'll soon see, history's direction did change.

Congress Shall Have the Power to Declare War

World War II was the last war declared by Congress. What about the Korean War, the Vietnam War, the war in Grenada, and—still to come—the Persian Gulf War and the war in Afghanistan?

They were all begun by presidents who claimed special powers. But was that the intent of the Framers of the Constitution? The words of the Constitution are clear. Article 1, Section 8, says that "Congress shall have the power to declare war."

In 1983, President Reagan ordered 2,000 Marines into Lebanon to help restore order to that war-ravaged country. But Muslim leaders made it clear they didn't want U.S. help. In October, a terrorist drove a truck loaded with explosives into a U.S. Marine barracks, and 239 Marines died.

That same month, the United States invaded the small Caribbean island of Grenada, ousting an unfriendly government and responding to reports that Cuban communists were building an airfield there. Most Grenadians approved. Many Americans wondered if it was our business to be there.

American troops arrive in Grenada in October 1983. ▼

60

The End of the Cold War

In 1989, the Soviet Union broke into pieces.

Yes, the Soviet Union, the U.S.S.R., the land we called Russia—a nation composed of many states—fell apart. The Soviet Union's military power didn't collapse. Communism did. As a political system, communism had failed. It had begun with high hopes as a visionary experiment. The experiment hadn't worked. It had turned Russia into an unfree, tyrannical, clumsy nation. Karl Marx's economic ideas hadn't worked, either. Government ownership of land and products didn't bring efficiency and productivity. Finally, the burden of ever-growing military needs helped wreck Russia's economy. (Trying to keep up with the Reagan-era military might have helped do it.)

When the Russian people had had enough, they just threw communism out. It was stunning; it was peaceful; it meant that everything had changed in the world's politics. The Cold War was over. It was hard to believe. Now that Russia was a free nation, there was no giant to battle. At first we didn't seem to know what to do.

In 1989, the Soviet Union fell apart—a momentous event symbolized by the removal of this statue of Vladimir Lenin, the founder of Russian communism. ▶

270 PART 4 New Challenges, New Directions

But it was becoming clear to most people that we are all passengers on the same global spaceship. The European nations had joined together to form a Common Market—called the European Union. They began acting—economically—as if they were one giant nation. Japan was a major economic power. Nations like South Korea, China, India, and Indonesia were making big moves in business. The world's economies were all becoming linked, as nations that had once been communist began to change to free market economies—economies with little government control.

People all over the world wanted freedom. When students in China rebelled against their corrupt government, they paraded around with a statue of the "Goddess of Democracy" modeled after our Statue of Liberty. The Chinese government sent troops, who opened fire on civilians in Beijing's Tiananmen Square. Many students were killed.

The fall of Russian communism was giving oppressed peoples everywhere an awareness of possibilities. It gave us a new appreciation of our freedoms. Ronald Reagan championed those freedoms worldwide, but it was the 41st president, Republican George Bush, who was able to take us in a new direction. Bush was a practical fellow with a low-key manner and an ability to tackle details. The son of a Connecticut senator, Bush was the youngest pilot in the navy during World War II and a genuine war hero. After the war, he moved west to Texas and became an oilman. But it was government that fascinated him, and he served in a series of important jobs—right up to the vice presidency under Ronald Reagan. In 1988, he became president himself.

He promised "no new taxes." But all those years of war preparation had been hard on us as well as on Russia. Bush became president at a time when cities were in decay, schools were

When thousands of Chinese students demonstrated and raised a statue of the "Goddess of Democracy" in Tiananmen Square in the capital of China, the government broke up the demonstrations and killed many of the rebels. ▼

▲ A U.S. F-117A, known as the stealth fighter

behind those of many other nations, crime was epidemic, and the huge national debt was making many Americans fearful of the future. So President Bush worked out an agreement with Congress—which was controlled by a Democratic Party majority—to raise taxes. It may have helped restrain the debt and thus take a step toward prosperity that was coming; it didn't help George Bush with the American people. But his foreign policy did win approval.

When Saddam Hussein, dictator of Iraq, sent troops into neighboring Kuwait and took over that nation, Bush led a forceful response. The United States, with the United Nations, stopped Hussein's aggression in the powerful, short Persian Gulf War.

President Bush led a military response (from August 1990 to February 1991) that would be known as the First Gulf War, or Operation Desert Storm. Working with the United Nations, the president put together a coalition of nations that quickly drove Iraq out of Kuwait. Air strikes on well-defined targets were coordinated with an effective ground force that raced through Kuwait and into southern Iraq. President Bush and his military advisers achieved their goal: an independent Kuwait. They resisted pressure to capture Baghdad and remove Saddam Hussein for two reasons: Iran, they thought, was an

U.S. Marines advance during the ground war in Operation Desert Storm. ▼

◄ A Serbian woman grieves in a makeshift cemetery during the ethnic and religious civil war in the former Yugoslavia.

even more dangerous threat than Iraq and a strong Iraq was necessary to contain Iran. The second reason for holding back? They understood that occupation of a defeated Iraq would be costly and dangerous. Some criticized President Bush for that decision, because it left Saddam Hussein in power in Iraq.

The next time President Bush called out American forces, it was to help starving people in Somalia. That nation, which elbows out into the Indian Ocean from the east coast of Africa, was in a state of crisis. Crops failed. Armed thugs were terrorizing and killing. There was no effective government. Our marines brought food and some help. We worked with the United Nations. Our aim was to make peacekeeping a whole-world venture.

But good intentions don't always matter. In the former Eastern European nation of Yugoslavia—which had been split into several different nations, some of them claiming the same land—Serbs and Croats and Muslims began killing each other, partly because their religions were different. That horrendous war, with "ethnic cleansing" or mass killings, finally ended with an agreement negotiated in Dayton, Ohio, in 1995.

In the face of such calamities, we started asking ourselves some hard questions: does the United States have a responsibility to try to solve the problems of other nations? Is it done best with armies or with negotiators? Or should we concentrate on creating a just society at home and hope that the rest of the world will take notice?

There are some 1,290 different religions practiced in the United States. In this country people of all faiths live together in relative harmony. *We have never fought a war over religion.* Most people agree that is because of our First Amendment—it separates church and state, which means that our government keeps its hands off when it comes to religion. That isn't true in most other countries. At the beginning of the 1990s, more than 30 religious wars were being fought around the globe.

A Boy from Hope

That a small-town boy from one of the poorest of states could make it to the nation's top job is what America is all about. William Jefferson Clinton, from Hope, Arkansas, became our 42nd president and, at the age of 46, the third-youngest in American history. He was the first Democratic president in 12 years.

Few men have arrived at the presidency with a background to match Clinton's. A graduate of Georgetown University's School of Foreign Service, he had been a Rhodes scholar at Oxford University in England, received a law degree from Yale University, and for 12 years served as governor of Arkansas. Everywhere he left an impression of vigor, compassion, and astonishing ability—along with troublesome stories of about-faces under pressure from wealthy interests and other less-than-principled actions.

Bill Clinton, seen here with his wife, Hillary, proved to be a brilliant campaigner who could connect with people of all backgrounds. ▼

The woman who would become Clinton's wife, Hillary Rodham, also awed people with her intellect and ability. As a lawyer, she held a series of jobs where her intensity and intelligence made her stand out. She served on the legal staff that investigated Watergate. She devoted much of her career to issues of health and child care. With Bill Clinton, she became half of an incredible political partnership.

What kind of president was Bill Clinton? For a Democratic president, he pursued many goals most often associated with conservatives. He cut welfare, put more police on the streets, built prisons, stepped up the war on drugs, expanded the death penalty, and, after passage of a deficit reduction bill (without any Republican votes), balanced the budget. For the first time in 30 years, instead of a budget deficit, the country had a surplus! All that helped bring about a stock-market surge, low unemployment, minimal inflation, and general prosperity.

▲ President Clinton brought Israeli Prime Minister Yitzhak Rabin (left) and PLO Chairman Yasser Arafat together for a historic handshake after the signing of the Israeli-PLO peace accord at the White House in 1993. Not since the Camp David accords of 1978 had people felt such hope for peace in the Middle East.

But Clinton was unable to get health insurance for all Americans, or change the way we paid for political campaigns, or do much for public schools. The gap between the rich and the middle class grew wider.

In foreign affairs, the Clinton administration brought warring parties from Serbia, Croatia, and Bosnia to Dayton, Ohio, where they sat down and agreed to stop killing each other. Former president Jimmy Carter was sent to Haiti and helped that impoverished island get its first fairly elected president, Jean-Bertrand Aristide, into office. In the Middle East, Clinton helped negotiate agreements between Israel and its Arab neighbors. In Ireland, where Protestants and Catholics had been fighting for centuries, the administration again acted as a mediator in the effort to achieve a historic peace agreement. Trade treaties—lowering tariffs and bolstering international free trade—were negotiated by the administration and ratified by Congress. And Clinton made a historic trip to China, where he charmed the Chinese with his willingness to answer hard questions.

▲ President Clinton arrives in Bosnia to spend Christmas with American troops stationed there.

▲ A humbled President Clinton vows to complete his term after the House of Representatives voted to impeach him. He was later acquitted of the impeachment charges by the Senate.

Despite his gifts of unusual intelligence and charm, Bill Clinton threw away the chance to be a great president. Clinton's presidency, begun with so much promise, turned into a personal and national disaster.

Even before he took office, Bill Clinton was accused of all kinds of wrongdoing. A special prosecutor was appointed to investigate questions about a real-estate investment (called Whitewater) in Arkansas that Clinton had made while he was that state's governor.

The special prosecutor—who ignored long-cherished legal traditions (such as the privacy of lawyer-and-client confidences)—found no evidence of wrongdoing connected with Whitewater, but he did find Clinton's flaw.

Bill Clinton was president when television and films were bombarding us with images that had once been seen only in private. In the past we hadn't known much about the private lives of politicians, but by Clinton's time the media were spreading opinions and information (and misinformation) everywhere—and quickly.

In the case of President William Jefferson Clinton, we learned details of his private life that no one wanted to know. The special prosecutor and the press went far beyond the bounds of legal necessity in describing the president's relations with a woman who worked in the White House. When faced with disturbing accusations about his personal life, Clinton was not honest. He lied to the American public and he lied to members of his administration. He wounded himself, his family, and the nation.

In December 1998, Bill Clinton was impeached in the House of Representatives. In the Senate trial that followed, the president was found not to have committed "high crimes and misdemeanors." His private behavior was not deemed a constitutional offense (no matter how inappropriate). It was an example of constitutional democracy at work.

To impeach is to accuse a public official of wrong conduct before a proper tribunal (a place of judgment, usually a court). The Constitution gives the House of Representatives power to impeach the president. Then the Senate must conduct a trial to consider the charges brought by the House. Only two presidents have been impeached: Andrew Johnson and Bill Clinton. Neither was found guilty of the "high crimes and misdemeanors" necessary for removal from office.

A Quilt, Not a Blanket

Orestes Lorenzo Perez, a Cuban military pilot, stepped into his Soviet-built jet fighter plane and flew toward the United States. He was risking his life, but he believed the risk was worthwhile. He wanted to live in a land that was free.

Lorenzo kept his plane low, just over the water, so it would not be detected by radar. There was no way his wife, Victoria, and his sons, Reyniel and Alejandro, could go with him. "Don't worry," he told his wife. "I will come back for you."

As soon as he arrived in the United States, Orestes Lorenzo Perez tried to get his family out of Cuba. He tried all the legal means. He lobbied members of Congress; he founded an organization called Parents for Freedom—but nothing worked. His wife and children were hostages of Fidel Castro, Cuba's dictator. Castro would not let them out of the country.

In the Little Havana section of Miami, Florida, children perform a traditional dance at a parade. ▼

In the meantime, Lorenzo became part of the flourishing Cuban American community. He learned to fly American planes and became a licensed American pilot. He came up with a plan, and he got a secret message to his wife. The message told of a spot on a highway near a beach. Then he borrowed a plane and called his wife on the telephone. They spoke of children's clothing, of his father, of the sunset. It was all a code. He said, "I'll send money to buy a TV."

"Already?" she asked, startled. Those code words meant he was coming the next day. He needed to know exactly when the sun set in Cuba. He asked about the children's shoe sizes. She said they were 5½ and 6½. The sun set between 5:30 and 6:30 p.m.

The next day, Victoria packed a lunch and she and the boys went to the beach. They spread out their towels and sat down. Two policemen were nearby. Victoria had brought a Bible. She read it. She tried to look like any other mother out for

▲ Cuban pilot Orestes Lorenzo Perez and his family were welcomed at the White House after their daring arrival in the United States.

a day on the beach with her children. But Reyniel, who was 11, wanted to go home. He didn't want to swim. She hadn't told the boys of the plans. "Go swim," she whispered. "This is a matter of life and death." Reyniel knew something important was happening. He swam.

At five o'clock, casually, they got up to leave. At 5:45, they were standing beside the highway when they saw a plane landing two blocks away. "Run, run!" said Victoria. "It's Daddy!" The plane missed a car, a bus, a huge rock, and a traffic sign. It came to a stop about 10 yards from a truck. The startled driver managed to hit his brakes just in time. The plane's pilot, Orestes Lorenzo, stayed on the ground for about 40 seconds, which was enough time to pick up his wife and boys. Then he turned the plane around and took off. He had told his wife, in the secret message, not to talk or hug him; he would need all his powers of concentration. Twenty-one minutes and forty-three seconds later, he shouted out, "We did it!" They were in United States territory. It was December 1992, and they were free.

Bang Huy Le's mother shook his bed. He got up sleepily. Two strange men were in his house. Bang Huy, who was seven years old, was soon squeezed beside his 14-year-old sister in a small, open boat with 50 other Vietnamese. Out at sea, they were attacked by pirates, who took their few possessions. But they were lucky; they made it to Indonesia, and, six months later, to the United States. Four years after that, when Bang Huy had almost forgotten the Vietnamese language, his parents, his grandmother, his younger sister, and his two brothers all joined him in America.

The Lorenzos and the Les were part of a long immigrant tradition in America. It began tens of thousands of years ago, when the first immigrants came from Asia—on foot or by dogsled or in small boats.

The people spread out over the two great American continents. Then, just 500 years ago—an eyeblink in the long view of time—new immigrants arrived from lands across the Atlantic Ocean. It was a meeting of two worlds; each had been unaware of the other.

At first, those who settled in the region that became the United States came mostly from Great Britain (England, Scotland, Wales, and Ireland) and from Africa. The Africans came unwillingly. They were forced to become workers in a society that needed them badly.

A new nation was founded—the United States of America. It was an unusual nation—a nation of free citizens (except, of course, for those who were slaves) in a world that was mostly unfree. It was born with the idea that people could govern themselves. It was a democracy.

Freedom, and the opportunities of a big, rich land, were like a magnet. People came. Lots of different people came. Many—like many of the English before them—were failures or outcasts in their old world. Comfortable people don't usually leave their homes.

No matter where they came from, everyone wanted all the freedoms and rights that were in the U.S. Constitution. They wanted to be Americans. But some of them, being human, became jealous of the next group of newly arriving immigrants.

So, when the 19th century began to turn into the 20th, and more new people came—this time speaking Italian and Polish and Russian and Greek and Turkish and Yiddish—the earlier immigrants worried. They said the newcomers would never learn English. They said they were poor people and uneducated. They said they were outcasts. All that had been

Figures from the 2000 U.S. Census Ethnicity	
White	211,460,626
Hispanic or Latino	35,305,818
Mexican	20,640,711
Puerto Rican	3,406,178
Cuban	1,241,685
Other Hispanic or Latino	10,017,244
African American	34,658,190
Asian	10,242,998
Chinese	2,432,585
Filipino	1,850,314
People from India	1,678,765
Vietnamese	1,122,528
Korean	1,076,672
Native Hawaiian and Other Pacific Islander	874,414
Japanese	796,700
Other Asian	1,285,234
American Indian and Alaska Native	2,475,956
Others	18,521,486

Figures from the 2000 U.S. Census Total Population	
Total	281,421,906
Male	138,053,563
Female	143,368,343
Median age	35.3

▲ South Vietnamese refugees approach a U.S. warship in the South China Sea near Saigon.

said before, and much of it was true. But they had forgotten that in America something happened when people were given opportunity and freedom. The new immigrants worked hard. They invented. They built. They achieved. They learned. Soon those people from southern and eastern Europe were successful Americans, and old-timers themselves.

Then, near the end of the 20th century, another group of new immigrants began arriving. Many spoke Spanish. Some people worried that they wouldn't bother to learn English and that the United States would become a two-language nation. But it wasn't likely. Their children were like all the children before them—eager to learn.

It was the same with Asians, who now arrived in force. (Until 1965, laws restricted Asian immigration.) The Asians, like Bang Huy Le and his family, were searching for opportunity and freedom. They would find it.

People came from Africa now because they wanted to be Americans. And, like all the immigrants who had arrived before them, they brought talent and energy. Other African Americans—whose ancestors had been in America for a long, long time—were finally permitted to achieve success in large numbers. Civil rights laws had opened doors to schools and jobs that for too long had been shut.

Jesse Jackson, a 20th-century political leader, said that "America is not like a blanket—one piece of unbroken cloth, the same color, the same texture, the same size. America is more like a quilt—many pieces, many colors, many sizes, all woven and held together by a common thread."

The United States counts its citizens every 10 years when it takes a census, or poll of the population. That's when we get to see the threads and colors that make up the American quilt and compare them with quilts of the past.

In 1820, which was the first year the United States kept statistics on immigration, 8,395 foreigners entered the country with the intention of becoming citizens. Most were English, Scotch-Irish, or German, but they also included 20 Danes, 14 Russians, 6 Asians, 5 Poles, and 1 Mexican.

The 2000 census was the first in which Americans could list themselves as multiracial (but only if they wanted to). Nearly 7 million people took that option (that's 2.4 percent of the nation).

The Hispanic population more than doubled in the 10 years between 1990 and 2000, making Hispanics, at 35.3 million, about equal in number to African Americans. (By 2001, Hispanics had become the nation's largest minority.)

The 21st century's first census told us there were 281.4 million people in the United States. It showed the largest number growth in our history—we added 32.7 million between 1990 and 2000. (Many industrial nations had declining birthrates and populations in those same years.) We were adding one person every 14 seconds, or about

Figures from the 2010 U.S. Census

Here are some statistics from the most recent census data available at the time this book was printed. How has the population changed since 2000? How can this information be useful? What kinds of people and organizations might use census data?

- The U.S. population in 2010 was 308.7 million people.
- New York, Los Angeles, Chicago, Dallas, Philadelphia, and Houston were our largest cities.
- Palm Coast, Florida, was the fastest-growing city in the United States.
- The population center of the United States continues to move southwest and in 2010 was in Texas County, Missouri.
- The West grew by 13.8 percent, the South by 14.3 percent, the Midwest by 3.9 percent, and the Northeast by 3.2 percent.

America is made up of people of many races and ethnicities. ▶

6,300 every day. Of that daily gain, about 4,400 came from the larger number of births than deaths in the U.S. (10,600 over 6,200). The rest of the increase came from immigration. We added one immigrant every 35 seconds (and one person left the country every three minutes). The population increased in every state—from a half-percent in North Dakota to 66 percent in Nevada.

Here are some of the things we learned from the 2000 census:

- People were moving back to cities (a few years ago they were fleeing them).

- Four out of five Americans lived in cities or suburbs.

- New York, Los Angeles, Chicago, Houston, Philadelphia, and Phoenix were our largest cities in the 2000 census.

- Eight of our 10 largest cities gained population (only Philadelphia and Detroit shrank).

The population center of the nation shifted 40 miles southwest, from DeSoto, Missouri, (in 1990) to Edgar Springs, Missouri, (in 2000). If you imagine a flat map of the country and then have all 281.4 million Americans stand on it where they live (and assume that they all weigh exactly the same), the spot where the map balances is the population center. In 1790, the population center was in Charlestown, Maryland. It has moved steadily westward.

Other things we learned: The West grew by 19.7 percent, the South by 17.3 percent, the Midwest by 7.9 percent, and the Northeast by 5.5 percent.

Four out of five Americans live in cities or suburbs. ▼

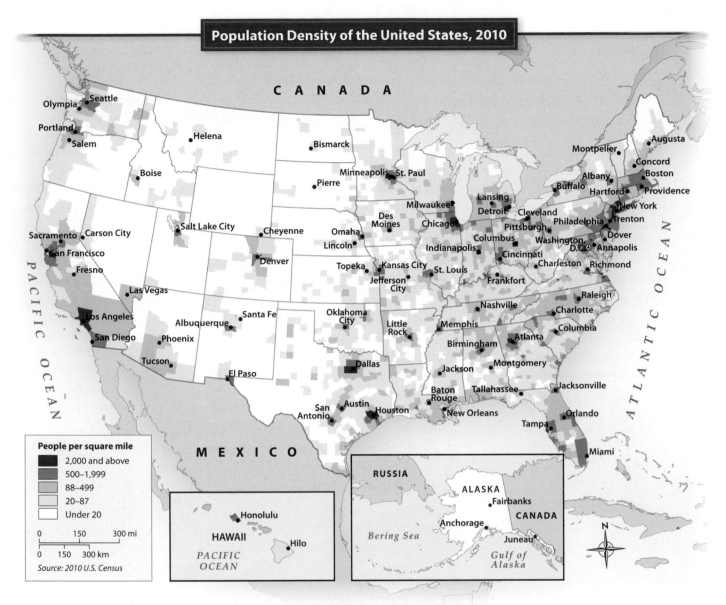

Population Density of the United States, 2010

CANADA

Olympia · Seattle
Portland · Salem
Helena
Bismarck
Boise
Minneapolis · St. Paul
Pierre
Milwaukee · Lansing
Des Moines · Detroit · Cleveland
Salt Lake City · Cheyenne
Sacramento · Carson City
San Francisco
Fresno
Omaha
Lincoln
Chicago
Columbus
Indianapolis · Cincinnati
Denver
Topeka · Kansas City · St. Louis
Jefferson City
Las Vegas
Santa Fe
Los Angeles
Albuquerque
San Diego · Phoenix
Tucson
El Paso
San Antonio · Austin · Houston
Dallas
Oklahoma City
Little Rock
Memphis
Birmingham · Atlanta
Jackson · Montgomery
Baton Rouge · Tallahassee
New Orleans
Montpelier · Augusta
Concord
Albany · Boston
Buffalo · Hartford · Providence
Pittsburgh · Philadelphia · New York · Trenton
Washington · Dover
D.C. · Annapolis
Charleston · Richmond
Frankfort
Nashville
Raleigh
Charlotte
Columbia
Jacksonville
Orlando
Tampa
Miami
Nashville

PACIFIC OCEAN

ATLANTIC OCEAN

MEXICO

RUSSIA

ALASKA
Fairbanks
Anchorage
CANADA
Bering Sea
Juneau
Gulf of Alaska

People per square mile
- 2,000 and above
- 500–1,999
- 88–499
- 20–87
- Under 20

0   150   300 mi
0   150   300 km

Source: 2010 U.S. Census

HAWAII
Honolulu
Hilo
PACIFIC OCEAN

For the first time in our history, we were evenly divided into age groups. Earlier census graphs looked like pyramids with a big, young population on the bottom and a small peak of older folk on top. The 2000 census was more like a Santa Claus with a fat stomach: 32 percent of our population was under the age of 25; 54 percent was between 25 and 60; and 14 percent was over 60.

Each census is used to reapportion seats in Congress. Shifting populations can make a political difference. New York and Pennsylvania each lost two seats in the House of Representatives. Texas, Georgia, Florida, and Arizona each gained two House members.

▲ The U.S. Constitution requires that a census of the nation be taken every 10 years. The census counts the growing and changing American population and pinpoints areas with very dense populations and areas where people are not so close together.

The New Technology

ENIAC—the name stands for *electronic numerical integrator and calculator*. ENIAC was the first all-electronic computer, which in 1946 meant that it had thousands of vacuum tubes.

ENIAC could perform numerical calculations much faster than the brains of any team of human mathematicians, but its vacuum tubes got hot; it had to be cooled down regularly.

With a machine as huge and hot as ENIAC, it didn't seem likely that computers would ever reach ordinary people. But the invention of the transistor changed all that. Scientists at Bell Telephone's research laboratory developed a device that didn't look like much—just a little piece of matter with a few wires in it—but it could do everything the vacuum tube could, and more. It boosted electrical current, produced no heat, didn't burn out, eliminated miles of wiring, was very, very small, and was very cheap to produce.

Even with transistors, you just couldn't make computers or other electronic devices small, because one transistor had to be wired to another, and that wire took up space. It was a big problem. Two American engineers, working separately, solved it. They figured out that you could etch transistors and their connections onto bits of silicon. Out of that idea came the microchip and today's technology, including pocket-sized video games, handheld and desktop computers, and other electronic wonders.

Operators of the ENIAC computer programmed the massive machine by plugging in and unplugging cables. ▼

Modern microchips made it possible to shrink computers from room-sized machines to handheld devices. ▶

▲ Communications satellites are used in television, radio, and telephone transmissions.

In the late 1970s, Californians Steven Jobs and Stephen Wozniak, operating out of Jobs's garage, developed a small computer. By 1977, sales of that computer, the Apple II, had reached $118 million. The personal computer was just getting started. Bill Gates saw its future. He imagined a computer on every desk in every office and every home, everywhere. He founded Microsoft Corporation and started selling software for computers. By 1990, he was one of the world's richest men. (By 2001, Gates had given away nearly $7.9 billion—more than any other living American philanthropist.)

▲ Steve Jobs, founder of Apple Computers Inc. (left); Microsoft Corporation's founder, Bill Gates (right)

And computers were only part of the story. They were joined by fiber optics, cable TV, satellites, fax machines, copiers, scanners, cellular phones, the Internet, automatic teller machines (ATMs, or cash machines), and an array of imaginative services. The new technology quickly became inexpensive enough for ordinary people to have in their homes and businesses.

Electing the 21st Century's First President

Democratic presidential nominee Vice President Al Gore addresses delegates at the 2000 Democratic National Convention. ▼

T he year 2000 brought a new century and a new millennium—and a presidential election. The two candidates were George Walker Bush and Albert Gore. Both came from privileged backgrounds, but otherwise they weren't much alike.

Al Gore grew up in Washington, D.C., where his father served as a Democratic senator from Tennessee. A serious kid, he went to St. Albans (a select prep school), and to Harvard, and then to Vanderbilt Law School. Gore worked himself up the political ladder from congressman to senator to vice president. He was an early voice on environmental issues like global warming.

George W. Bush was descended from a patrician New England family with substantial wealth and a tradition of public service. Young George grew up in West Texas amid oil rigs, desert dust, and wildcat oilmen. He attended Phillips Academy in Andover, Massachusetts (where his father, the former president, had gone to school), Yale (where all the Bushes went), and Harvard Business School.

Texas governor George W. Bush, son of President George H. W. Bush, campaigns in 2000. ▶

Despite the impressive schools, he failed in several business ventures (until he bought a baseball team and did well), and then he lost in his first foray into politics, running for Congress from Texas. But he had more political savvy than his critics understood.

His relaxed, affable personality made him easy to underestimate. He ran for governor of Texas, won and won again, and, at a time when the American people were looking for new faces, decided to run for president. He became the Republican candidate, and Al Gore the Democratic.

It was the longest and most expensive campaign in the history of the nation up to that time. How did it turn out? In a dead heat. It took 36 days to find out who had won. To understand what happened, you need to know about how the Electoral College works.

The Electoral College is not part of a university. It has nothing to do with a school. It has no buildings. But when the members of the Electoral College vote, it is a weighty occasion. Those college members are called "electors." Their vote decides who will be president.

Every four years, each state chooses its electors. The number of electors in a state equals its number of representatives and senators in Congress. Electors never actually get together. What they do is send their votes for president and vice president to Washington. They vote for the rest of us. This is how they do it:

In each state, the electors check the popular vote—that is, the number of votes by eligible voters for each candidate. Then—even if the vote is very close—usually all the electors' votes in that state go to the winning candidate. Although some states are reconsidering how they distribute their electoral votes, in general it's a winner-takes-all system. So, imagine you are running for president. You come in a close second in all the big states and win

TV viewing (along with the popularity of "talk" radio) has changed politics. Campaigning now takes lots of money. If you can't buy TV time (which is very expensive), it is almost impossible to win. Where do candidates get all their money? They have to woo and win the support of the rich and powerful. This reduces the political clout of ordinary citizens, who are supposed to be the foundation of a democracy.

If you want to run for Congress, where will you get money to pay for commercials? Do you see a problem if officeholders are beholden to money-givers?

▲ The 2000 presidential race remained undecided for more than a month.

most of the small states. Across the nation, you get the largest total popular vote—but you may still lose the election because your opponent gets more electoral votes.

Why do we elect our chief executives that way? We do it because that's what the Constitution says to do. (See Article 2, Section 1.)

In the year 2000, Al Gore won the popular vote, nationwide, by about half a million votes out of about 100 million cast. Gore's margin of victory was a tiny 0.5% or half of one percent of the total, though if you count numbers of voters, not percentage, it was the largest margin since Ronald Reagan won in 1984.

The electoral vote was split, with Florida's 25 electors holding the key to the election. Whoever got those 25 votes would become president. George Bush seemed the winner by a slight majority, but Florida's votes were being disputed. Substantial numbers of voters—especially African Americans—had been turned away from the polls for reasons that were later found to be invalid. Besides that, outdated voting machines had failed in many locales. And thousands of

The Electoral College

The decision to have electors came, in part, because of jealousies between the North and South at the time the Constitution was written. A direct popular vote—with only free males voting—would have given the North the choice of the president because it had a much greater free population. So the Founders came up with a system for picking electors similar to that for picking senators and representatives. That way the South was able to more than hold its own in selecting presidents. Having an Electoral College had a lot to do with balancing power.

Do you think we should have an Electoral College or should we vote directly for the president? No one knows what would happen if we abolish the Electoral College. It has helped mold the American political system. It forces politicians to pay attention to small states. But sometimes it seems to thwart the will of the people. What should we do? It's not an easy decision. It's one that needs to be considered.

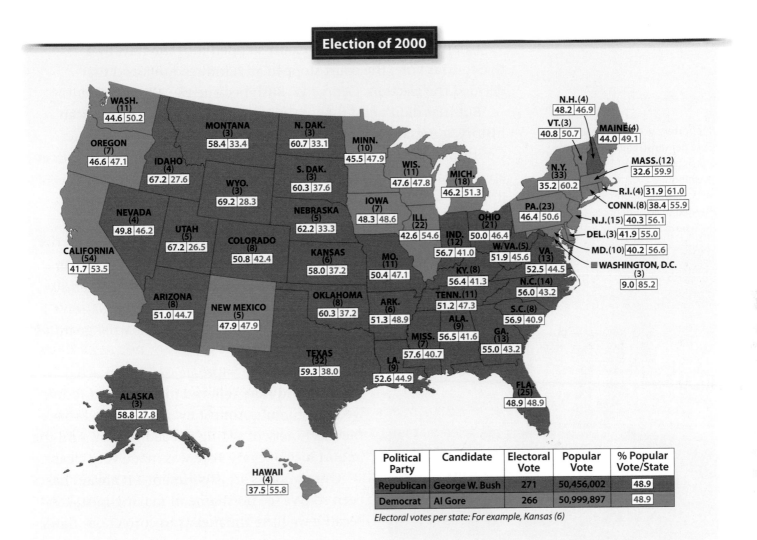

Political Party	Candidate	Electoral Vote	Popular Vote	% Popular Vote/State
Republican	George W. Bush	271	50,456,002	48.9
Democrat	Al Gore	266	50,999,897	48.9

Electoral votes per state: For example, Kansas (6)

absentee ballots (ballots sent in by voters who were not in the state at the time of the election) had been treated in different ways in different parts of the state. Election night coverage on TV made the problem worse. The major networks predicted a winner before all the polls were closed, then changed their minds, then changed again. That may have influenced many voters.

In brief, the situation in Florida was a mess.

The first thing both sides did was to bring in armies of lawyers. The Democrats wanted to recount votes by hand in several disputed counties (especially where they thought they could gain votes). The Republicans didn't want any hand recounts. Both sides sent protesters to Florida. Things got nasty.

▲ George W. Bush was the fourth candidate in United States history to lose the popular vote but win the electoral vote and, therefore, the presidency.

Finally, the U.S. Supreme Court stepped into the fray. By a five-to-four vote, the court stopped all hand recounts and that decided the election. George W. Bush became the 43rd president.

But that didn't end the turmoil. For the first time in American history, a presidential election had been decided by the Supreme Court—and by one vote. That court—with its nine unelected justices appointed for life—is the most powerful court in the world. Did it have a sound legal basis for this decision? Or had the system gone awry? One of the four dissenting justices, John Paul Stevens, wrote, "Although we may never know with complete certainty the identity of the winner of this year's presidential election, the identity of the loser is perfectly clear. It is the Nation's confidence in the judge as an impartial guardian of the rule of law."

Others felt the Supreme Court had acted properly and were relieved to see an end to five weeks of tumult. Almost everyone agreed that the machinery of voting needed reform. And the importance of every vote was made very clear.

Our nation is an experiment—it always has been so. We see no shame in making mistakes because we have the means to correct our flaws.

Supporters of both Bush and Gore demonstrated outside the U.S. Supreme Court building in Washington, D.C., as the nine justices of the Supreme Court listened to arguments by lawyers from both sides. ▼

George W. Bush shakes hands with Chief Justice William Rehnquist after being sworn in as president. In the American system of government, there can be hotly contested elections, lawsuits, and protests, but still power changes hands peacefully. ▶

Catastrophe, War, and a New Century

When the 21st century emerged, Americans were optimistic, energetic, more free than any people anywhere, and dedicated to that freedom. We were enjoying a breezy, confident, promising time of affluence and achievement. After a long and tortuous Cold War, it seemed to the average American as if the world's problems were on the way to being solved and that democracy would soon be universal. How could there be a contest? How could oppression triumph over freedom?

People flee the scene near New York's World Trade Center on September 11, 2001. ▼

Most of us were very sure of ourselves, but we were underestimating the power of demons: of anger, jealousy, poverty, and ignorance. We were the world's superpower, and often so self-absorbed that we hardly paid attention to what was going on in the rest of the world (aside from wanting global customers). We knew that a worldwide terrorist network, al-Qaeda (pronounced "al-kay-duh"), was training a generation of young men in tactics of violence, but we didn't do much about it. We'd forgotten that freedom is a delicate flower that needs nurturing or rough feet will trample it.

On September 11, 2001, something happened that jolted us from our complacency, and we and the whole world shuddered. That day, 19 terrorists hijacked four airliners, ramming two of them into the World Trade Center in New York City, one into the Pentagon in Washington, D.C., while the fourth crashed in a Pennsylvania field after a heroic takeover

Terrorists crashed two planes into the twin towers of the 110-story World Trade Center. Here, the North Tower burns as the second plane flies toward the South Tower. ▶

by passengers and crew. Officially, more than 3,000 people died (including citizens from 80 nations), and thousands of others were injured, many seriously. Most were just ordinary people—but very special to the children, parents, friends, and lovers they left behind.

It was, as President George W. Bush announced, a declaration of war by international terrorists based in the Muslim world. "This is the world's fight," said the president. The "civilized world," he said, was pitted against a terrorist network intent on "remaking the world—and imposing its radical beliefs on people everywhere."

Making September 11th still worse, we learned that the hijackers blamed us, and the world's free nations, for most of their problems. And they hated us so much they were willing to die themselves in order to kill our citizens. Being hated isn't easy to take. Especially as it was our deep beliefs—the freedom and pluralism and religious openness we so cherish—that they especially abhorred. Terrorist organizations (al-Qaeda, the political/religious Taliban in Afghanistan, and others) were teaching armies of followers to be haters, too.

These people were using the language of the Islamic religion to justify murder. They were preaching that we were Satan's children, that only they and their followers knew the truth about God, and that God would reward them for murdering us. They were religious zealots and—history shows—zealotry is uncompromising.

> A *zealot* is a person fanatically devoted to a cause.

The terrorists' message was a perversion of Islam, which rests on a foundation of peacefulness and respect for others. It was also a smokescreen that was hiding the real problems of a portion of the world where people were hurting. Much of the Middle East, despite oil riches, was an economic disaster. It was a region aching for answers.

The terrorists were destroyers, not builders. They said the killing of innocent people was a tribute to Allah (God). Around the world, religious leaders, including Muslims, recoiled in horror.

The al-Qaeda leader, a Saudi named Osama bin Laden, had been disowned by his family and kicked out of his own country. He had defiled the spirit of Islam's holy book, the *Qur'an* (also written *Koran*), with other acts of terror. Three years earlier, he had issued an unholy edict that said: "To kill Americans and their allies, both civil and military, is an

This screen shot from a training video shows recruits of Islamic militant Osama bin Laden raising their weapons at an undisclosed location in Afghanistan. ▼

individual duty of every Muslim who is able, in any country, where this is possible…." Bin Laden was calling for what he said was a *jihad*, or holy war, against America. But there is nothing holy about war (though it is sometimes necessary for protection or to end criminality).

Many Muslim leaders made it clear that bin Laden did not speak for them and that their religion is respectful of life and of all peoples and that, according to Islamic teachings, it is unholy to start a war or to kill the innocent. More than that, some Islamic scholars insist that the word *jihad* is often misused. It means to strive or struggle for a worthwhile purpose. To call killing innocent people a jihad is a distortion of its meaning, say many Muslims. (But others, throughout Islamic history, have called for jihads against nonbelievers. Words are important and disagreement over them often leads to conflict.)

One religious duty for Muslims is to make a pilgrimage to Mecca, the holiest city of Islam, in Saudi Arabia. Here, thousands of Muslims worship at sunset at the Grand Mosque in Mecca. ▼

Because we are free to read history, we know about witch burnings, crusades, and false jihads. We also know of Europe's Dark Ages when Islam was the leading world civilization and Christians and Jews participated in its affluent, tolerant multicultural cities and universities. It was Islamic scholars who preserved Greek art and science when Western nations had discarded them. And all the world became richer for it. And then something happened, and fairly quickly, so that, today, most Islamic nations are poor and troubled.

When things go wrong you can do two things: blame others, or face problems and do something about them. The killers who destroyed the World Trade Center blamed the West for troubles in their nations. Many voices, Islamic and others, saw that as cowardly. Why is there misery in so many Muslim nations? Most experts tie it to the absence of freedom.

Why did the terrorists pick on New York? Walk down New York's streets and you'll rub elbows with Pakistanis, Puerto Ricans, Japanese, Scots, Poles, Afghans, and Nigerians (many on their way to citizenship) as well as American citizens of every hue and faith and origin. Name any country you want, and you'll find someone from there in New York. And all those diverse people manage to live and work together in a free society with astonishing harmony. What a marvelous example for the world. And that's just what the zealots were attempting to destroy. Their narrow vision said there is only one way to live: their way.

We Americans reacted to the mass murders of September 11th with forceful, effective action. President George W. Bush immediately made it clear that we have no tolerance for terrorism and wrongdoing. Citizens gave him their overwhelming support.

Almost unnoticed was our astonishing response to the unprecedented emergency. New Yorkers and volunteers from around the nation responded without hesitation. Firefighters rushed to the World Trade Center and 343 died heroically trying to save others. Subways, water pipes, electricity, phone lines, and other elements of the city's infrastructure were hard

After the attack on the World Trade Center, New York firefighters struggled heroically to save lives and find victims. Three hundred forty-three firefighters died, leaving more than 600 children behind. ▼

▲ A "Tribute in Light" shines brightly over the lower Manhattan skyline to mark where the twin towers of the World Trade Center once stood.

hit, but workers quickly repaired them. A U.S. Navy hospital ship pulled into New York Harbor and provided meals, medicine, and care. Hospitals set up emergency trauma units. Schoolchildren made sandwiches for rescue and cleanup crews. Donors lined up to give blood. So many volunteer workers turned up that most had to be sent away.

Perhaps most poignant was the platform erected at ground zero so that families and others could visit the site, pray, and pay respects. Those who came left messages and notes:

"Andrew—I've been here twice looking for your beautiful smile and that twinkle in your eyes and both times God has let me know you are with Him in a safer place."

"To my dearest love, life has no meaning without you, Angela, you were appropriately named. Kind, sweet and gentle. Love you forever, Elliott"

"Daddy, a piece of me died with you on Sept. 11. You were the most important man in my life. You were my strong point. You were my daddy."

"What lies behind us and what lies before us are tiny matters compared to what lies within us," wrote the 19th-century philosopher, Ralph Waldo Emerson. After September 11th we knew that what lies within us is civic spirit, compassion, unselfishness, love, and a large measure of heroism.

▲ In the days after the 9/11 attacks, in towns and cities all over the United States and around the world, vigils were held to honor victims and show solidarity in the face of terrorism.

A Very Brief History of a Very Complex Place

In Afghanistan, Osama bin Laden, leader of the terrorist organization al-Qaeda, claimed credit for the destruction of New York's twin towers. (Much of the actual planning for 9/11 was carried out by an al-Qaeda group in Hamburg, Germany.) United States officials knew bin Laden. In the 1970s, when Afghans were fighting Russia, bin Laden had trained Muslim volunteers to fight the Russians, with American support. Some background here might help.

Afghanistan is located at a crossroads, between India, Iran, and Central Asia, where Europe and Asia find passageway to each other. Alexander the Great and his mighty Greek army marched from Persia (today's Iran) into Afghanistan in 320 B.C.E. There, Alexander faced his fiercest battles and gravest losses.

Even then, Afghanistan was a country with an ancient heritage: some of the world's first farming communities had appeared there tens of thousands of years earlier. Alexander's army learned what others would learn later: Afghans will fight foreign forces just because they are foreign.

Its people have a tradition of taking what they want from invaders—there have been many—and using it in their own ways.

After the attacks of September 11, 2001, Osama bin Laden became the world's most wanted criminal. ▼

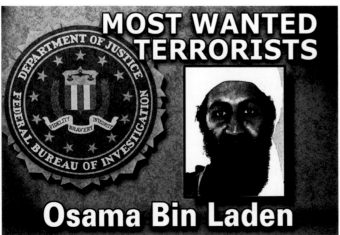

Some left their languages: Pashto (Afghan) and Farsi (Persian). An Arab-Muslim conquest in the 7th century made Islam the common religion of the region, wiping out a Greek, Hindu, Buddhist, Mongol past.

In 1747 a Pashtun leader, Ahmad Shah, established an Afghan state in the south and east; that state gradually conquered nearby Tajik, Hazara, and Uzbek areas to the north and west. Today Pashtuns make up about half of the population, Tajiks about 25 percent. (Statistics are shaky as there has been no official census in Afghanistan since 1979.)

During the 19th century Britain and Russia, fighting for dominance in Asia, sent armies and set up power bases in the region (the Persian/Iranians sent warriors, too). The British tried to rule the unruly Pashtuns, which led to disaster after disaster. On August 19, 1919, the British finally left, and today Afghans celebrate that as their independence day. In the 20th century Pashtuns led a modern monarchy; periods of corruption alternated with moderately representative government.

Then, in 1978, in a big coup, Afghanistan became what was labeled a democratic republic (most Americans called it communism). In some regions, men were forced to cut their beards, women couldn't wear the traditional long dress called a *burqa*, and many mosques were closed. Thousands were arrested and imprisoned. Devout Muslims were soon fighting liberal Muslims in a civil war over issues of modernization, power, and foreign influence. The Soviet Union sent troops and money with the hope of gaining power in the region. The U.S., under President Jimmy Carter, sent massive aid to support anti-Russian guerrilla efforts.

Osama bin Laden, a Saudi living in Afghanistan, was among those whose efforts were financed by the U.S. No one realized that he would form a terrorist group: al-Qaeda. Other anti-Russian fighters included the Taliban, an organization led by conservative Muslim scholars and religious leaders with a medieval agenda (they thought women should have almost no rights and everyone should pray to Allah exactly as

Al-Qaeda is a terrorist network, a group that operates between nations but has no national home. Its members are fundamentalist Sunni Muslims (most Sunnis don't approve of its terrorist ways) whose goal is global jihad that would remove all foreign influences from Muslim countries.

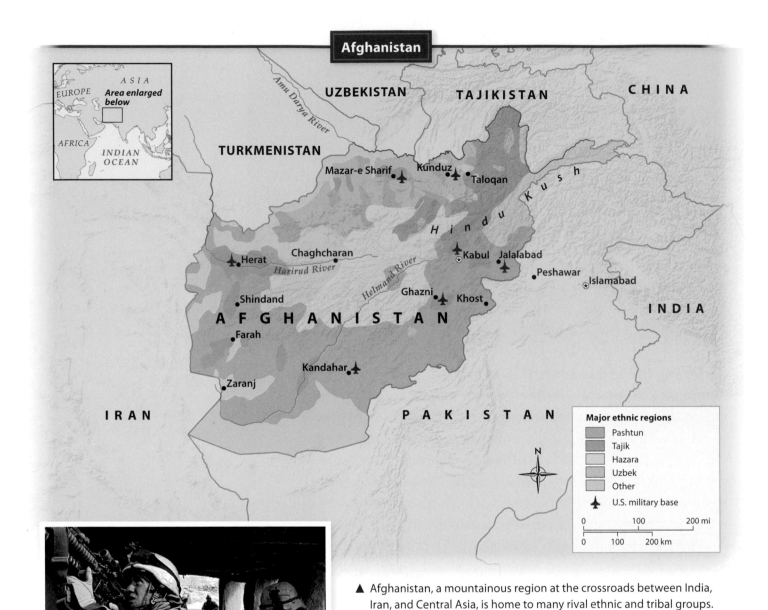

▲ Afghanistan, a mountainous region at the crossroads between India, Iran, and Central Asia, is home to many rival ethnic and tribal groups.

Major ethnic regions
- Pashtun
- Tajik
- Hazara
- Uzbek
- Other
- ✈ U.S. military base

0   100   200 mi

0   100   200 km

▲ American soldiers secure an Afghan house near al-Qaeda and Taliban strongholds.

ancient Afghans did). The Taliban's radical extremists learned how to be terrorists. The Russians, expecting to rule Afghanistan, stayed for a decade (1979–89), finally leaving in defeat, having lost 15,000 soldiers.

By the year 2000, the Taliban controlled 90 percent of the country, providing free schooling for Afghan boys (not girls) in schools called *madrassas*, where students were taught to memorize the Qur'an and hate all things "Western" or "democratic." In early 2001, Taliban militia destroyed all statues in the nation, including two ancient giant Buddhas in Bamiyan, near Kabul. Taliban religious

leaders said the figures were idolatrous and un-Islamic; much of the international community, including some Islamic nations, said they were historic treasures.

After 9/11, the United States and its allies invaded Afghanistan. We were determined to capture Osama bin Laden. But bin Laden, who wasn't Afghan and had only a small following there, soon moved to neighboring Pakistan, a nation with nuclear weapons and an unstable government. Suicide warfare and extremist tactics began to threaten Pakistan as the Taliban spread there, too.

It didn't take long for the U.S.-led coalition forces to topple the Taliban in Afghanistan. But remember, Afghanistan has a long history of resisting outside forces. The effort to bring political stability to Afghanistan would confront the U.S. and its partners with ongoing challenges and no apparent reasonable alternatives.

▲ In the dry, mountainous borderlands of Afghanistan, U.S. troops faced great challenges in trying to find and combat Taliban and al-Qaeda forces.

Osama bin Laden, who claimed responsibility for 9/11, was killed on May 2, 2011, in a raid authorized by President Barack Obama. A team of U.S. Navy SEALs and CIA agents helicoptered into bin Laden's hideout, a three-story compound behind a high wall in Abbottabad, Pakistan, where they shot him. They took his body to Afghanistan for identification; then they buried it at sea.

War in Iraq

In December 2002, a little more than a year after the September 11th attacks, the nation of Iraq delivered a 12,000-page report to the United Nations. It claimed that Iraq did *not* possess nuclear bombs or other weapons of mass destruction (known as WMDs).

Was it true? No one knew. And no one trusted Saddam Hussein, Iraq's dictator. Saddam lived in opulent palaces and ruled brutally, killing Iraqis who opposed him or whom he viewed as a threat, often just because they were from a different ethnic group. No one could predict what he might do, especially if he had WMDs.

The United States was fighting one war in the Middle East after 9/11, targeting the terrorist al-Qaeda and Taliban militias in Afghanistan, both of which operated under the influence of the radical Osama bin Laden, who had funded and developed training camps for terrorists. Bin Laden was still at large, but now President George W. Bush was turning his attention to Iraq and what he and his administration viewed as a major threat to the world: the possibility that Saddam Hussein had deadly weapons of mass destruction and a willingness to share them with terrorists.

President Bush challenged Saddam Hussein to let UN investigators into Iraq to search for WMDs. But Saddam wasn't cooperating. More than two decades earlier, Iraq had built a nuclear reactor with help from France. The reactor was not yet "hot" (operational) in June 1981 when Israel carried out a carefully planned bombing attack that destroyed the reactor and with it Iraq's nuclear program. Had Saddam rebuilt that program? There was no information that said he had. But it was known that Iraq had experimented with chemical and biological weapons. Did Saddam still have them? No one seemed to know. Much of the information concerning Saddam's capabilities and intent was classified and not available to the public. Among American government officials there was a raging debate and no agreement as to whether Iraq had the capability and the intent to use WMDs.

After Iraq invaded Kuwait in 1990, the peace terms called for Iraq to destroy (under UN supervision) all world-threatening weapons. UN inspectors entered Iraq and found and dismantled some biological facilities, but Saddam kicked them out before they could be sure there

Iraqi dictator Saddam Hussein poses with a gun for his personal photographer. ▼

was no nuclear program. Because of this lack of cooperation, the United Nations imposed sanctions, which kept Iraq from buying and selling a variety of goods on the world market, especially military supplies. Under President Clinton, the U.S. dropped bombs on targets in Iraq.

In September 2002, Iraq said that UN inspectors could return, but then wouldn't agree to the UN's conditions. Three months later, Iraq produced the 12,000-page report. The UN inspectors said there was nothing new in it, but asked for more time to negotiate. President George W. Bush wasn't willing to wait.

On March 20, 2003, a U.S.-led force invaded Iraq. Baghdad fell 21 days later, on April 9, 2003. On April 15, Saddam's hometown, Tikrit, surrendered. On May 1, President Bush declared that "In the battle of Iraq, the United States and our allies have prevailed." On December 13, a bearded, bedraggled Saddam Hussein was captured. He'd been hiding in a hole in the ground on a relative's farm.

As for those WMDs, the U.S. troops couldn't find any. It was all baffling, especially to the British and American leaders.

Iraq has a long history of tribal and religious conflict and a distaste for foreign invaders. At the end of World War I, after a long period of colonial rule, when the modern Iraqi nation was formed, it brought together various peoples that seemed to have little in common.

Americans disagreed about whether we were right to invade Iraq. Senator Robert C. Byrd of West Virginia said, "This Administration has directed all of the anger, fear, and grief which emerged from the ashes of the twin towers and the twisted metal of the Pentagon towards a tangible villain [Saddam Hussein], one we can see and hate and attack. And villain he is. But, he is the wrong villain."

The second night of war in Iraq brings heavy bombing in Baghdad and the start of the U.S. "Shock and Awe" military campaign. ▼

▲ A statue of the brutal Iraqi dictator is toppled in Baghdad on April 9, 2003.

Sunni and Shi'a (or Shi'ite)—what's the difference? Briefly, it's about leadership and the way their holy book, the Qur'an, is to be understood. Sunnis are a majority (about 85 percent of all Muslims) in most Muslim nations, except in Iran and Iraq. Sunnis usually believe in a literal interpretation of the Qur'an. Shi'as look to their religious leaders, the Imams, as God's infallible voice on religious truth.

The Sunnis and the Shi'as (competing branches of Islam) each wanted to dominate the other. The Kurds (mostly Sunni Muslim, and not Arabs) wanted independence from their Arab neighbors.

So, almost as soon as President George W. Bush declared the battle of Iraq officially over in May 2003, another battle began. This was not army vs. army, it was suicide bombers and car bombs blowing up innocent bystanders. It was an insurgents' war, which is a rebellion against those in control.

The American and British forces were trying to establish a democracy in Iraq and turn the nation over to Iraqi leaders. But, like most wars, this one didn't go as intended.

For the most part the insurgents were Sunni extremists, who were a minority in Iraq but, under Saddam, had been a ruling elite. They were caught up in anti-American and anti-Western hatreds as well as centuries-old religious and regional conflicts and a desire to regain power. Complicating things was the oil, and its riches, that went to those in power. U.S. and coalition forces, hampered by poor intelligence and little knowledge of Islamic culture, made some bad mistakes, which didn't help.

As to the war in Iraq, some people were calling it a clash of cultures. But that was too simplistic. Most Muslims clearly preferred peace to war and freedom to tyranny.

Oil complicated matters in Iraq. Here, waste gas is burned off at an Iraqi oil plant. ▼

A woman mourns as victims of a suicide bomber are brought to a hospital morgue in Baqouba, Iraq. ▶

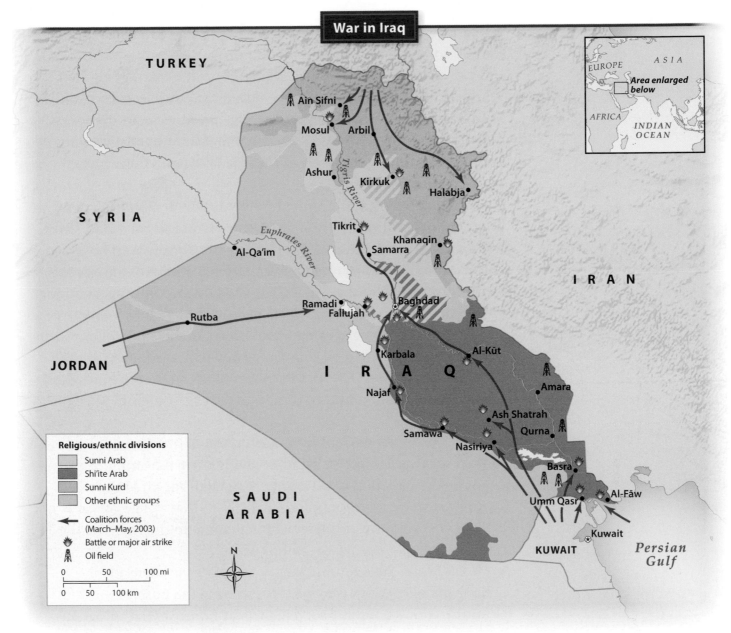

▲ Iraq, situated on the Tigris and Euphrates Rivers, where civilization began, is a complex country divided by religious and ethnic conflict. Shortly after achieving a quick military victory in 2003, coalition forces faced a difficult insurgency.

This was about terrorists, people with a fervent belief that they want to impose on others usually by violent means. It was a civil war with religious groups fighting for power and old anti-Western feelings complicating things.

For the United States and its allies there was a timely question: How do we deal with cultures that have completely different traditions, laws, and ways of organizing themselves from ours? And, should we impose our treasured concepts of freedom and democracy on others?

Blowing in the Wind

Almost all of the 20th-century presidents, starting with Franklin D. Roosevelt, attempted to acquire executive power beyond that described in the Constitution. Usually the claim was that national security, or war, or other emergencies made enhanced executive power necessary.

Back in April 1952 the United Steel Workers demanded a raise in wages for its workers; the steel industry refused, and a steel strike was called. Harry S. Truman was fighting the Korean War; he issued an executive order directing the secretary of commerce to seize the steel mills to prevent the strike. The president said, during a national emergency (in this case, a war), the executive branch becomes supreme and does not need approval from Congress for actions in the national interest. The steel companies were outraged; they went to court in protest. The U.S. Supreme Court decided that the president is not all-powerful even in wartime and that he could not seize the steel industry.

In 2004, President George W. Bush claimed that he had the power to hold suspected terrorists without giving them a hearing. Supreme Court Justice Sandra Day O'Connor disagreed. She cited the steel seizure case. "We have long since made clear that a state of war is not a blank check for the president when it comes to the rights of the nation's citizens," Justice O'Connor wrote.

In 2005 and 2006, during Bush's second term as president, congressional hearings were held to examine the Bush administration's domestic surveillance (at-home spying) programs. Again, the steel seizure case was cited. Again, our nation faced the thorny question: How much power and flexibility should the chief executive have in a crisis or an emergency?

Before that question got answered, some fast-blowing winds made Americans focus on state and local issues. In August 2005, a hurricane formed over the Bahama Islands. Named Katrina, it moved over Florida as a moderate Category 1 hurricane causing a few deaths and some flooding. Any hurricane means serious winds, damage, and usually floods. A Category 1 is the mildest; a Category 3 can be really bad; a Category 5 is the worst. After leaving Florida, Katrina picked up speed and strength as it traveled over unusually warm currents in the Gulf of Mexico. Roaring and blowing, it headed for a swath of land stretching from Texas to Louisiana.

Katrina, still over the Gulf, became a Category 5. More than a million people left New Orleans in the largest mass evacuation from a major American city ever.

But not everyone left. For some there was no transportation; others, who didn't understand the urgency, thought they could make it through the storm; a few, without radios, never realized what was coming. Looters, with criminal intent, thought they could outwit the storm.

New Orleans sits in a bowl at the mouth of the Mississippi River (the delta), stretching from the river to big, round Lake Pontchartrain. The original city was built on rare high land at the river's edge. As the city grew, waterways were opened to Pontchartrain to promote boat commerce. Then, in the 1940s, the state filled those waterways, and homes and buildings were put on the filled land. Further low

◄ This meteorological image reveals the deadly swirls of Hurricane Katrina.

land got developed when large areas of marshland and swamp were drained. Meanwhile, the town's underlying water table fell drastically. So New Orleans began to sink. By 2001, 51 percent of the land surface in greater New Orleans subdivisions (called "parishes") was at or below sea level.

Federally built levees were designed to keep the water out and the city dry, but over time there were many warnings that in a major storm the levees might not hold. Almost everyone knew they needed to be strengthened. Flooding was not unusual in parts of the city.

Katrina hit Gulf Coast communities east of New Orleans early Monday, August 29, as a Category 3 fury with sustained winds that reached 125 mph (205 km/h). At 9 a.m., the eye passed slightly to the east of New Orleans, over Lake Pontchartrain. Lake water surged 15 feet above the norm and the levee walls, meant to protect New Orleans, weren't able to hold back Katrina's wrath. Water poured through breaks in the levees, quickly flooding the city.

By late afternoon, New Orleans is dark, it has no electricity, and there is no fresh water to drink. Bodies of drowned people and animals float in what, the day before, had been city streets. Some people have

Floodwaters engulfed much of New Orleans after the historic city's defenses were breached by Hurricane Katrina. ▼

climbed onto rooftops to escape flooded homes and are calling for help. The Louisiana Superdome is an evacuation center, but Katrina has torn two holes in its roof and wind and water damage make it a stinking mess.

FEMA (the Federal Emergency Management Agency) is slow to respond to the disaster in New Orleans. Meanwhile, oil refineries (there are lots of them in Louisiana) are sloshing oily ooze into the water. They stop refining oil, which sends oil prices up around the globe.

By Tuesday, floodwaters cover 80 percent of New Orleans and they don't recede. Houses, shops, restaurants, and office buildings are stuck inside a deep, dirty, toxic moat. The water will stay for weeks. Now evacuation helicopters begin rescuing people from rooftops and buildings. Rescuers in rowboats bang on rooftops and wait for a response.

At least 1,836 people die in what is one of the deadliest natural disasters in American history. It is the costliest. New Orleans in 2005 produces incredible examples of heroism and selflessness, but there is also looting and criminal disorder.

Slowly, New Orleans begins to recover: its heroes are mostly ordinary people who roll up their sleeves and help their neighbors. Downed trees, wet mattresses, destroyed homes, decayed food, and noxious mold clutter the soggy city; before there can be any rebuilding the debris has to be collected and bagged. From across the nation, and the world, people respond to the city's tragedy with astonishing generosity. Some come to New Orleans to do what they can to help. Many communities, like Houston, open their homes and halls to Katrina refugees.

Eventually the president approves more than $110 billion in disaster relief funds and visits the Gulf region more than a dozen times. But the slow response to Katrina becomes a public relations disaster for the administration. For those in New Orleans, it is a human and city disaster; for the nation as a whole, it is a devastating example of the cost of bureaucratic indifference to known problems. And four years later, thousands of Katrina victims in Mississippi and Louisiana are still living in temporary trailers.

▲ The Coast Guard hoists a man to safety from the top of a vehicle in the flooded streets of New Orleans.

The Iraq War Continues

The Iraq War, which was supposed to be quick and clean with no cost to the American taxpayer (oil revenue was expected to pay for it), goes on and on. By 2007, it has lasted longer than World War II. By the end of 2009, it has cost more than the Vietnam War. More than 4,000 American soldiers have been killed, More than 100,000 Iraqis are dead, hundreds of thousands in the Middle East are displaced, and the war's cost—hundreds of billions of dollars—begins to hurt the American economy.

Information emerges, slowly making it clear that there were no links between the 9/11 terrorists and Iraq. Saddam Hussein's cruel dictatorship had one plus: he kept terrorist groups out of Iraq. Now terrorists are setting off roadside bombs with regularity. While the addition of thousands of American soldiers (called "the surge") does bring some safety to Iraqi streets, for the most part, at home and abroad, things aren't going well.

The Bush administration suspends the basic constitutional right of habeas corpus for prisoners of war. Some prisoners are being held, without access to lawyers or free trials, at an American-run prison in

A young boy runs past victims and burning debris after bomb blasts in a densely populated section of Karbala, Iraq. ▶

Iraq called Abu Ghraib, at the Guantánamo Bay Naval Base on the island of Cuba, and elsewhere.

Administration spokespersons say that the war on terror has changed global ground rules and that new tactics are essential. But nations that had once looked to the United States for inspiration and moral leadership are beginning to produce suicide bombers eager to kill Americans.

In the United States, polls show that most Americans are tired of the war and its many costs. Needs at home, like health care and education funding, are being neglected.

The end of the Cold War left us as the most powerful country the world has known. We took on a role as the world's peacekeeper—but is that something that Americans really want? Americans were beginning to ask: Can we afford the expense of a huge global military empire? Should other wealthy nations be sharing costs when there is a crisis that demands military intervention? Does an American military presence create conflict inside nations that resent foreign troops? Do our troops truly act as peacekeepers?

In late 2008 and early 2009, the nation and the world were gripped by a paralyzing financial crisis. The crisis was sparked by the collapse of the housing market in the United States. The collapse of the housing market would have been bad enough, but then the nation's major investment banks began to falter. In Detroit, General Motors and Chrysler, two of the three American automakers, declared bankruptcy, costing tens of thousands of workers their jobs. By the fall of 2009, the nation's unemployment rate had climbed to 10 percent, meaning that one out of every 10 adults was out of work.

By 2009, the United States was fighting two major wars (in Iraq and Afghanistan), the debt was astronomical, and the economy was in the worst tailspin since the Great Depression. Where was the nation heading? Where should it head? No one seemed to know.

The financial crisis of 2008 was spurred by the failure of major automakers and banks and by the collapse of the housing market. ▼

CHAPTER 69

Both Lucky and Ready

Barack Hussein Obama, a mostly unknown Illinois state legislator, is running for a seat in the U.S. Senate when he gets a telephone call from John Kerry's campaign manager asking if he will deliver the keynote speech at the Democratic convention in 2004. Obama thinks for a few minutes and says, "I know exactly what I want to say…I really want to talk about my story as part of the larger American story."

And that's exactly what he does a few months later when he tells those at the convention, and a larger audience watching on television, about his Kenyan father who herded goats as a child, about his Kansas-born mother, his grandfather who enlisted in Patton's army during World War II, and his grandmother who worked on a bomber assembly line.

I stand here knowing that my story is part of the larger American story, that I owe a debt to all of those who came before me, and that, in no other country on earth, is my story even possible.

Barack Obama, then a candidate for the United States Senate from Illinois, delivers the keynote address at the 2004 Democratic National Convention. ▼

By 2004, many Americans are tired of war and tired of divisive politics; the speech focuses on what we all share: a belief in the ideas that have made the United States unique. It is a speech full of ringing oratory and patriotism. Obama affirms:

> *There's not a liberal America and a conservative America; there's the United States of America. There's not a black America and white America and Latino America and Asian America; there's the United States of America.*

Even before Barack Obama finishes it is clear that with this powerful speech he has catapulted himself onto the national scene. Just four years later, he will win the Democratic nomination for president.

▲ New York senator Hillary Clinton campaigns for the 2008 Democratic nomination for president. She lost to Senator Barack Obama of Illinois.

In the race for the Democratic nomination, Obama began well behind the Democratic Party front-runner, Hillary Clinton. Many expected, and hoped, that she would become the first woman president.

Obama has been a community organizer in Chicago, a law school professor, an Illinois congressman, and, briefly, a U.S. senator. It isn't a whole lot of experience, but that is part of his appeal. He doesn't seem to be part of the Washington scene at a time when most Americans disapprove of what has been going on in the capital city.

Obama campaigns as a candidate of change. He puts together a talented and disciplined campaign staff; they will try to bring as many new people to the polls as possible. They register millions of potential voters, especially young people, and are successful in expanding the electorate. Using the Internet effectively, they raise money from a broad swath of Americans. Obama finds a catchphrase to inspire his followers: "Yes, we can!" he shouts.

The Republican candidate, John McCain, is an experienced senator who calls himself a "maverick." McCain was a prisoner of war in Hanoi during the Vietnam War and responded to torture and other indignities with strength and integrity. He seems to represent

Veteran Republican senator John McCain of Arizona lost ground as Election Day approached. ▼

the best when it comes to traditional American values. But in 2008 most Americans aren't looking for traditions; they want new faces and new ideas and it is McCain's running mate, Alaska's governor Sarah Palin, who begins to draw cheering crowds that rival those of Barack Obama. Palin is controversial and she doesn't have much background in national politics, but she adds fire and excitement to the campaign.

A year earlier most pundits didn't think Obama had a chance to capture the Democratic nomination. Hillary Clinton was a formidable candidate. After that, John McCain fought in what was a tight race, but the seemingly endless Iraq War, the erupting financial crisis, and the appeal of a candidate who focused on change began to swing undecided voters. By Election Day, November 4, it is the size of the Obama victory that many believe is uncertain.

Yet only as the voting returns are tabulated, does what is happening seem to hit TV commentators and people across the country. The United States, with its lofty ideals, has lived with a nasty reality that it has often tried to ignore, but the awfulness of racism and other prejudices has affected America since its beginnings.

The First Hispanic Supreme Court Justice

In August 2009, Judge Sonia Sotomayor is confirmed by the U.S. Senate as the first Hispanic justice on the Supreme Court.

Sonia Sotomayor, raised by a single, widowed parent (her mom) in a Bronx housing project (a stone's throw from Manhattan's Harlem), worked hard in high school, got into an Ivy League college (Princeton), became a lawyer (at Yale Law School), and then a judge. She has conquered towering obstacles to make it to the top of the legal world. President Barack Obama says, "With this historic vote the Senate has affirmed that Judge Sotomayor has the intellect, the temperament, the history, the integrity and the independence of mind to ably serve on our nation's highest court." He calls it another step that moves the nation closer "to a more perfect union."

▲ Supreme Court Justice Sonia Sotomayor

▲ President-elect Barack Obama, with his wife and daughters, greets an enormous and exuberant Chicago crowd on election night.

Now the United States is electing an African American as chief executive. That means that any American, whatever his or her background, has a chance to rise to the top. Can that really be true?

After John McCain graciously concedes defeat, President-elect Barack Obama, his wife, Michelle, and their daughters stand onstage at Chicago's Grant Park. To an excited crowd of well-wishers he says, "If there is anyone out there who still doubts that America is a place where all things are possible, who still wonders if the dream of our founders is alive in our time, who still questions the power of our democracy, tonight is your answer."

"A Call to Action"

In 2009, Barack Obama was awarded the Nobel Peace Prize for his "extraordinary efforts to strengthen international diplomacy and cooperation between peoples." The committee praised "Obama's vision of and work for a world without nuclear weapons." Most Americans were proud, but some felt he hadn't been president long enough to have solid achievements in the field. Obama himself said:

To be honest, I do not feel that I deserve to be in the company of so many of the transformative figures who've been honored by this prize—men and women who've inspired me and inspired the entire world through their courageous pursuit of peace.

But I also know that throughout history the Nobel Peace Prize has not just been used to honor specific achievement; it's also been used as a means to give momentum to a set of causes. That is why I've said that I will accept this award as a call to action, a call for all nations and all peoples to confront the common challenges of the 21st century. These challenges won't all be met during my presidency, or even my lifetime. But I know these challenges can be met so long as it's recognized that they will not be met by one person or one nation alone.

This award—and the call to action that comes with it—does not belong simply to me or my administration; it belongs to all people around the world who have fought for justice and for peace. And most of all, it belongs to you, the men and women of America, who have dared to hope and have worked so hard to make our world a little better.

So today we humbly recommit to the important work that we've begun together. I'm grateful that you've stood with me thus far, and I'm honored to continue our vital work in the years to come.

In January 2009, flags wave at President Obama's inauguration in Washington, D.C. ▼

APPENDIX:
SOME PRIMARY
SOURCES

From Franklin D. Roosevelt, First Inaugural Address (1933)

On a bleak March day, Franklin D. Roosevelt took the oath of office as president and assured the public that "the only thing we have to fear is fear itself." With words of optimism and hope, Roosevelt backed an active role for government in addressing the Great Depression. He pledged "to wage war against the emergency as great as the power that would be given me if we were...invaded by a foreign foe."

The Depression demanded action to revive the economy and calm the public's fears. With his infectious optimism and self-assurance, Roosevelt succeeded in restoring people's hopes. In his inaugural address he promised decisive action, and during the first 100 days of his administration he pushed 15 major bills through Congress. The federal government provided insurance to protect bank deposits, federal regulations to protect stock-market investors, jobs programs, and subsidies to farmers.

consecration: blessing

induction: installation

candor: honesty

impels: demands

pre-eminently: overwhelmingly

assert: strongly state

President Hoover, Mr. Chief Justice, my friends:

This is a day of national consecration, and I am certain that my fellow-Americans expect that on my induction into the Presidency I will address them with a candor and a decision which the present situation of our nation impels.

This is pre-eminently the time to speak the truth, the whole truth, frankly and boldly. Nor need we shrink from honestly facing conditions in our country today. This great nation will endure as it has endured, will revive and will prosper.

So first of all let me assert my firm belief that the only thing we have to fear is fear itself—nameless, unreasoning, unjustified terror which paralyzes needed efforts to convert retreat into advance.

In every dark hour of our national life a leadership of frankness and vigor has met with that understanding and support of the people themselves which is essential to victory.

I am convinced that you will again give that support to leadership in these critical days.

In such a spirit on my part and on yours we face our common difficulties. They concern, thank God, only material things. Values have shrunken to fantastic levels; taxes have risen; our ability to pay has fallen, government of all kinds is faced by serious curtailment of income; the means of exchange are frozen in the currents of trade; the withered leaves of industrial enterprise lie on every side; farmers find no markets for their produce; the savings of many years in thousands of families are gone.

curtailment: lowering

More important, a host of unemployed citizens face the grim problem of existence, and an equally great number toil with little return. Only a foolish optimist can deny the dark realities of the moment.

Yet our distress comes from no failure of substance. We are stricken by no plague of locusts. Compared with the perils which our forefathers conquered because they believed and were not afraid, we have still much to be thankful for. Nature still offers her bounty and human efforts have multiplied it. Plenty is at our doorstep, but a generous use of it languishes in the very sight of the supply.

stricken: hit by

plague of locusts: biblical disaster

perils: dangers

languishes: wastes away

Primarily, this is because the rulers of the exchange of mankind's goods have failed through their own stubbornness and their own incompetence, have admitted their failure and abdicated. Practices of the unscrupulous money changers stand indicted in the court of public opinion, rejected by the hearts and minds of men.

True, they have tried, but their efforts have been cast in the pattern of an outworn tradition. Faced by failure of credit, they have proposed only the lending of more money.

Stripped of the lure of profit by which to induce our people to follow their false leadership, they have resorted to exhortations, pleading tearfully for restored confidence. They know only the rules of a generation of self-seekers.

abdicated: given up

unscrupulous money changers: selfish bankers; a New Testament reference

outworn: outgrown

credit: loans

lure: appeal

induce: coax

exhortations: pleas

They have no vision, and when there is no vision the people perish.

The money changers have fled from their high seats in the temple of our civilization. We may now restore that temple to the ancient truths.

The measure of the restoration lies in the extent to which we apply social values more noble than mere monetary profit.

Happiness lies not in the mere possession of money; it lies in the joy of achievement, in the thrill of creative effort.

The joy and moral stimulation of work no longer must be forgotten in the mad chase of evanescent profits. These dark days will be worth all they cost us if they teach us that our true destiny is not to be ministered unto but to minister to ourselves and to our fellow-men.

Recognition of the falsity of material wealth as the standard of success goes hand in hand with the abandonment of the false belief that public office and high political position are to be valued only by the standards of pride of place and personal profit; and there must be an end to a conduct in banking and in business which too often has given to a sacred trust the likeness of callous and selfish wrongdoing.

Small wonder that confidence languishes, for it thrives only on honesty, on honor, on the sacredness of obligations, on faithful protection, on unselfish performance. Without them it cannot live.

Restoration calls, however, not for changes in ethics alone. This nation asks for action, and action now.

Our greatest primary task is to put people to work. This is no unsolvable problem if we face it wisely and courageously.

It can be accomplished in part by direct recruiting by the government itself, treating the task as we would treat the emergency of a war, but at the same time, through this employment, accomplishing greatly needed projects to stimulate and reorganize the use of our natural resources.

Hand in hand with this, we must frankly recognize the overbalance of population in our industrial centers and, by engaging on a national scale in the redistribution, endeavor to provide a better use of the land for those best fitted for the land.

The task can be helped by definite efforts to raise the values of agricultural products and with this the power to purchase the output of our cities.

It can be helped by preventing realistically the tragedy of the growing loss, through foreclosure, of our small homes and our farms.

foreclosure: when banks repossess (take back) something because the owner cannot pay back a loan

It can be helped by insistence that the Federal, State and local governments act forthwith on the demand that their cost be drastically reduced.

It can be helped by the unifying of relief activities which today are often scattered, uneconomical and unequal. It can be helped by national planning for and supervision of all forms of transportation and of communications and other utilities which have a definitely public character.

There are many ways in which it can be helped, but it can never be helped merely by talking about it. We must act, and act quickly.

Finally, in our progress toward a resumption of work we require two safeguards against a return of the evils of the old order; there must be a strict supervision of all banking and credits and investments; there must be an end to speculation with other people's money, and there must be provision for an adequate but sound currency.

These are the lines of attack. I shall presently urge upon a new Congress in special session detailed measures for their fulfillment, and I shall seek the immediate assistance of the several States....

I am prepared under my constitutional duty to recommend the measures that a stricken nation in the midst of a stricken world may require.

These measures, or such other measures as the Congress may build out of its experience and wisdom, I shall seek, within my constitutional authority, to bring to speedy adoption.

But in the event that the Congress shall fail to take one of these two courses, and in the event that the national emergency is still critical, I shall not evade the clear course of duty that will then confront me.

I shall ask the Congress for the one remaining instrument to meet the crisis—broad executive power to wage a war against the emergency as great as the power that would be given me if we were in fact invaded by a foreign foe.

For the trust reposed in me I will return the courage and the devotion that befit the time. I can do no less.

We face the arduous days that lie before us in the warm courage of national unity; with the clear consciousness of seeking old and precious moral values; with the clean satisfaction that comes from the stern performance of duty by old and young alike.

We aim at the assurance of a rounded and permanent national life.

We do not distrust the future of essential democracy. The people of the United States have not failed. In their need they have registered a mandate that they want direct, vigorous action.

They have asked for discipline and direction under leadership. They have made me the present instrument of their wishes. In the spirit of the gift I take it.

In this dedication of a nation we humbly ask the blessing of God. May He protect each and every one of us! May He guide me in the days to come!

evade: avoid, escape from

instrument: legal tool

arduous: difficult

mandate: order

Emma Lazarus, "The New Colossus" (1935)

A gift from France in 1884, the Statue of Liberty was originally meant to symbolize the friendship and commitment to liberty shared by the French and American people. But for millions of immigrants it has been a beacon of freedom and opportunity. Emma Lazarus gave powerful expression to this idea in her poem "The New Colossus." The poem's title refers to the Colossus of Rhodes, a giant bronze statue of the sun god Helios that stood near the harbor of the Greek island of Rhodes. As a young woman who was born to a privileged New York City family, Lazarus wrote poems that brought her to the attention of Ralph Waldo Emerson and Henry Wadsworth Longfellow. Attacks on Jews in Russia in 1881 and 1882 inspired Lazarus, who was Jewish, to become an ardent defender of Jews fleeing anti-Semitism in Czarist Russia. She wrote "The New Colossus" for an auction that raised money for the statue's pedestal. Lazarus died of cancer at the age of 38, just a few years after writing her famous poem.

Not like the brazen giant of Greek fame,
With conquering limbs astride from land to land,
Here at our sea-washed, sunset gates shall stand
A mighty woman with a torch, whose flame
Is the imprisoned lightning, and her name
Mother of Exile. From her beacon-hand
Glows world-wide welcome; her mild eyes command
The air-bridged harbor that twin cities frame.
"Keep, ancient lands, your storied pomp!" cries she
With silent lips. "Give me your tired, your poor,
Your huddled masses yearning to breathe free,
The wretched refuse of your teeming shore.
Send these, the homeless, tempest-tost to me,
I lift my lamp beside the golden door!"

brazen: made of brass

From Franklin D. Roosevelt, "The Four Freedoms": Message to Congress (1941)

In 1941, in his annual State of the Union message, President Franklin D. Roosevelt called for "a world founded on four essential freedoms. Freedom of speech and expression, freedom of worship, freedom from want, and freedom from fear." The United States would not enter World War II for another 11 months. But in his speech, the president contrasted American values with those of Nazi Germany, which emphasized racial purity and military conquest. Roosevelt used his State of the Union address to urge support for nations such as Britain that were fighting to preserve democratic values. He requested a "lend-lease" program to supply Britain with war equipment to fight Germany. After hearing Roosevelt's address, the country's foremost illustrator, Norman Rockwell, began to paint images of the president's Four Freedoms. These images became powerful national symbols during World War II.

To the Congress of the United States:

I address you, the Members of the Seventy-Seventh Congress, at a moment unprecedented in the history of the Union. I use the word "unprecedented," because at no previous time has American security been as seriously threatened from without as it is today....

unprecedented: something that has not happened before

It is true that prior to 1914 the United States often had been disturbed by events in other Continents. We had even engaged in two wars with European nations and in a number of undeclared wars in the West Indies, in the Mediterranean and in the Pacific for the maintenance of American rights and for the principles of peaceful commerce. In no case, however, had a serious threat been raised against our national safety or our independence.

convey: express

What I seek to convey is the historic truth that the United States as a nation has at all times maintained opposition to any attempt to lock us in behind an ancient Chinese wall while the procession of civilization went past. Today, thinking of our children and their children, we oppose enforced isolation for ourselves or for any part of the Americas.

Even when the World War broke out in 1914, it seemed to contain only small threat of danger to our own American future. But, as time went on, the American people began to visualize what the downfall of democratic nations might mean to our own democracy.

We need not over-emphasize imperfections in the Peace of Versailles. We need not harp on failure of the democracies to deal with problems of world deconstruction. We should remember that the Peace of 1919 was far less unjust than the kind of "pacification" which began even before Munich, and which is being carried on under the new order of tyranny that seeks to spread over every continent today. The American people have unalterably set their faces against that tyranny.

Every realist knows that the democratic way of life is at this moment being directly assailed in every part of the world— assailed either by arms, or by secret spreading of poisonous propaganda by those who seek to destroy unity and promote discord in nations still at peace. During sixteen months this assault has blotted out the whole pattern of democratic life in an appalling number of independent nations, great and small. The assailants are still on the march, threatening other nations, great and small.

Therefore, as your President, performing my constitutional duty to "give to the Congress information of the state of the Union," I find it necessary to report that the future and the safety of our country and of our democracy are overwhelmingly involved in events far beyond our borders.

Armed defense of democratic existence is now being gallantly waged in four continents. If that defense fails, all the population and all the resources of Europe, Asia, Africa and Australasia will be dominated by the conquerors. The total of those populations and their resources greatly exceeds the sum total of the population and resources of the whole of the Western Hemisphere—many times over.

Peace of Versailles: the 1919 treaty that ended World War I

pacification: making peace with an enemy by giving up more than is wise

tyranny: rule by a single, all-powerful leader

propaganda: information, often untrue, spread to make people believe something

gallantly: heroically

In times like these it is immature—and incidentally untrue—for anybody to brag that an unprepared America, single-handed, and with one hand tied behind its back, can hold off the whole world....

First, by an impressive expression of the public will and without regard to partisanship, we are committed to all-inclusive national defense.

Second, by an impressive expression of the public will and without regard to partisanship, we are committed to full support of all those resolute peoples, everywhere, who are resisting aggression and are thereby keeping war away from our Hemisphere. By this support, we express our determination that the democratic cause shall prevail; and we strengthen the defense and security of our own nation.

Third, by an impressive expression of the public will and without regard to partisanship we are committed to the proposition that principles of mortality and considerations for our own security will never permit us to acquiesce in a peace dictated by aggressors and sponsored by appeasers. We know that enduring peace cannot be bought at the cost of other people's freedom.

In the recent national election there was no substantial difference between the two great parties in respect to that national policy. No issue was fought out on this line before the American electorate. Today, it is abundantly evident that American citizens everywhere are demanding and supporting speedy and complete action in recognition of obvious danger. Therefore, the immediate need is a swift and driving increase in our armament production....

Our most useful and immediate role is to act as an arsenal for them as well as for ourselves. They do not need man power. They do need billions of dollars worth of the weapons of defense....

Let us say to the democracies: "We Americans are vitally concerned in your defense of freedom. We are putting forth our energies, our resources and our organizing powers to give

partisanship: party politics inside the country

mortality: death

acquiesce: go along with

you the strength to regain and maintain a free world. We shall send you, in ever-increasing numbers, ships, planes, tanks, guns. This is our purpose and our pledge."...

As men do not live by bread alone, they do not fight by armaments alone. Those who man our defenses, and those behind them who build our defenses, must have the stamina and courage which come from an unshakable belief in the manner of life which they are defending. The mighty action which we are calling for cannot be based on a disregard of all things worth fighting for.

armament: weapons

stamina: long-term strength

The Nation takes great satisfaction and much strength from the things which have been done to make its people conscious of their individual stake in the preservation of democratic life in America. Those things have toughened the fibre of our people, have renewed their faith and strengthened their devotion to the institutions we make ready to protect. Certainly this is no time to stop thinking about the social and economic problems which are the root cause of the social revolution which is today a supreme factor in the world.

fibre: basic character

There is nothing mysterious about the foundations of a healthy and strong democracy. The basic things expected by our people of their political and economic systems are simple. They are: equality of opportunity for youth and for others; jobs for those who can work; security for those who need it; the ending of special privilege for the few; the preservation of civil liberties for all; the enjoyment of the fruits of scientific progress in a wider and constantly rising standard of living.

These are the simple and basic things that must never be lost sight of in the turmoil and unbelievable complexity of our modern world. The inner and abiding strength of our economic and political systems is dependent upon the degree to which they fulfill these expectations.

turmoil: confusion

Many subjects connected with our social economy call for immediate improvement. As examples: We should bring more citizens under the coverage of old age pensions and unemployment insurance. We should widen the opportunities

social economy: parts of the economic life of the country that affect people's well-being

for adequate medical care. We should plan a better system by which persons deserving or needing gainful employment may obtain it.

I have called for personal sacrifice. I am assured of the willingness of almost all Americans to respond to that call....

In the future days, which we seek to make secure, we look forward to a world founded upon four essential human freedoms.

The first is freedom of speech and expression—everywhere in the world.

The second is freedom of every person to worship God in his own way—everywhere in the world.

The third is freedom from want—which, translated into world terms, means economic understandings which will secure to every nation a healthy peace time life for its inhabitants—everywhere in the world.

The fourth is freedom from fear—which, translated into world terms, means a worldwide reduction of armaments to such a point and in such a thorough fashion that no nation will be in a position to commit an act of physical aggression against any neighbor—anywhere in the world.

That is no vision of a distant millennium. It is a definite basis for a kind of world attainable in our own time and generation. That kind of world is the very antithesis of the so-called new order of tyranny which the dictators seek to create with the crash of a bomb.

To that new order we oppose the greater conception—the moral order. A good society is able to face schemes of world domination and foreign revolutions alike without fear.

Since the beginning of our American history we have been engaged in change—in a perpetual peaceful revolution—a revolution which goes on steadily, quietly adjusting itself to changing conditions—without the concentration camp or the quick-lime in the ditch. The world order which we seek is the cooperation of free countries, working together in a friendly, civilized society.

millennium: time of perfect happiness, far in the future

antithesis: opposite

quick-lime: substance that eats away and dissolves organic matter

This nation has placed its destiny in the hands and heads and hearts of its millions of free men and women; and its faith in freedom under the guidance of God. Freedom means the supremacy of human rights everywhere. Our support goes to those who struggle to gain those rights or keep them. Our strength is in our unity of purpose.

To that high concept there can be no end save victory.

supremacy: overall importance

John F. Kennedy, "Ask Not What Your Country Can Do for You": Inaugural Address (1961)

John F. Kennedy was the first president born in the 20th century and the youngest man ever elected to the presidency. During the 1960 presidential campaign, Kennedy promised to "get the country moving again." He called for greater federal aid for education, medical care for the elderly, support for public housing, and aggressive steps to fight poverty. In his inaugural address, however, he largely ignored domestic issues and concentrated on foreign policy, especially the need to contain communist expansion. "Let every nation know," the new president declared, that the United States "shall pay any price… to assure the survival and success of liberty." Even though his address focused on foreign affairs, his stirring language—"Ask not what your country can do for you—ask what you can do for your country"— inspired idealism and hope, especially among young Americans.

Vice-President Johnson, Mr. Speaker, Mr. Chief Justice, President Eisenhower, Vice-President Nixon, President Truman, Reverend Clergy, Fellow Citizens:

We observe today not a victory of party but a celebration of freedom—symbolizing an end as well as a beginning— signifying renewal as well as change. For I have sworn before you and Almighty God the same solemn oath our forebearers prescribed nearly a century and three-quarters ago.

forebearers: ancestors

The world is very different now. For man holds in his mortal hands the power to abolish all forms of human life. And yet the same revolutionary beliefs for which our forebearers fought are still at issue around the globe—the belief that the rights of man come not from the generosity of the state but from the hand of God.

We dare not forget today that we are the heirs of that first revolution. Let the word go forth from this time and place, to friend and foe alike, that the torch has been passed to a new generation of Americans—born in this century, tempered by war, disciplined by a hard and bitter peace, proud of our ancient heritage—and unwilling to witness or permit the slow undoing of those human rights to which this nation has always been committed, and to which we are committed today at home and around the world.

Let every nation know, whether it wishes us well or ill, that we shall pay any price, bear any burden, meet any hardship, support any friend, oppose any foe to assure the survival and the success of liberty.

To those old allies whose cultural and spiritual origins we share, we pledge the loyalty of faithful friends. United, there is little we cannot do in a host of co-operative ventures. Divided, there is little we can do—for we dare not meet a powerful challenge at odds and split asunder.

To those new states whom we welcome to the ranks of the free, we pledge our word that one form of colonial control shall not have passed away merely to be replaced by a far more iron tyranny. We shall not always expect to find them supporting our view. But we shall always hope to find them strongly supporting their own freedom—and to remember that, in the past, those who foolishly sought power by riding the back of the tiger ended up inside.

To those people in the huts and villages of half the globe struggling to break the bonds of mass misery, we pledge our best efforts to help them help themselves, for whatever period is required—not because the Communists may be doing it,

asunder: apart

not because we seek their votes, but because it is right. If a free society cannot help the many who are poor, it cannot save the few who are rich.

To our sister republics south of our border, we offer a special pledge—to convert our good words into good deeds—in a new alliance for progress—to assist free men and free governments in casting off the chains of poverty. But this peaceful revolution of hope cannot become the prey of hostile powers. Let all our neighbors know that we shall join with them to oppose aggression or subversion anywhere in the Americas. And let every other power know that this hemisphere intends to remain the master of its own house.

subversion: attempts to destroy quietly or from the inside

To that world assembly of sovereign states, the United Nations, our last best hope in an age where the instruments of war have far outpaced the instruments of peace, we renew our pledge of support—to prevent it from becoming merely a forum for invective—to strengthen its shield of the new and the weak—and to enlarge the area in which its writ may run.

instruments of war: weapons

instruments: tools

invective: angry words

Finally, to those nations who would make themselves our adversary, we offer not a pledge but a request: that both sides begin anew the quest for peace, before the dark powers of destruction unleashed by science engulf all humanity in planned or accidental self-destruction.

engulf: surround and overwhelm

We dare not tempt them with weakness. For only when our arms are sufficient beyond doubt can we be certain beyond doubt that they will never be employed.

But neither can two great and powerful groups of nations take comfort from our present course—both sides overburdened by the cost of modern weapons, both rightly alarmed by the steady spread of the deadly atom, yet both racing to alter that uncertain balance of terror that stays the hand of mankind's final war.

So let us begin anew—remembering on both sides that civility is not a sign of weakness, and sincerity is always subject to proof. Let us never negotiate out of fear. But let us never fear to negotiate.

belaboring: making a big deal out of

invoke: call forth

eradicate: destroy

beachhead: a position opening the way for further development

tribulation: times of difficulty

tyranny: rule by a single, all-powerful leader

Let both sides explore what problems unite us instead of belaboring those problems which divide us.

Let both sides, for the first time, formulate serious and precise proposals for the inspection and control of arms—and bring the absolute power to destroy other nations under the absolute control of all nations.

Let both sides seek to invoke the wonders of science instead of its terrors. Together let us explore the stars, conquer the deserts, eradicate disease, tap the ocean depths, and encourage the arts and commerce.

Let both sides unite to heed in all corners of the earth the command of Isaiah—to "undo the heavy burdens…[and] let the oppressed go free."

And if a beachhead of co-operation may push back the jungle of suspicion, let both sides join in creating a new endeavor, not a new balance of power, but a new world of law, where the strong are just and the weak secure and the peace preserved.

All this will not be finished in the first one hundred days. Nor will it be finished in the first one thousand days, nor in the life of this administration, nor even perhaps in our lifetime on this planet. But let us begin.

In your hands, my fellow citizens, more than mine, will rest the final success or failure of our course. Since this country was founded, each generation of Americans has been summoned to give testimony to its national loyalty. The graves of young Americans who answered the call to service surround the globe.

Now the trumpet summons us again—not as a call to bear arms, though arms we need—not as a call to battle, though embattled we are—but a call to bear the burden of a long twilight struggle, year in and year out, "rejoicing in hope, patient in tribulation"—a struggle against the common enemies of man: tyranny, poverty, disease, and war itself.

Can we forge against these enemies a grand and global alliance, North and South, East and West, that can assure a more fruitful life for all mankind? Will you join in that historic effort?

In the long history of the world, only a few generations have been granted the role of defending freedom in its hour of maximum danger. I do not shrink from this responsibility—I welcome it. I do not believe that any of us would exchange places with any other people or any other generation. The energy, the faith, the devotion which we bring to this endeavor will light our country and all who serve it—and the glow from that fire can truly light the world.

And so, my fellow Americans: ask not what your country can do for you—ask what you can do for your country.

My fellow citizens of the world: ask not what America will do for you, but what together we can do for the freedom of man.

Finally, whether you are citizens of America or citizens of the world, ask of us here the same high standards of strength and sacrifice which we ask of you. With a good conscience our only sure reward, with history the final judge of our deeds, let us go forth to lead the land we love, asking His blessing and His help, but knowing that here on earth God's work must truly be our own.

Martin Luther King, Jr., "I Have a Dream": Address at the March on Washington (1963)

In 1941, A. Philip Randolph, the president of the Brotherhood of Sleeping Car Porters, proposed a march on Washington to protest segregation in the armed forces and discrimination in government employment and defense industries. Randolph called off the march when President Franklin D. Roosevelt issued an executive order creating the Fair Employment Practices Committee with the power to end discrimination in war industries. In 1962, Randolph renewed his call for a march on Washington. He believed that a massive march might provide the pressure necessary to convince Congress to pass legislation that would guarantee all Americans "access to public accommodations, decent housing, adequate and integrated education, and the right to vote." At that time, African Americans earned just half as much on average as white Americans and were a third as likely to attend college. Fewer than 100 black Americans held elected office.

On August 28, 1963, more than 200,000 people gathered around the Washington Monument and marched 8/10 of a mile to the Lincoln Memorial. They carried signs reading: "Jobs! Justice! Peace!" and sang the civil rights anthem, "We Shall Overcome." Ten speakers addressed the crowd, but the event's highlight was an address by the Rev. Dr. Martin Luther King, Jr. After he finished his prepared text, he launched into his legendary closing words: "I have a dream that one day this nation will rise up and live out the true meaning of its creed...that all men are created equal."

In his speech, King appealed to our country's noblest principles and showed how the nation's mistreatment of African Americans contradicted our ideals of justice and equality. He presented an inspiring vision of an America undivided by barriers of social caste, color, gender, religion, or region. King's eloquent plea for a color-blind America created momentum for passage of the 1964 Civil Rights Act, which outlawed white-only restaurants and hotels.

I am happy to join with you today in what will go down in history as the greatest demonstration for freedom in the history of our nation.

Fivescore years ago, a great American, in whose symbolic shadow we stand today, signed the Emancipation Proclamation. This *momentous* decree came as a great beacon light of hope to millions of Negro slaves who had been seared in the flames of withering injustice. It came as a joyous daybreak to end the long night of their captivity.

But one hundred years later, the Negro still is not free; one hundred years later, the life of the Negro is still sadly crippled by the *manacles* of segregation and the chains of discrimination; one hundred years later, the Negro lives on a lonely island of poverty in the midst of a vast ocean of

momentous: historically important

manacles: chains

material prosperity; one hundred years later, the Negro is still languished in the corners of American society and finds himself in exile in his own land.

So we've come here today to dramatize a shameful condition. In a sense we've come to our nation's capital to cash a check. When the architects of our republic wrote the magnificent words of the Constitution and the Declaration of Independence, they were signing a promissory note to which every American was to fall heir. This note was the promise that all men, yes, black men as well as white men, would be guaranteed the unalienable rights of life, liberty, and the pursuit of happiness.

It is obvious today that America has defaulted on this promissory note in so far as her citizens of color are concerned. Instead of honoring this sacred obligation, America has given the Negro people a bad check; a check which has come back marked "insufficient funds."

We refuse to believe that there are insufficient funds in the great vaults of opportunity of this nation. And so we've come to cash this check, a check that will give us upon demand the riches of freedom and the security of justice.

We have also come to this hallowed spot to remind America of the fierce urgency of now. This is no time to engage in the luxury of cooling off or to take the tranquilizing drug of gradualism. Now is the time to make real the promises of democracy; now is the time to rise from the dark and desolate valley of segregation to the sunlit path of racial justice; now is the time to lift our nation from the quicksands of racial injustice to the solid rock of brotherhood; now is the time to make justice a reality for all God's children. It would be fatal for the nation to overlook the urgency of the moment. This sweltering summer of the Negro's legitimate discontent will not pass until there is an invigorating autumn of freedom and equality.

languished: left in a weakened, impoverished, undignified state

promissory note: promise to pay back

unalienable: cannot be separated from

hallowed: sacred

tranquilizing: calming

gradualism: doing things slowly, one at a time

desolate: lifeless, gloomy, deserted

Nineteen sixty-three is not an end, but a beginning. And those who hope that the Negro needed to blow off steam and will now be content, will have a rude awakening if the nation returns to business as usual.

There will be neither rest nor tranquility in America until the Negro is granted his citizenship rights. The whirlwinds of revolt will continue to shake the foundations of our nation until the bright day of justice emerges.

But there is something that I must say to my people who stand on the warm threshold which leads into the palace of justice. In the process of gaining our rightful place we must not be guilty of wrongful deeds.

Let us not seek to satisfy our thirst for freedom by drinking from the cup of bitterness and hatred. We must forever conduct our struggle on the high plane of dignity and discipline. We must not allow our creative protest to degenerate into physical violence. Again and again we must rise to the majestic heights of meeting physical force with soul force.

The marvelous new militancy which has engulfed the Negro community must not lead us to a distrust of all white people, for many of our white brothers, as evidenced by their presence here today, have come to realize that their destiny is tied up with our destiny and they have come to realize that their freedom is inextricably bound to our freedom. This offense we share mounted to storm the battlements of injustice must be carried forth by a biracial army. We cannot walk alone.

And as we walk, we must make the pledge that we shall always march ahead. We cannot turn back. There are those who are asking the devotees of civil rights, "When will you be satisfied?" We can never be satisfied as long as the Negro is the victim of the unspeakable horrors of police brutality.

We can never be satisfied as long as our bodies, heavy with fatigue of travel, cannot gain lodging in the motels of the

degenerate: break down

militancy: political activism

inextricably: inseparably

highways and the hotels of the cities. We cannot be satisfied as long as the Negro's basic mobility is from a smaller ghetto to a larger one.

We can never be satisfied as long as our children are stripped of their selfhood and robbed of their dignity by signs stating "for whites only." We cannot be satisfied as long as a Negro in Mississippi cannot vote and a Negro in New York believes he has nothing for which to vote. No, we are not satisfied, and we will not be satisfied until justice rolls down like waters and righteousness like a mighty stream.

I am not unmindful that some of you have come here out of excessive trials and tribulation. Some of you have come fresh from narrow jail cells. Some of you have come from areas where your quest for freedom left you battered by the storms of persecution and staggered by the winds of police brutality. You have been the veterans of creative suffering. Continue to work with the faith that unearned suffering is redemptive.

Go back to Mississippi; go back to Alabama; go back to South Carolina; go back to Georgia; go back to Louisiana; go back to the slums and ghettos of the northern cities, knowing that somehow this situation can, and will be changed. Let us not wallow in the valley of despair.

So I say to you, my friends, that even though we must face the difficulties of today and tomorrow, I still have a dream. It is a dream deeply rooted in the American dream that one day this nation will rise up and live out the true meaning of its creed—we hold these truths to be self evident, that all men are created equal.

I have a dream that one day on the red hills of Georgia, sons of former slaves and sons of former slave-owners will be able to sit down together at the table of brotherhood.

I have a dream that one day, even the state of Mississippi, a state sweltering with the heat of injustice, sweltering with the heat of oppression, will be transformed into an oasis of freedom and justice.

mobility: ability to move

tribulation: time of trouble

redemptive: brings its own reward

oasis: green and welcoming refuge in a desert

I have a dream my four little children will one day live in a nation where they will not be judged by the color of their skin but by content of their character. I have a dream today!

I have a dream that one day, down in Alabama, with its vicious racists, with its governor having his lips dripping with the words of interposition and nullification, that one day, right there in Alabama, little black boys and black girls will be able to join hands with little white boys and white girls as sisters and brothers. I have a dream today!

I have a dream that one day every valley shall be exalted, every hill and mountain shall be made low, the rough places shall be made plain, and the crooked places shall be made straight and the glory of the Lord will be revealed and all flesh shall see it together.

This is our hope. This is the faith that I go back to the South with.

With this faith we will be able to hew out of the mountain of despair a stone of hope. With this faith we will be able to transform the jangling discords of our nation into a beautiful symphony of brotherhood.

With this faith we will be able to work together, to pray together, to struggle together, to go to jail together, to stand up for freedom together, knowing that we will be free one day. This will be the day when all of God's children will be able to sing with new meaning— "my country 'tis of thee; sweet land of liberty; of thee I sing; land where my fathers died, land of the pilgrim's pride; from every mountain side, let freedom ring"—and if America is to be a great nation, this must become true.

So let freedom ring from the prodigious hilltops of New Hampshire.

Let freedom ring from the mighty mountains of New York.

Let freedom ring from the heightening Alleghenies of Pennsylvania.

interposition: some Southern states' attempt to use states' rights strategies against desegregation in the 1960s

nullification: states' rights strategy used unsuccessfully by Southern states in 1832–33

every valley shall be exalted…: a phrase from the Bible's description of the coming of God

hew: cut

prodigious: impressive

Let freedom ring from the snow-capped Rockies of Colorado.

Let freedom ring from the curvaceous slopes of California. But not only that.

Let freedom ring from Stone Mountain of Georgia.

Let freedom ring from Lookout Mountain of Tennessee.

Let freedom ring from every hill and molehill of Mississippi, from every mountainside, let freedom ring.

And when we allow freedom to ring, when we let it ring from every village and hamlet, from every state and city, we will be able to speed up that day when all of God's children—black men and white men, Jews and Gentiles, Catholics and Protestants—will be able to join hands and to sing in the words of the old Negro spiritual, "Free at last, free at last; thank God Almighty, we are free at last."

curvaceous: rounded

hamlet: small village

Gentiles: non-Jews

The Fifty States

Alabama
Population 4,779,736*
State capital Montgomery
Statehood December 14, 1819
State bird Yellowhammer
State flower Camellia
State tree Southern pine
Land area 50,744 square miles

Alaska
Population 710,231
State capital Juneau
Statehood January 3, 1959
State bird Willow ptarmigan
State flower Forget-me-not
State tree Sitka spruce
Land area 571,951 square miles

Arizona
Population 6,392,017
State capital Phoenix
Statehood February 14, 1912
State bird Cactus wren
State flower Saguaro (giant cactus)
State tree Palo verde
Land area 113,635 square miles

Arkansas
Population 2,915,918
State capital Little Rock
Statehood June 15, 1836
State bird Mockingbird
State flower Apple blossom
State tree Pine tree
Land area 52,068 square miles

California
Population 37,253,956
State capital Sacramento
Statehood September 9, 1850
State bird California valley quail
State flower Golden poppy
State tree California redwood
Land area 155,959 square miles

Colorado
Population 5,029,196
State capital Denver
Statehood August 1, 1876
State bird Lark bunting
State flower White and lavender columbine
State tree Colorado blue spruce
Land area 103,718 square miles

Connecticut
Population 3,574,097
State capital Hartford
Statehood January 9, 1788
State bird Robin
State flower Mountain laurel
State tree White oak
Land area 4,845 square miles

Delaware
Population 897,934
State capital Dover
Statehood December 7, 1787
State bird Blue hen chicken
State flower Peach blossom
State tree American holly
Land area 1,954 square miles

Florida
Population 18,801,310
State capital Tallahassee
Statehood March 3, 1845
State bird Mockingbird
State flower Orange blossom
State tree Sabal palm
Land area 53,927 square miles

Georgia
Population 9,687,653
State capital Atlanta
Statehood January 2, 1788
State bird Brown thrasher
State flower Cherokee rose
State tree Live oak
Land area 57,906 square miles

Hawaii
Population 1,360,301
State capital Honolulu
Statehood August 21, 1959
State bird Nene (Hawaiian goose)
State flower Yellow hibiscus
State tree Kukui
Land area 6,423 square miles

Idaho
Population 1,567,582
State capital Boise
Statehood July 3, 1890
State bird Mountain bluebird
State flower Mock orange
State tree Western white pine
Land area 82,747 square miles

Illinois
Population 12,830,632
State capital Springfield
Statehood December 3, 1818
State bird Cardinal
State flower Native violet
State tree Oak
Land area 55,584 square miles

Indiana
Population 6,483,802
State capital Indianapolis
Statehood December 11, 1816
State bird Cardinal
State flower Peony
State tree Tulip tree
Land area 35,867 square miles

Iowa
Population 3,046,355
State capital Des Moines
Statehood December 28, 1846
State bird Eastern goldfinch
State flower Wild rose
State tree Oak
Land area 55,869 square miles

Kansas

Population 2,853,118
State capital Topeka
Statehood January 29, 1861
State bird Western meadowlark
State flower Sunflower
State tree Cottonwood
Land area 81,815 square miles

Kentucky

Population 4,339,367
State capital Frankfort
Statehood June 1, 1792
State bird Kentucky cardinal
State flower Goldenrod
State tree Kentucky coffee tree
Land area 39,728 square miles

Louisiana

Population 4,533,372
State capital Baton Rouge
Statehood April 30, 1812
State bird Brown pelican
State flower Magnolia
State tree Bald cypress
Land area 43,562 square miles

Maine

Population 1,328,361
State capital Augusta
Statehood March 15, 1820
State bird Chickadee
State flower White pine cone and flower
State tree White pine
Land area 30,862 square miles

Maryland

Population 5,773,552
State capital Annapolis
Statehood April 28, 1788
State bird Baltimore oriole
State flower Black-eyed Susan
State tree White oak
Land area 9,774 square miles

Massachusetts

Population 6,547,629
State capital Boston
Statehood February 6, 1788
State bird Chickadee
State flower Mayflower
State tree American elm
Land area 7,840 square miles

Michigan

Population 9,883,640
State capital Lansing
Statehood January 26, 1837
State bird Robin
State flower Apple blossom
State tree White pine
Land area 56,804 square miles

Minnesota

Population 5,303,925
State capital St. Paul
Statehood May 11, 1858
State bird Common loon
State flower Pink and white lady slipper
State tree Norway pine
Land area 79,610 square miles

Mississippi

Population 2,967,297
State capital Jackson
Statehood December 10, 1817
State bird Mockingbird
State flower Magnolia
State tree Magnolia
Land area 46,907 square miles

Missouri

Population 5,988,927
State capital Jefferson City
Statehood August 10, 1821
State bird Eastern bluebird
State flower Hawthorn
State tree Flowering dogwood
Land area 68,886 square miles

Montana

Population 989,415
State capital Helena
Statehood November 8, 1889
State bird Western meadowlark
State flower Bitterroot
State tree Ponderosa pine
Land area 145,552 square miles

Nebraska

Population 1,826,341
State capital Lincoln
Statehood March 1, 1867
State bird Western meadowlark
State flower Goldenrod
State tree Cottonwood
Land area 76,872 square miles

Nevada

Population 2,700,551
State capital Carson City
Statehood October 31, 1864
State bird Mountain bluebird
State flower Sagebrush
State tree Pine nut
Land area 109,826 square miles

New Hampshire

Population 1,316,470
State capital Concord
Statehood June 21, 1788
State bird Purple finch
State flower Purple lilac
State tree White birch
Land area 8,968 square miles

New Jersey

Population 8,791,894
State capital Trenton
Statehood December 18, 1787
State bird Eastern goldfinch
State flower Purple violet
State tree Red oak
Land area 7,417 square miles

New Mexico

Population 2,059,179
State capital Santa Fe
Statehood January 16, 1912
State bird Roadrunner
State flower Yucca flower
State tree Pine nut
Land area 121,356 square miles

New York

Population 19,378,102
State capital Albany
Statehood July 26, 1788
State bird Bluebird
State flower Rose
State tree Sugar maple
Land area 47,214 square miles

North Carolina

Population 9,535,483
State capital Raleigh
Statehood November 21, 1789
State bird Cardinal
State flower Flowering dogwood
State tree Pine
Land area 48,711 square miles

North Dakota

Population 672,591
State capital Bismarck
Statehood November 2, 1889
State bird Western meadowlark
State flower Wild prairie rose
State tree American elm
Land area 68,976 square miles

Ohio

Population 11,536,504
State capital Columbus
Statehood March 1, 1803
State bird Cardinal
State flower Scarlet carnation
State tree Buckeye
Land area 40,948 square miles

Oklahoma

Population 3,751,351
State capital Oklahoma City
Statehood November 16, 1907
State bird Scissor-tailed flycatcher
State flower Mistletoe
State tree Redbud
Land area 68,667 square miles

Oregon

Population 3,831,074
State capital Salem
Statehood February 14, 1859
State bird Western meadowlark
State flower Oregon grape
State tree Douglas fir
Land area 95,997 square miles

Pennsylvania

Population 12,702,379
State capital Harrisburg
Statehood December 12, 1787
State bird Ruffed grouse
State flower Mountain laurel
State tree Hemlock
Land area 44,817 square miles

Rhode Island

Population 1,052,567
State capital Providence
Statehood May 29, 1790
State bird Rhode Island red
State flower Violet
State tree Red maple
Land area 1,045 square miles

South Carolina

Population 4,625,364
State capital Columbia
Statehood May 23, 1788
State bird Carolina wren
State flower Carolina jessamine
State tree Palmetto
Land area 30,109 square miles

South Dakota

Population 814,180
State capital Pierre
Statehood November 2, 1889
State bird Ring-necked pheasant
State flower American pasqueflower
State tree Black Hills spruce
Land area 75,885 square miles

Tennessee

Population 6,346,105
State capital Nashville
Statehood June 1, 1796
State bird Mockingbird
State flower Iris
State tree Tulip poplar
Land area 41,217 square miles

Texas

Population 25,145,561
State capital Austin
Statehood December 29, 1845
State bird Mockingbird
State flower Bluebonnet
State tree Pecan
Land area 261,797 square miles

Utah

Population 2,763,885
State capital Salt Lake City
Statehood January 4, 1896
State bird Seagull
State flower Sego lily
State tree Blue spruce
Land area 82,144 square miles

Vermont

Population 625,741
State capital Montpelier
Statehood March 4, 1791
State bird Hermit thrush
State flower Red clover
State tree Sugar maple
Land area 9,250 square miles

Virginia

Population 8,001,024
State capital Richmond
Statehood June 25, 1788
State bird Cardinal
State flower Dogwood flower
State tree Dogwood
Land area 39,594 square miles

Washington

Population 6,724,540
State capital Olympia
Statehood November 11, 1889
State bird Willow goldfinch
State flower Coast rhododendron
State tree Western hemlock
Land area 66,544 square miles

West Virginia

Population 1,852,994
State capital Charleston
Statehood June 20, 1863
State bird Cardinal
State flower Rhododendron
State tree Sugar maple
Land area 24,078 square miles

Wisconsin

Population 5,686,986
State capital Madison
Statehood May 29, 1848
State bird Robin
State flower Wood violet
State tree Sugar maple
Land area 54,310 square miles

Wyoming

Population 563,626
State capital Cheyenne
Statehood July 10, 1890
State bird Meadowlark
State flower Indian paintbrush
State tree Cottonwood
Land area 97,100 square miles

*population statistics based on 2010 U.S. Census

Presidents of the United States

	Born–Died	Years in Office	Political Party	Home State	Vice President
1 George Washington	1732–1799	1789–1797	None	Virginia	John Adams
2 John Adams	1735–1826	1797–1801	Federalist	Massachusetts	Thomas Jefferson
3 Thomas Jefferson	1743–1826	1801–1809	Republican*	Virginia	Aaron Burr George Clinton
4 James Madison	1751–1836	1809–1817	Republican	Virginia	George Clinton Elbridge Gerry
5 James Monroe	1758–1831	1817–1825	Republican	Virginia	Daniel D. Tompkins
6 John Quincy Adams	1767–1848	1825–1829	Republican	Massachusetts	John C. Calhoun
7 Andrew Jackson	1767–1845	1829–1837	Democratic	Tennessee	John C. Calhoun Martin Van Buren
8 Martin Van Buren	1782–1862	1837–1841	Democratic	New York	Richard M. Johnson
9 William Henry Harrison	1773–1841	1841	Whig	Ohio	John Tyler
10 John Tyler	1790–1862	1841–1845	Whig	Virginia	None
11 James K. Polk	1795–1849	1845–1849	Democratic	Tennessee	George M. Dallas
12 Zachary Taylor	1784–1850	1849–1850	Whig	Louisiana	Millard Fillmore
13 Millard Fillmore	1800–1874	1850–1853	Whig	New York	None
14 Franklin Pierce	1804–1869	1853–1857	Democratic	New Hampshire	William R. King
15 James Buchanan	1791–1868	1857–1861	Democratic	Pennsylvania	John C. Breckenridge
16 Abraham Lincoln	1809–1865	1861–1865	Republican	Illinois	Hannibal Hamlin Andrew Johnson
17 Andrew Johnson	1808–1875	1865–1869	Democratic (nominated for vice president on the Republican ticket)	Tennessee	None
18 Ulysses S. Grant	1822–1885	1869–1877	Republican	Illinois	Schuyler Colfax Henry Wilson
19 Rutherford B. Hayes	1822–1893	1877–1881	Republican	Ohio	William A. Wheeler
20 James A. Garfield	1831–1881	1881	Republican	Ohio	Chester A. Arthur

*The Republican Party of the early 1800s evolved into the modern Democratic Party. Today's Republican Party was founded in 1854.

	Born–Died	Years in Office	Political Party	Home State	Vice President
21 Chester A. Arthur	1829–1886	1881–1885	Republican	New York	None
22 Grover Cleveland	1837–1908	1885–1889	Democratic	New York	Thomas A. Hendricks
23 Benjamin Harrison	1833–1901	1889–1893	Republican	Indiana	Levi P. Morton
24 Grover Cleveland	1837–1908	1893–1897	Democratic	New York	Adlai E. Stevenson
25 William McKinley	1843–1901	1897–1901	Republican	Ohio	Garret A. Hobart Theodore Roosevelt
26 Theodore Roosevelt	1858–1919	1901–1909	Republican	New York	Charles W. Fairbanks
27 William Howard Taft	1857–1930	1909–1913	Republican	Ohio	James S. Sherman
28 Woodrow Wilson	1856–1924	1913–1921	Democratic	New Jersey	Thomas R. Marshall
29 Warren G. Harding	1865–1923	1921–1923	Republican	Ohio	Calvin Coolidge
30 Calvin Coolidge	1872–1933	1923–1929	Republican	Massachusetts	Charles G. Dawes
31 Herbert Hoover	1874–1964	1929–1933	Republican	California	Charles Curtis
32 Franklin D. Roosevelt	1882–1945	1933–1945	Democratic	New York	John Nance Garner Henry Wallace Harry S. Truman
33 Harry S. Truman	1884–1972	1945–1953	Democratic	Missouri	Alben W. Barkley
34 Dwight D. Eisenhower	1890–1969	1953–1961	Republican	Kansas	Richard M. Nixon
35 John F. Kennedy	1917–1963	1961–1963	Democratic	Massachusetts	Lyndon B. Johnson
36 Lyndon B. Johnson	1908–1973	1963–1969	Democratic	Texas	Hubert H. Humphrey
37 Richard M. Nixon	1913–1994	1969–1974	Republican	California	Spiro T. Agnew Gerald R. Ford
38 Gerald R. Ford	1913–2006	1974–1977	Republican	Michigan	Nelson A. Rockefeller
39 James Earl "Jimmy" Carter	1924–	1977–1981	Democratic	Georgia	Walter F. Mondale
40 Ronald Reagan	1911–2004	1981–1989	Republican	California	George H. W. Bush
41 George H. W. Bush	1924–2018	1989–1993	Republican	Texas	J. Danforth Quayle
42 William J. Clinton	1946–	1993–2001	Democratic	Arkansas	Albert Gore, Jr.
43 George W. Bush	1946–	2001–2009	Republican	Texas	Richard Cheney
44 Barack Obama	1961–	2009–2017	Democratic	Hawaii	Joseph Biden
45 Donald J. Trump	1946–	2017–	Republican	New York	Michael R. Pence

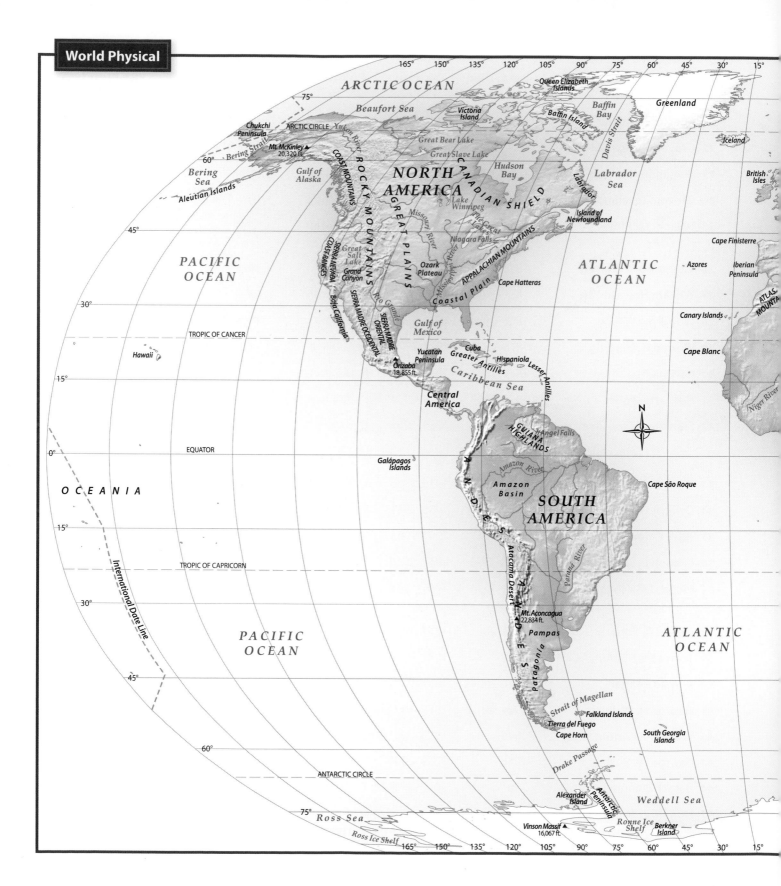

ARCTIC OCEAN

Beaufort Sea

Queen Elizabeth Islands

Baffin Bay

Greenland

75°

Chukchi Peninsula

ARCTIC CIRCLE

Victoria Island

Baffin Island

Iceland

60°

Bering Strait

Mt. McKinley ▲ 20,320 ft.

Yukon River

Great Bear Lake

Great Slave Lake

Davis Strait

Bering Sea

Gulf of Alaska

COAST MOUNTAINS

NORTH AMERICA

CANADIAN SHIELD

Hudson Bay

Labrador Sea

British Isles

Aleutian Islands

ROCKY MOUNTAINS

Lake Winnipeg

Labrador

Island of Newfoundland

45°

PACIFIC OCEAN

GREAT PLAINS

Missouri River

The Great Lakes

Niagara Falls

ATLANTIC OCEAN

Cape Finisterre

30°

SIERRA NEVADA

COAST RANGES

Great Salt Lake

Grand Canyon

Ozark Plateau

Mississippi River

APPALACHIAN MOUNTAINS

Coastal Plain

Cape Hatteras

Azores

Iberian Peninsula

ATLAS MOUNTA

TROPIC OF CANCER

Hawaii

SIERRA MADRE OCCIDENTAL

Baja California

Rio Grande

SIERRA MADRE ORIENTAL

Gulf of Mexico

Canary Islands

Cape Blanc

15°

Yucatan Peninsula

Orizaba 18,855 ft.

Cuba

Greater Antilles

Hispaniola

Lesser Antilles

Caribbean Sea

Central America

0° EQUATOR

OCEANIA

Galápagos Islands

ANDES

GUIANA HIGHLANDS

Angel Falls

Amazon River

Cape São Roque

N

Niger River

Amazon Basin

SOUTH AMERICA

15°

Paraná River

TROPIC OF CAPRICORN

30°

Atacama Desert

ANDES

Mt. Aconcagua ▲ 22,834 ft.

Pampas

ATLANTIC OCEAN

PACIFIC OCEAN

Patagonia

45°

International Date Line

Strait of Magellan

Falkland Islands

Tierra del Fuego

Cape Horn

South Georgia Islands

60°

ANTARCTIC CIRCLE

Drake Passage

Alexander Island

Antarctic Peninsula

Weddell Sea

75°

Ross Sea

Ross Ice Shelf

Vinson Massif ▲ 16,067 ft.

Ronne Ice Shelf

Berkner Island

165° 150° 135° 120° 105° 90° 75° 60° 45° 30° 15°

ARCTIC OCEAN

15° 30° 45° 60° 75° 90° 105° 120° 135° 150° 165°

Svalbard
Barents Sea
Novaya Zemlya
Kara Sea
North Land
Laptev Sea
East Siberian Sea
75°

Norwegian Sea
Scandinavia
Kola Peninsula
Yenisey River
Ob River
Central Siberian Plateau
S I B E R I A
ARCTIC CIRCLE
Chukchi Peninsula

Ob River
West Siberian Plain
A S I A
60°
Sea of Okhotsk
Kamchatka Peninsula
Bering Sea

North Sea
Northern European Plain
URAL MOUNTAINS
The Steppes
Sakhalin
Date Line

Rhine R.
EUROPE
Volga River
Aral Sea
Mongolian Plateau
Gobi
Hokkaido
45°

Danube River
CARPATHIAN MOUNTAINS
Elbrus 18,510 ft.
Caspian Sea
TIAN SHAN
Huang He R.
Sea of Japan
Honshu
PACIFIC OCEAN

ALPS
Balkan Peninsula
Black Sea
CAUCASUS MOUNTAINS
Taklimakan Desert
KUNLUN MOUNTAINS
K2 28,251 ft.
Plateau of Tibet
Kyushu
Sea of Japan
30°

Mediterranean Sea
Anatolia
Mt. Ararat 16,854 ft.
Syrian Desert
ZAGROS MOUNTAINS
HIMALAYA
Mt. Everest 29,035 ft.
Yangtze River
East China Sea
TROPIC OF CANCER

Sinai Peninsula
Libyan Desert
Red Sea
Arabian Peninsula
Great Indian Desert
Ganges River
Deccan Plateau
Taiwan
Philippine Sea
15°

SAHARA
S u d a n
Nile River
Arabian Sea
Bay of Bengal
Indochina Peninsula
South China Sea
Philippine Islands

AFRICA
ETHIOPIAN HIGHLANDS
Cape Gwardafuy
Somali Peninsula
Cape Comorin
Malay Peninsula
EQUATOR
0°

Congo River
Congo Basin
Lake Victoria
Kilimanjaro 19,340 ft.
Sumatra
Borneo
New Guinea
OCEANIA

Lake Tanganyika
INDIAN OCEAN
Celebes
Java
Arafura Sea
15°

Katanga Plateau
Lake Malawi
Coral Sea

Namib Desert
Victoria Falls
Madagascar
Mozambique Channel
Réunion
TROPIC OF CAPRICORN
Great Sandy Desert
Western Plateau
AUSTRALIA
Great Victoria Desert
Darling River
GREAT DIVIDING RANGE

Kalahari Desert
Murray R.
Tasman Sea
North Island
30°

Cape of Good Hope
New Zealand
South Island
45°

Kerguelen Is.
Tasmania

0   1000   2000 mi
0 1000 2000 km
Scale at equator

60°

ANTARCTIC CIRCLE

ANTARCTICA
TRANSANTARCTIC MOUNTAINS
Ross Ice Shelf
75°

15° 30° 45° 60° 75° 90° 105° 120° 135° 150° 165°

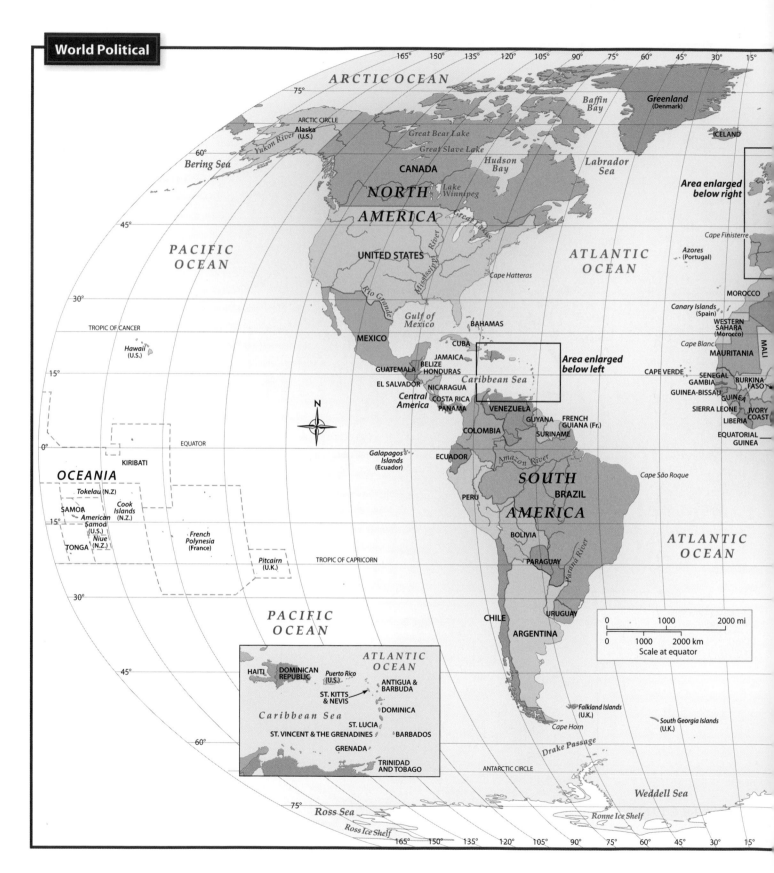

ARCTIC OCEAN

75°

Baffin
Bay

Greenland
(Denmark)

ARCTIC CIRCLE

Great Bear Lake

ICELAND

Alaska
(U.S.)

Yukon River

60°

Great Slave Lake

Hudson
Bay

Labrador
Sea

Bering Sea

CANADA

**NORTH
AMERICA**

Lake
Winnipeg

45°

Great Lakes

PACIFIC
OCEAN

UNITED STATES

**Area enlarged
below right**

Cape Finisterre

Mississippi River

ATLANTIC
OCEAN

Azores
(Portugal)

30°

Rio Grande

Cape Hatteras

MOROCCO

TROPIC OF CANCER

Canary Islands
(Spain)

Gulf of
Mexico

BAHAMAS

Hawaii
(U.S.)

WESTERN
SAHARA
(Morocco)

MEXICO

CUBA

Cape Blanc

15°

JAMAICA

BELIZE

GUATEMALA HONDURAS

**Area enlarged
below left**

MAURITANIA

MALI

CAPE VERDE

EL SALVADOR   NICARAGUA

Caribbean Sea

SENEGAL

BURKINA

**Central
America**

COSTA RICA

GAMBIA

FASO

PANAMA

GUINEA-BISSAU

GUINEA

N

VENEZUELA

SIERRA LEONE

IVORY
COAST

GUYANA

FRENCH
GUIANA (Fr.)

LIBERIA

COLOMBIA

SURINAME

EQUATORIAL
GUINEA

0°

EQUATOR

Galapagos
Islands
(Ecuador)

ECUADOR

Amazon River

KIRIBATI

Cape São Roque

OCEANIA

PERU

**SOUTH
AMERICA**

BRAZIL

Tokelau (N.Z)

Cook
Islands
(N.Z.)

BOLIVIA

ATLANTIC
OCEAN

SAMOA

American
Samoa
(U.S.)

Niue
(N.Z.)

15°

Paraná River

TONGA

French
Polynesia
(France)

PARAGUAY

Pitcairn
(U.K.)

TROPIC OF CAPRICORN

PACIFIC
OCEAN

30°

CHILE

URUGUAY

0	1000		2000 mi
0	1000	2000 km	

Scale at equator

ARGENTINA

Falkland Islands
(U.K.)

45°

HAITI

DOMINICAN
REPUBLIC

Puerto Rico
(U.S.)

ATLANTIC
OCEAN

ANTIGUA &
BARBUDA

ST. KITTS
& NEVIS

South Georgia Islands
(U.K.)

Caribbean Sea

DOMINICA

Cape Horn

ST. LUCIA

ST. VINCENT & THE GRENADINES

BARBADOS

Drake Passage

60°

GRENADA

TRINIDAD
AND TOBAGO

ANTARCTIC CIRCLE

Weddell Sea

75°

Ross Sea

Ronne Ice Shelf

Ross Ice Shelf

165° 150° 135° 120° 105° 90° 75° 60° 45° 30° 15°

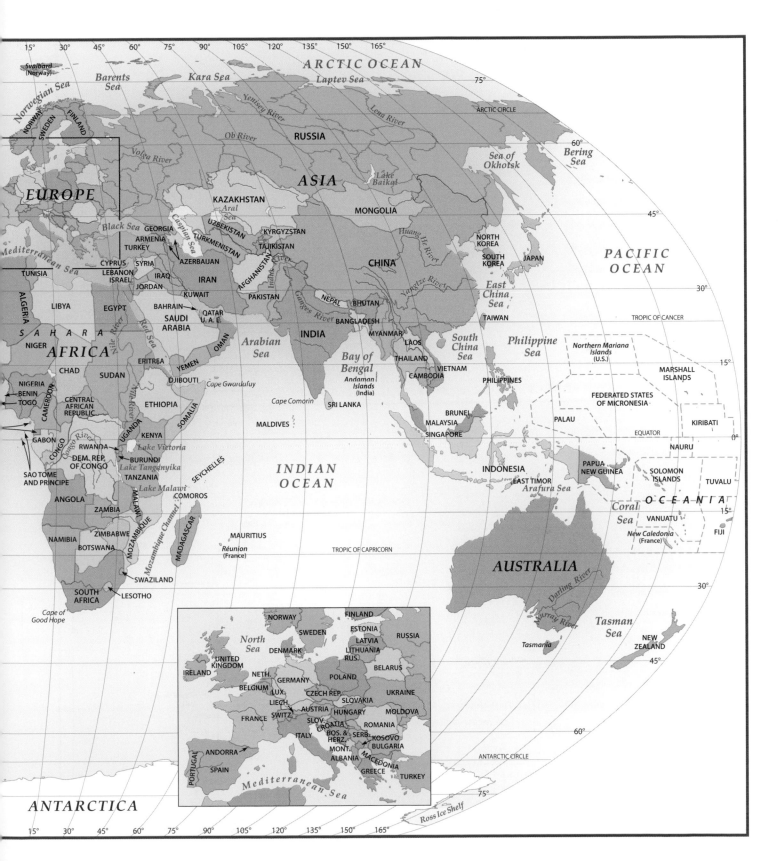

ARCTIC OCEAN

Svalbard (Norway)

Norwegian Sea   Barents Sea   Kara Sea   Laptev Sea   75°

ARCTIC CIRCLE

Yenisey River   Lena River

NORWAY   SWEDEN   FINLAND

Ob River   RUSSIA   Sea of Okhotsk   60°   Bering Sea

EUROPE   ASIA   Lake Baikal   45°

Volga River

KAZAKHSTAN   Aral Sea   MONGOLIA

Black Sea   GEORGIA   UZBEKISTAN   KYRGYZSTAN   NORTH KOREA   PACIFIC OCEAN

Caspian Sea   ARMENIA   TURKMENISTAN   TAJIKISTAN   Huang He River   SOUTH KOREA   JAPAN

Mediterranean Sea   TURKEY   AZERBAIJAN   CHINA   East China Sea   30°

CYPRUS   SYRIA   AFGHANISTAN   Yangtze River

TUNISIA   LEBANON   IRAQ   Indus River   PACIFIC OCEAN

ISRAEL   JORDAN   IRAN   PAKISTAN   NEPAL   BHUTAN   TAIWAN   TROPIC OF CANCER

ALGERIA   LIBYA   EGYPT   KUWAIT   BANGLADESH

BAHRAIN   QATAR   SAUDI ARABIA   U.A.E.   Ganges River   MYANMAR   South China Sea   Philippine Sea   Northern Mariana Islands (U.S.)   MARSHALL ISLANDS   15°

S A H A R A   Nile River   OMAN   INDIA   LAOS   THAILAND

NIGER   AFRICA   Red Sea   Arabian Sea   Bay of Bengal   VIETNAM   CAMBODIA   PHILIPPINES   FEDERATED STATES OF MICRONESIA

CHAD   SUDAN   ERITREA   YEMEN   Andaman Islands (India)   PALAU   KIRIBATI

NIGERIA   CENTRAL AFRICAN REPUBLIC   DJIBOUTI   Cape Gwardafuy   Cape Comorin   SRI LANKA   BRUNEI   EQUATOR   0°

BENIN   TOGO   ETHIOPIA   SOMALIA   MALDIVES   MALAYSIA   NAURU

GABON   UGANDA   SINGAPORE

CONGO   RWANDA   Lake Victoria   INDONESIA   PAPUA NEW GUINEA   SOLOMON ISLANDS

SAO TOME AND PRINCIPE   DEM. REP. OF CONGO   BURUNDI   Lake Tanganyika   INDIAN OCEAN   EAST TIMOR   TUVALU

TANZANIA   SEYCHELLES   Arafura Sea   OCEANIA

ANGOLA   MALAWI   Lake Malawi   COMOROS   Coral Sea   15°

ZAMBIA   VANUATU   New Caledonia (France)   FIJI

NAMIBIA   ZIMBABWE   MADAGASCAR   MAURITIUS   TROPIC OF CAPRICORN   AUSTRALIA

BOTSWANA   Réunion (France)

SWAZILAND   Darling River   Tasman Sea   NEW ZEALAND

SOUTH AFRICA   LESOTHO   Tasmania   Murray River   30°

Cape of Good Hope

45°

60°

ANTARCTICA   ANTARCTIC CIRCLE

Ross Ice Shelf   75°

NORWAY   FINLAND

North Sea   SWEDEN   ESTONIA   RUSSIA

DENMARK   LATVIA   LITHUANIA

UNITED KINGDOM   RUS.   BELARUS

IRELAND   NETH.   GERMANY   POLAND

BELGIUM   LUX.   CZECH REP.   SLOVAKIA   UKRAINE

LIECH.   AUSTRIA   HUNGARY   MOLDOVA

FRANCE   SWITZ.   SLOV.   CROATIA   ROMANIA

ITALY   BOS. & HERZ.   SERB.   KOSOVO

MONT.   BULGARIA

PORTUGAL   ANDORRA   ALBANIA   MACEDONIA

SPAIN   GREECE   TURKEY

Mediterranean Sea

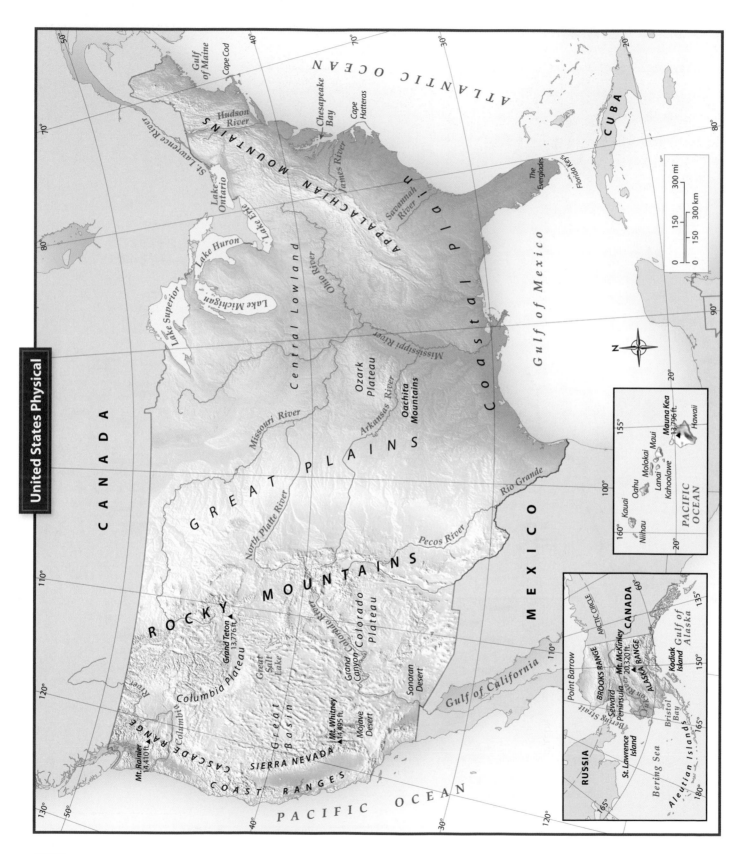

United States Physical

CANADA

PACIFIC OCEAN

ATLANTIC OCEAN

Gulf of Maine
Cape Cod
Hudson River
St. Lawrence River
Lake Ontario
Lake Erie
Lake Huron
Lake Superior
Lake Michigan

Chesapeake Bay
Cape Hatteras
James River
Savannah River

APPALACHIAN MOUNTAINS

Central Lowland

Ohio River

Mississippi River

Ozark Plateau
Arkansas River
Oachita Mountains

Coastal Plain

The Everglades
Florida Keys

Gulf of Mexico

CUBA

GREAT PLAINS

Missouri River
North Platte River

ROCKY MOUNTAINS

Grand Teton 13,776 ft.
Great Salt Lake
Columbia Plateau
Columbia River
Snake River

Great Basin

Grand Canyon
Colorado River
Colorado Plateau

Sonoran Desert

Mt. Whitney 14,495 ft.
Mojave Desert

SIERRA NEVADA

CASCADE RANGE

COAST RANGES

Mt. Rainier 14,410 ft.

Rio Grande
Pecos River

Gulf of California

MEXICO

PACIFIC OCEAN

N

50°
40°
70°
30°
20°
80°
70°
80°
90°
100°
110°
120°
130°
50°
40°
30°
120°

300 mi
150
0
300 km
150
0

Mauna Kea 13,796 ft.
Hawaii
Oahu
Molokai
Maui
Lanai
Kahoolawe
Kauai
Niihau
PACIFIC OCEAN
155°
160°
20°

Point Barrow
ARCTIC CIRCLE
BROOKS RANGE
Mt. McKinley 20,320 ft.
CANADA
ALASKA RANGE
Kodiak Island
Gulf of Alaska
Seward Peninsula
St. Lawrence Island
Bering Strait
RUSSIA
Bristol Bay
Bering Sea
Aleutian Islands
60°
135°
150°
110°
165°
180°
165°

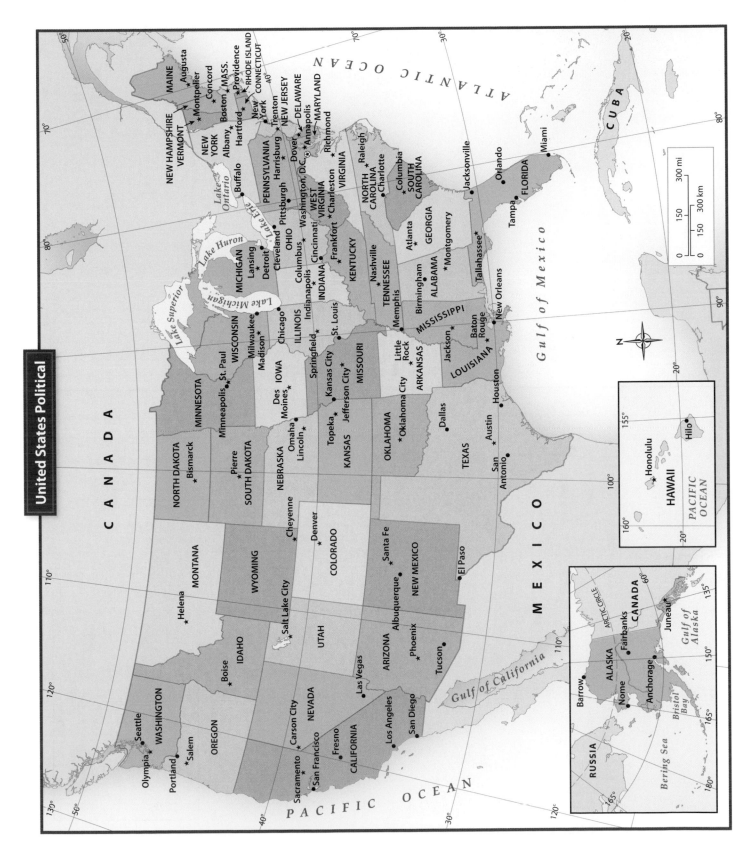

United States Political

ATLANTIC OCEAN

CANADA

MAINE
Augusta ★
Montpelier ★
Concord ★ MASS.
NEW HAMPSHIRE   Boston
VERMONT   Providence — RHODE ISLAND
NEW YORK   Hartford — CONNECTICUT
Albany ★   New York — NEW JERSEY
Buffalo   Trenton
Lake Ontario   PENNSYLVANIA   DELAWARE
Lake Erie   Harrisburg ★   Dover
MICHIGAN   Pittsburgh   Washington, D.C. ✪   MARYLAND
Lansing ★   OHIO   Annapolis ★
Detroit   Columbus ★   WEST   Richmond ★
Cleveland   Cincinnati   VIRGINIA   VIRGINIA
Lake Huron   Frankfort ★   Charleston ★   Raleigh ★
Lake Superior   INDIANA   KENTUCKY   NORTH CAROLINA   Charlotte
Lake Michigan   Indianapolis ★   Nashville ★   Columbia ★
MICHIGAN   ILLINOIS   TENNESSEE   SOUTH CAROLINA
Milwaukee   Chicago   Memphis   Atlanta ★   Jacksonville
WISCONSIN   Springfield ★   Birmingham   GEORGIA   Orlando
Madison ★   St. Louis   MISSISSIPPI   ALABAMA   FLORIDA
St. Paul ★   IOWA   Jackson ★   Montgomery ★   Tampa   Miami
Minneapolis   Des Moines ★   Little Rock ★   Baton Rouge ★   Tallahassee ★
MINNESOTA   Kansas City   ARKANSAS   New Orleans
NORTH DAKOTA   Jefferson City ★   LOUISIANA   Gulf of Mexico
Bismarck ★   MISSOURI
Pierre ★   Topeka ★   OKLAHOMA
SOUTH DAKOTA   KANSAS   Oklahoma City ★
NEBRASKA   Omaha   Dallas   Houston
Lincoln ★   Cheyenne ★   Austin ★   TEXAS
Denver ★   COLORADO   San Antonio
MONTANA   Santa Fe ★   MEXICO
Helena ★   WYOMING   NEW MEXICO   El Paso
IDAHO   Salt Lake City ★   Albuquerque   Gulf of California
Boise ★   UTAH   ARIZONA   Phoenix ★
NEVADA   Las Vegas   Tucson
WASHINGTON   Carson City ★   Los Angeles
Seattle   Sacramento ★   San Diego
Olympia ★   San Francisco   CALIFORNIA   Fresno
Portland   Salem ★
OREGON   PACIFIC OCEAN

N

Gulf of Mexico

HAWAII
Honolulu ★   Hilo
PACIFIC OCEAN

ALASKA
ARCTIC CIRCLE
CANADA
RUSSIA   Fairbanks
Nome   Anchorage   Juneau ★
Barrow   Gulf of Alaska
Bering Sea   Bristol Bay

CUBA

300 mi
300 km
150   150
0   0

ATLAS **349**

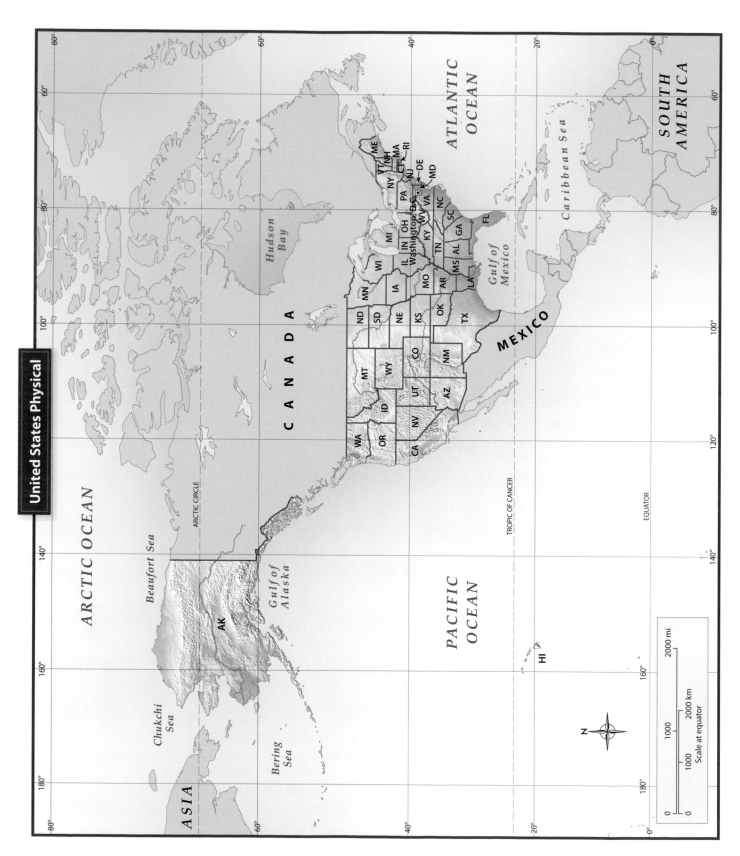

United States Physical

ATLANTIC OCEAN

SOUTH AMERICA

ARCTIC OCEAN

Beaufort Sea

Chukchi Sea

Bering Sea

ASIA

Gulf of Alaska

PACIFIC OCEAN

Hudson Bay

CANADA

MEXICO

Gulf of Mexico

Caribbean Sea

ME
VT NH
MA
CT RI
NY
PA NJ
DE
OH MD
IN WV VA
MI KY NC
IL SC
WI TN GA
Washington, D.C.
MS AL
IA MO AR LA
MN
ND SD NE KS OK TX
FL
MT WY CO NM
ID UT AZ
WA OR NV CA

AK

HI

ARCTIC CIRCLE

TROPIC OF CANCER

EQUATOR

2000 mi
1000
2000 km
1000
Scale at equator

N

Glossary

allies   people or countries united for a specific purpose; during World War II, the countries that united to fight Germany

amendment   a change, addition, or correction; specifically, a change or addition to the U.S. Constitution

anti-Semitism   hatred of and prejudice against Jews

appeal   request for a higher court to review a case

armada   Spanish word used to describe a great fleet of armed ships

assassin   a murderer, especially someone who kills a public figure for political reasons

baby boom   an increase in the U.S. birth rate that began after World War II and continued through the mid-1960s

bigotry   intolerance, prejudice

Bill of Rights   first 10 amendments to the U.S. Constitution

blitzkrieg   German word used to describe sudden warfare intended to surprise the enemy and win a quick victory

blockade   closing off a place (such as a harbor or port) to prevent entering or leaving an area

boycott   to refuse to deal with a nation, company, or organization in order to show disapproval or force a change

cabinet   officially chosen group of advisers to the president

candidate   someone running for political office

capitalism   economic system based on private ownership of land and resources, in which individuals and businesses produce goods and services to make money; also known as the free enterprise (or free market) system

census   official count of people

citizen   someone with all the rights, protections, and responsibilities guaranteed under a nation's government

civil disobedience   opposing a law as a matter of principle by refusing to obey it

civil rights   rights guaranteed to all citizens by the Constitution and acts of Congress

Civil Rights Act of 1964   law prohibiting discrimination in public places and employment

coalition   union of groups with a common objective

colony   land controlled by a distant or foreign nation

commune   group of people living together who share resources and responsibilities

communism   economic and political system in which the state owns most of the land and property and which in theory is dedicated to social equality

concentration camp   place where Nazis imprisoned, tortured, and killed people during World War II

Constitution   the document that outlines the plan of government in the United States

containment   policy to stop the spread of communism

counterculture   culture with values that are very different from those of established society

crusade   expedition or war motivated by religious beliefs

democracy   government by the people, either directly or through elected representatives

depression   time of severe economic decline, including high unemployment and falling prices

dictator   ruler with complete authority and no accountability

discrimination   showing favor toward or prejudice against people because they belong to a particular group

dove   someone who takes an antiwar position

economy   management and flow of resources and money in a community

emancipation   granting of freedom

Emancipation Proclamation   document written and signed by President Abraham Lincoln that freed all slaves living in Confederate states during the Civil War

embargo   ban on commerce and trade

empire   group of cities, states, or territories under the rule of one person

equality   having the same rights, privileges, and status

executive branch   the branch of government that carries out the laws; in the U.S. the president is its head

exile   to banish someone from his or her home or country

fascism   political system, usually led by a dictator, characterized by extreme national and racial pride and suppression of opposition

feminists   people who believe that women deserve the same rights and opportunities as men

free trade   business between nations that is carried out without major restrictions

fundamentalism   belief in the literal truth of religious texts and in strict adherence to religious laws

genocide   deliberate murder of an entire nation or ethnic group or the destruction of its culture

ghetto   a city neighborhood where poor people live crowded together, usually in bad conditions

guerrilla   a soldier who fights by using surprise tactics to bring down the enemy

habeas corpus, writ of   a court order requiring proof that a prisoner is being justly held

hawks   people who advocate war or the use of force against other nations

hippies   young people of the 1960s who rebelled against traditional values

Hoovervilles   settlements of makeshift houses built by homeless people during the Great Depression

hostage   someone held prisoner as a bargaining chip in a conflict

immigrants   people who move to a new country or region

impeach   to charge a public official with crimes or misconduct

imperialism   expanding a nation by taking other lands

inauguration   ceremony that ushers a new president into office

infidels   nonbelievers in a dominant religion, according to the believers

inflation   the process by which the prices of goods and services increase

integration   bringing together different racial and ethnic groups

internment   confinement, especially in wartime

isolationism   a national policy of withdrawal from world affairs

Jim Crow   system of laws beginning in the late 1800s that segregated blacks and forced them to use separate and inferior facilities

Ku Klux Klan   an organization formed in the South in 1866 that used lynching and violence to intimidate and control blacks and others

labor unions   associations of workers formed to promote and protect the rights of members

League of Nations   an organization proposed by President Woodrow Wilson after World War I to unite nations in working for peace and security

lobby   to attempt to influence lawmakers

lynching   kidnapping and execution of a person by a mob

martyr   someone who chooses to die rather than give up a religious belief or political principle

migration   movement of a group from one country or region to another

national debt   total amount of money the federal government owes to lenders

nationalism   strong feeling of pride in one's country

Native Americans   the first peoples of North America, including those called Eskimos and Indians

nativism   the practice of favoring native-born citizens over immigrants

Nazis the German political party led by Adolf Hitler

nonconformist person who follows his or her own beliefs instead of what may be traditional or popular

nonviolent resistance peaceful protest that avoids the use of physical force

orator an effective public speaker

pacifism opposition to the use of force under any circumstance

pardon official forgiveness for a crime

parliament a legislature

peninsula a piece of land almost entirely surrounded by water

perjury lying under oath

poll tax tax (that has been found to be unconstitutional) that people in some states used to have to pay before they were allowed to vote

Quakers a Christian group, officially called the Society of Friends, that opposes war and believes in respecting the rights of other people

quota limit on the number of people from an ethnic, religious, or other group who will be allowed into a nation, institution, or organization

radical someone who favors extreme changes in existing laws or conditions

ratify to formally approve a suggested action

reparations payments made for damages suffered

reservation public land set aside for special use, especially land set aside for Indian peoples after European Americans took over Indian land

revenues income, especially from city, state, or national taxes

revolution overthrow of a government

riots violent disturbances of the peace

segregation the practice of separating one racial, ethnic, or religious group from another, especially in public places

self-determination the right of citizens to choose the form of government under which they will live

sit-in organized demonstration by protesters who sat down in segregated establishments and refused to leave

socialism government ownership of factories and services with wages determined by workers' needs

speculation financial risks taken in order to make a large profit

stock exchange trading center where shares of stock are bought and sold

stock market the stock exchange and associated businesses for the buying and selling of stocks

suburb a residential community on the outskirts of a city

tariff tax on imports or exports

tax money that citizens and businesses are required to contribute to pay for the cost of government and the services it provides

technology application of scientific ideas for practical purposes

Third Reich Germany under Adolf Hitler, 1933 to 1945

totalitarian form of dictatorship that has total control over all aspects of life and that suppresses all political or cultural opposition

treaty formal agreement between nations

truce agreement to stop fighting

tyranny absolute power, especially when it is unjustly or cruelly used

U-boats German submarines

United Nations an international organization formed in 1945 to promote peace, security, and economic development among nations

white-collar job office job

Illustrations Credits

Index

Page references in **bold** refer to maps.